Research-Based Approaches for Assessment

John Wills Lloyd

University of Virginia

Timothy J. Landrum

University of Louisville

Bryan G. Cook

University of Hawaii

Melody Tankersley

Kent State University

PEARSON

Boston   Columbus   Indianapolis   New York   San Francisco   Upper Saddle River
Amsterdam   Cape Town   Dubai   London   Madrid   Milan   Munich   Paris   Montreal   Toronto
Delhi   Mexico City   São Paulo   Sydney   Hong Kong   Seoul   Singapore   Taipei   Tokyo

Vice President and Editorial Director: Jeffery W. Johnston
Executive Editor: Ann Castel Davis
Editorial Assistant: Andrea Hall
Vice President, Director of Marketing: Margaret Waples
Marketing Manager: Joanna Sabella
Senior Managing Editor: Pamela D. Bennett
Project Manager: Sheryl Glicker Langner
Senior Operations Supervisor: Matthew Ottenweller
Senior Art Director: Diane C. Lorenzo

Cover Designer: Candace Rowley
Cover Image: Background: © Lora liu/Shutterstock;
Photo: © iofoto/Shutterstock
Full-Service Project Management: S4Carlisle Publishing
Services
Composition: S4Carlisle Publishing Services
Printer/Binder: Edwards Brothers Malloy
Cover Printer: Phoenix-Lehigh Color/Hagerstown
Text Font: Times LT Std

Credits and acknowledgments for material borrowed from other sources and reproduced, with permission, in this textbook appear on the appropriate page within the text.

Photo Credits: Chapter-opening photo: © iofoto/Shutterstock. Design images (from left to right): © Orange Line Media/Shutterstock; © kali9/iStockphoto; © Nailia Schwarz/Shutterstock; © iofoto/Shutterstock; © Jaren Jai Wicklund/Shutterstock.

Every effort has been made to provide accurate and current Internet information in this book. However, the Internet and information posted on it are constantly changing, so it is inevitable that some of the Internet addresses listed in this textbook will change.

Library of Congress Cataloging-in-Publication Data is available upon request.

10 9 8 7 6 5 4 3 2 1

ISBN 10:   0-13-703485-7
ISBN 13: 978-0-13-703485-7

Dedication

In memory of a superb teacher and wonderful friend, Patricia L. Pullen—JWL, TJL, BGC, and MT

Preface

Research-Based Approaches for Assessment was born of discussions over many years between special education practitioners and researchers regarding the need for a reliable and practical guide to highly effective, research-based practices in special education. Providing this type of information is a primary focus of the Council for Exceptional Children's Division for Research (CEC-DR), which the Division has pursued in many ways—sometimes with considerable success, sometimes with disappointment. At a meeting of the Executive Board of CEC-DR, then President Dr. Robin A. McWilliam suggested that the division consider producing a textbook to meet this need that would be unique in its emphasis on research-based practices. And so began concrete discussions that led to the book you are now reading.

You have probably read or heard something about the research-to-practice gap in special education—when practice is not based on research and, although less often emphasized in the professional literature, when research is not relevant to practice. This gap is not unique to special education; it occurs in general education and many other professional fields, including medicine. It is unlikely that the gap between research and practice will ever disappear entirely; indeed, it may not be desirable to thoroughly commingle the worlds of special education research and practice. However, when the gap between research and practice becomes a chasm, with practice being dictated more by tradition and personal trial-and-error than reliable research, the outcomes and opportunities of students suffer unnecessarily. Simply stated, special educators need to use the most effective instructional practices so that students with disabilities can reach their potentials; all too often, that does not occur.

We believe that this text is made all the more timely and important given the recent explosion of information on the Internet. The wealth of information available on the Internet (as well as from other, more traditional sources of recommendations on instructional practices such as professional development trainings, textbooks, and journals) can be an important asset in helping to determine what works. However, much of the information on the Internet and other sources is not research based and therefore is often inaccurate. Thus, although having thousands of pieces of information about various teaching techniques at one's fingertips may seem wonderful, it often has a stultifying effect, leaving many educators drowning in a sea of information overload, without the time or necessary information (i.e., research findings) to determine what is truly credible and what is not. Rather than unsubstantiated promotion of scores of techniques, special educators need in-depth information on the practices shown by reliable research to be most effective for improving important outcomes of learners with disabilities, which is our aim in this text. By focusing on practices with solid research support, such as those featured in this text, special educators can feel confident that they are implementing approaches that are reliable and are those most likely to work for learners with disabilities.

It is important to realize, though, that research support is not an iron-clad guarantee of effectiveness for each and every student. Even the most effective, research-based practices do not work for everyone (there are nonresponders to every practice); and contextual factors (e.g., school and classroom environments, student characteristics) found in practice seldom align perfectly with the research studies supporting most practices. Therefore, teachers will have to rely on their professional wisdom to select and adapt the research-based practices targeted in this text to make them work in their classrooms, for their students. Nonetheless, having practices identified as effective on the basis of sound research, knowing what the research says about those practices, and understanding how those practices work are the critical first steps in achieving effective special education practice.

We believe that *Research-Based Approaches for Assessment* will be counted as one of the considerable successes of CEC-DR because it provides researchers, teacher trainers, policy makers, practitioners, family members, and other stakeholders information about research-based practices shown to generally produce desirable outcomes in the core area of assessment.

Acknowledgments

Very little is accomplished in isolation, and that was certainly true for this text. It is important for us to acknowledge the many professionals whose hard work is responsible for this text. We first acknowledge the chapter authors. We were fortunate to have the participation of the foremost authorities in the topics of focus in this work. We thank them for sharing their expertise and working so diligently and agreeably with us throughout the entire process. We thank Ann Davis, our editor at Pearson, for her unflagging support and insightful assistance. We also express our appreciation to Dr. Christine Balan, Dr. Lysandra Cook, Luanne Dreyer Elliott, and Norine Strang for their excellent and professional editing. Thank you to our reviewers:

Mary E. Cronin, University of New Orleans, and E. Paula Crowley, Illinois State University. And most importantly, we acknowledge our families, without whose support and forbearance this work could not have been accomplished.

John Wills Lloyd
University of Virginia

Timothy J. Landrum
University of Louisville

Bryan G. Cook
University of Hawaii

Melody Tankersley
Kent State University

Contents

1 Introduction to Research-Based Approaches for Assessment   1

Bryan G. Cook and Melody Tankersley

Limitations of Traditional Methods
    for Determining What Works   1
Benefits of Using Research to Determine
    What Works   2
The Research-to-Practice Gap in Special
    Education   6
This Textbook and Addressing the
    Research-to-Practice Gap   6
Conclusion   7

2 Response to Intervention: School-Wide Prevention of Academic Difficulties   8

Matthew K. Burns and Sarah Scholin

Tier 1   9
Tier 2   9
Tier 3   10
Critical Elements of Response-to-
    Intervention Efforts   11
Effectiveness of School-Wide Prevention
    of Academic Difficulties   15
Conclusion   17

3 Data-Based Decision Making in Academics Using Curriculum-Based Measurement   18

Erica S. Lembke, David Hampton, and Elise Hendricker

What Does Progress Monitoring Contribute
    to Making Data-Based Decisions?   18

What Does Research Say About Using
    CBM in Reading and Mathematics?   21
Recommended Practices for Using CBM
    Progress-Monitoring Tools   26
Summary   31

4 Best Practices in Assessment for Eligibility Identification   32

Berttram Chiang, Suzanne L. Russ and Stacey N. Skoning

Historical, Legal, and Ethical Context
    of Eligibility Determination   32
Assessment Procedures for Eligibility
    Determination   34
Best Practices in Eligibility Determination
    for High-Incidence Disabilities   35
Conclusion   41

5 Parent Participation in Assessment and in Development of Individualized Education Programs   43

Katharine G. Shepherd, Michael F. Giangreco, and Bryan G. Cook

Parent Involvement and General Education   44
Historical, Legal, and Theoretical
    Underpinnings of Parent Participation
    in Special Educational Planning   44
Observed Levels of Parental Involvement
    and Observed Roadblocks   45
Examples of Family-Centered Practices   47
Conclusion   54

6 **Individualized Education Programs:** *Legal Requirements and Research Findings*   **56**

Christine A. Christle and Mitchell L. Yell

Legal Requirements   57
Developing Educationally Meaningful
    and Legally Sound IEPs   58
Research on IEP Compliance Issues   61

7 **Using Assessments to Determine Placement in the Least Restrictive Environment for Students with Disabilities**   **70**

Frederick J. Brigham and Jean B. Crockett

Contextual Bases for Making Instructional
    Placement Decisions   71
Tools in the Workshop   74
Using Assessments in Making
    Placement Decisions   80
Conclusion   82

8 **Curriculum-Based Assessment**   **84**

John Venn

Defining Curriculum-Based Assessment   84
Characteristics of Curriculum-Based
    Assessment   85

Reliability, Validity, and Fairness   86
Representative CBA Strategies
    and Procedures   86
Issues in Curriculum-Based Assessment   91
Recommendations for Teachers,
    Decision Makers, and Researchers   92
Summary   93

9 **Accommodations for Assessment**   **94**

Martha L. Thurlow, Sheryl S. Lazarus, and Laurene L. Christensen

Historical, Theoretical, Legal, and Policy
    Contexts for Accommodations   94
Research Base for Assessment
    Accommodations   97
Conclusion   103
Appendix 9.1   Extended Time:
    Study Descriptions   105
Appendix 9.2   Read-Aloud/Oral
    Administration Study Descriptions   107
Appendix 9.3   Computerized Testing
    Study Descriptions   109

References   **111**

Name Index   **133**

Subject Index   **139**

CHAPTER 1

Introduction to Research-Based Approaches for Assessment

Bryan G. Cook | *University of Hawaii*

Melody Tankersley | *Kent State University*

This is not a typical introductory textbook in special education that provides brief overviews of a large number of student characteristics and instructional practices. Textbooks with this focus serve important purposes. For example, individuals who are just beginning to explore the field of special education need to understand the breadth of student needs and corresponding instructional techniques that have been and are being used to teach students with disabilities. This text addresses a different need—the need for extensive information on selected, highly effective practices in special education. Stakeholders such as advanced preservice special educators, practicing special education and inclusive teachers, administrators, parents, and many teacher-educators are more directly involved with the instruction and learning of children and youth with disabilities and as a result need in-depth treatments of the most effective practices that they can use to meaningfully impact and improve the educational experiences of children and youth with and at risk for disabilities.

In this textbook we provide extensive (rather than cursory) information on selected, highly effective practices (rather than on many practices, some of which may be less than effective) in special education. This endeavor begs an important question: What are the most highly effective practices identified in special education?

That is, how do we tell "what works" for children and youth with and at risk for disabilities?

Traditionally, special educators have relied on sources such as personal experience, colleagues, tradition, and experts to guide their instructional decision making (e.g., B. G. Cook & Smith, 2012). These resources have served teachers well in many ways. Special education teachers are skilled professionals who learn from their personal experiences and refine their teaching accordingly. Traditions and custom represent the accumulated personal experiences of whole groups and cultures and therefore can be imbued with great wisdom. And experts most often know of which they speak (and write) and make many valid recommendations. Yet, just as in other aspects of life, the personal experiences that lie at the root of these sources of knowing are prone to error and can lead special educators to false conclusions about which practices work and should be implemented with students with disabilities.

Limitations of Traditional Methods for Determining What Works

Chabris and Simons (2010) described five everyday illusions documented in the psychological literature (i.e., illusions of attention, memory, confidence, knowledge, and cause) that cast doubt on whether teachers can use personal experiences (their own, or those of their colleagues) to determine reliably whether practices work for their students. Chabris and Simons noted that although people assume that they attend to everything within their perceptual field, in reality many stimuli—especially those that contrast with one's expectations—"often go completely unnoticed" (p. 7). That is, people tend to focus their attention on what they expect to happen. Moreover, even when people actively attend to phenomena, their memories are unlikely to be wholly accurate and also are biased by their preconceptions. "We cannot play back our memories like a DVD—each time we recall a memory, we integrate whatever details we do remember with our expectations for what we should remember" (p. 49). Moreover, people tend to hold false illusions of confidence (e.g., most people think of themselves as above-average drivers) and knowledge (e.g., people tend to falsely believe that they know how familiar tools and systems work). Finally, "Our minds are built to detect meaning in patterns, to infer causal relationships from coincidences, and to believe that earlier events cause later ones" (p. 153), even though many patterns are meaningless, many associations are coincidental, and earlier events often simply precede rather than cause later occurrences.

Special education teachers—just like other people in their professional and day-to-day lives—may, then, not attend to events in a classroom that they do not expect (e.g., when using preferred practices, teachers may be more likely to focus on students who are doing well but not recognize struggling students); may construct memories of teaching experiences that are influenced by their preconceptions of whether a practice is likely to work; may be more confident than warranted that a favored instructional approach works when they use it; may believe that they fully understand why and how a practice works when they do not; and may believe that a practice causes positive changes in student outcomes when it does not. We are not suggesting that special educators are more gullible or error prone than anyone else. Nonetheless, these documented illusions show that using one's perceptions of personal experiences is an error-prone method for establishing whether instructional practices cause improved student outcomes.

Traditional wisdom shares many important traits with scientific research (e.g., refining understanding based on empirical input over time; Arunachalam, 2001). Indeed, many traditional practices are shown to be valid when examined scientifically (Dickson, 2003). Yet, tradition and custom often are based on incomplete science or consist of inaccurate superstition and folklore. History is replete with examples of traditional thinking that science subsequently has shown to be incorrect—from

the flat-earth and geocentric models of the solar system to the direct inheritability of intelligence and ineducability of individuals with various disabilities. Accordingly, although many traditional instructional practices for students with disabilities may be effective, others have been passed down through generations of teachers even though they do not have a consistently positive effect on student outcomes. Basing instruction on the individual learning styles of students with disabilities, for example, is an accepted, traditional teaching practice despite the lack of supporting evidence (see Landrum & McDuffie, 2010).

As with personal experience and tradition, expert opinion is often faulty. Indeed, a common logical fallacy is the appeal to authority, in which one argues that a statement is true based on the authority of who said it. Not surprisingly, so-called authorities such as new-age gurus and celebrities often support less than effective products. But experts more commonly considered credible, such as textbook authors, also frequently provide inaccurate guidance. "The fact is, expert wisdom usually turns out to be at best highly contested and ephemeral, and at worst flat-out wrong" (Freedman, 2010, p. 7). In special education, "experts" have a long history of advocating for ineffective practices such as avoiding immunizations, facilitated communication, colored glasses or prism lenses, and patterning (e.g., Mostert, 2010; Mostert & Crockett, 2000). Thus, special educators need to be wary of basing instructional decisions on unverified expert recommendation.

Unlike their nondisabled peers, who often experience success in school while receiving mediocre or even poor instruction, students with disabilities require the most effective instruction to succeed (Dammann & Vaughn, 2001). As Malouf and Schiller (1995) noted, special education serves "students and families who are especially dependent on receiving effective services and who are especially vulnerable to fraudulent treatment claims" (p. 223). It appears, then, that those who teach and work with students with disabilities need a more reliable and trustworthy method for determining what works than personal experience, tradition, or expert opinion. Scientific research can provide a meaningful guide to special educators and other stakeholders when making decisions about what and how to teach learners with disabilities.

Benefits of Using Research to Determine What Works

It is the professional and ethical duty of special educators to implement the instructional techniques most likely to benefit the students they serve. Indeed, the Council for Exceptional Children's (CEC) standards for well-prepared special education teachers specify that special educators should keep abreast of research findings and implement

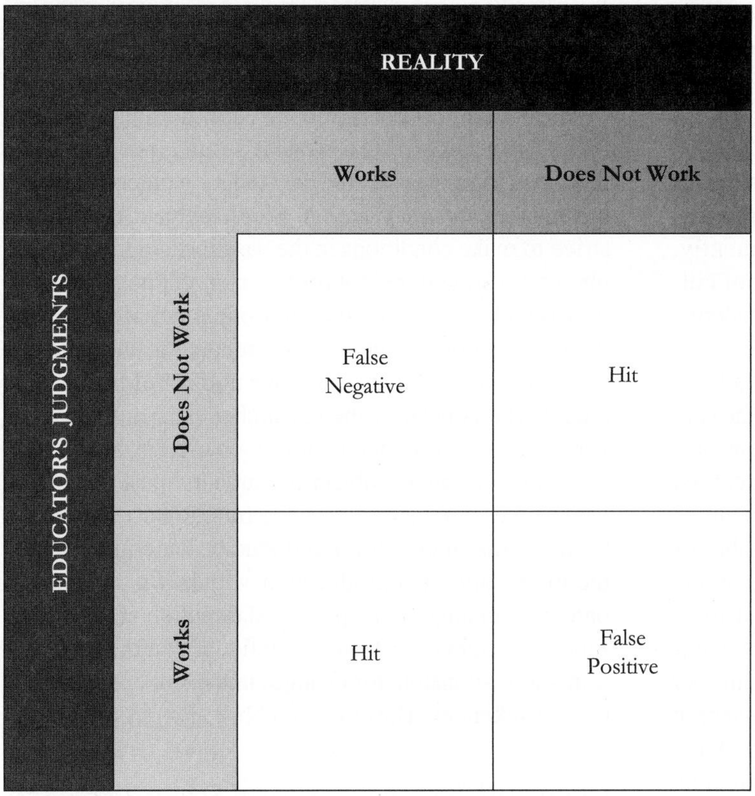

Figure 1.1 Relation between educator's judgments and reality regarding the effectiveness of instructional practices.

research-based practices with their students (CEC, 2009). Moreover, the No Child Left Behind Act and the Individuals with Disabilities Education Act of 2004 both place considerable emphasis on practices that are supported by scientifically based research (e.g., Hess & Petrilli, 2006; A. Smith, 2003; H. R. Turnbull, 2005). Using research as the preferred method to determine what and how to teach makes sense because research can address many of the shortcomings of other traditional approaches for identifying what works.

False Positives and False Negatives

When examining a practice's effectiveness, four possibilities exist to represent the relation between reality (Does the practice actually work for the children in question?) and educators' judgments (Do I believe that the practice works?) (see Figure 1.1). Educators can be right, or hit, in two ways: they can conclude that the practice (a) works, and it actually does, or (b) does not work, and it actually does not. They can also be wrong, or miss, in two ways. First, educators can commit a false positive by concluding that the practice works when it actually *is not* effective. Second, educators can commit a false negative by concluding that the practice does not work, when it actually *is* effective. The goal of any approach to determining what works is to maximize the number of hits while minimizing the likelihood of false positives and false negatives.

As discussed in the previous section, using personal experience, colleagues, tradition, and expert opinion leaves the door open to false positives and false negatives, which results in ineffective teaching and suboptimal outcomes for students with disabilities. Sound scientific research reduces the likelihood of false positives and false negatives in a number of ways, such as (a) using credible measures of student performance, (b) involving large and representative samples, (c) using research designs that rule out alternative explanations for change in student performance, and (d) engaging in the open and iterative nature of science (Lloyd, Pullen, Tankersley, & Lloyd, 2006).

Safeguards in Scientific Research
Credible Measures

Teachers' perceptions of students' behavior and academic performance are often based on subjective perceptions and unreliable measures and therefore do not correspond strictly with actual student behavior and performance (e.g., Madelaine & Wheldall, 2005). In contrast, sound scientific research uses trustworthy methods for measuring phenomena. Whether using direct observations of behavior, formal assessments, curriculum-based measures, or standardized rating scales, high-quality research utilizes procedures and instruments that are both reliable (i.e., consistent) and valid (i.e., meaningful) to accurately gauge student behavior and performance.

Large and Representative Samples

Educators typically interact with a limited number of students, whose performance and behavior may differ meaningfully from other students. Consequently, personal experience (as well as the experiences of colleagues or experts) may not generalize to other students. That is, just because a practice worked for a few students does not mean that it will work for most others. In contrast, research studies typically involve relatively large and often representative samples of student participants across multiple environments and educators. When research has shown that a practice has been effective for the vast majority of a very large number of students, the results are likely to generalize to others in the same population. It is true, however, that most single-subject research studies and some group experimental studies involve a relatively small number of participants. In these cases, confidence in research findings is obtained across a body of research, when multiple studies with convergent findings show that an intervention works for a substantial number of students within a population.

Ruling Out Alternative Explanations

When educators informally examine whether a practice works, they might implement the technique and observe whether students' outcomes subsequently improve. If outcomes do improve, it might seem reasonable to conclude that the intervention worked. However, this conclusion might be a false positive. The students may have improved because of their own development, or something else (e.g., a new educational assistant, a change in class schedule) may be responsible for improved outcomes. Group experimental and single-subject research studies are designed to rule out explanations for improved student outcomes other than the intervention being examined. In other words, causality (i.e., an intervention generally *causes* improved outcomes) can be inferred reasonably from these designs (B. G. Cook, Tankersley, Cook, & Landrum, 2008).

Group experimental research incorporates a control group (to which participants are randomly assigned in true experiments) that is as similar as possible to the experimental group. Ideally, the control and experimental groups comprise functionally equivalent participants and the only differences in their experiences are that the experimental group receives the intervention whereas the control group does not. Under these conditions, if the experimental group improves more than the control group, those improved

outcomes must logically be ascribed to the intervention (e.g., L. Cook, Cook, Landrum, & Tankersley, 2008).

In single-subject research studies, individuals provide their own control condition. A baseline measure (e.g., typical instruction) of a student's outcomes over time serves as a comparison for the student's outcomes in the presence of the intervention. Single-subject researchers strive to make conditions in the baseline and intervention phases equivalent, except for the intervention. Of course, it is possible that the student's outcomes improved in the presence of the intervention relative to the outcome trend during baseline because of a number of phenomena outside the control of the researcher (i.e., not the intervention; e.g., new medication, a change in home life). Accordingly, single-subject researchers must provide at least three demonstrations of a functional relationship between the intervention and student outcomes. When the intervention is introduced or withdrawn and student outcomes change in the predicted direction at least three times, educators can then be confident that the intervention was responsible for changes in the student outcomes (e.g., Tankersley, Harjusola-Webb, & Landrum, 2008).

Open and Iterative Nature of Science

Although many safeguards exist at the level of individual studies to protect against false positives and false negatives, scientific research is inevitably an imperfect enterprise. No study is ideal, and it is impossible for researchers to control for all possible factors that may influence student outcomes in the real world of schools. Furthermore, researchers can and sometimes do make mistakes, which may result in reporting misleading findings. The more general process and nature of scientific research protects against spurious findings in at least two additional ways: public examination of research and recognizing that knowledge is an iterative process.

When reporting a study, researchers must describe their research (e.g., sample, procedures, instruments) in detail. Additionally, before being published in a peer-reviewed journal (the most common outlet for research studies), research studies are evaluated by the journal editors and blind-reviewed (the reviewers' and authors' identities are confidential) by a number of experts in the relevant field. Authors also must provide contact information, which readers can use to make queries about the study or request the data for reevaluation. These processes necessitate that published research undergoes multiple layers of scrutiny, which are likely to (a) weed out most studies with serious errors before being published and (b) identify errors that do exist in published studies.

Finally, it is critical to recognize that research is an iterative process in which greater confidence in a practice is accrued as findings from multiple studies converge in its support. Even with the safeguard of peer review and public scrutiny of research, published studies do sometimes report inaccurate findings. However, the iterative nature of science suggests that conclusions are best examined across entire bodies of research literature made up of multiple studies. For truly effective practices, the possible erroneous conclusions of one or two studies will be shown to be incorrect by a far larger number of studies with accurate findings. Thus, in contrast to relying on personal experience or on expert opinions, science has built-in self-correction mechanisms for identifying spurious results (Sagan, 1996; Shermer, 2002).

Caveats

Research-based practices represent powerful tools for improving the educational outcomes of students with disabilities, yet special educators need to understand a number of associated caveats and limitations. Specifically, research-based practices (a) will not work for everyone, (b) need to be implemented in concert with effective teaching practices, (c) must be selected carefully to match the needs of targeted students, and (d) should be adapted to maximize their impact.

Special educators cannot assume that a practice shown by research to be *generally* effective will be automatically effective for *all* of their students. No number of research participants or studies translates into a guarantee that a practice will work for each and every student, especially for students with disabilities who have unique learning characteristics and needs. Nonresponders, or treatment resistors, will exist for even the most effective instructional approaches. Therefore, although research-based practices are highly likely to be effective and special educators should therefore prioritize these practices, special educators should also always systematically evaluate the effects of these practices through progress monitoring (e.g., Deno, 2006).

Furthermore, research-based practices do not constitute good teaching but represent one important component of effective instruction. Research on effective teaching indicates that effective instruction is characterized by a collection of teacher behaviors, such as pacing instruction appropriately, emphasizing academic instruction, previewing instruction and reviewing previous instruction, monitoring student performance, circulating around and scanning the instructional environment to identify learner needs, recognizing appropriate student behavior, exhibiting enthusiasm, displaying "withitness" (an awareness of what is happening throughout the classroom), and using wait time after asking questions (Brophy & Good, 1986; Doyle, 1986). When educators implement research-based practices in the context of generally *ineffective* instruction—instruction

that occurs in the absence of these hallmarks of effective teaching—the practices are unlikely to produce desired outcomes. As such, research-based practices cannot take the place of and should always be applied in the context of good teaching (B. G. Cook, Tankersley, & Harjusola-Webb, 2008).

Another important caveat is that a practice demonstrated by research studies to be effective for one group may not work for others. It is therefore important that special educators are aware of the student group for which a practice has been demonstrated to be effective when selecting instructional and assessment practices to use with their students. For example, although a practice may have been shown by research studies to be effective for elementary students with learning disabilities, it may not work or even be appropriate for high school students with autism. However, highly effective practices tend to be powerful and their effects robust, and as such, they typically work for more than one specific group of children. For example, the use of mnemonic strategies has been shown to be effective for nondisabled students, students with learning disabilities, students with emotional and behavioral disorders, and students with intellectual impairments at a variety of grade levels (Scruggs & Mastropieri, 2000). Therefore, when reading about a practice that has been validated by research as effective with, for example, students with learning disabilities, special educators working with children and youth with other disabilities should not simply assume that the practice will be similarly effective for their students. But neither should they automatically assume that the practice will be ineffective. Rather, we recommend that special educators use their unique insights and knowledge of their students to evaluate the supporting research, underlying theory, and critical elements of a practice to determine the likelihood that a research-based practice will work for them.

Furthermore, special educators will need to consider whether and how to adapt research-based practices to meet the unique needs of their students. Although implementing a practice as designed is important (e.g., if a practice is not implemented correctly, one cannot expect it to be as effective as it was in the supporting research), recent research has indicated that overly rigid adherence to research-based practices may actually reduce their effectiveness (e.g., Hogue et al., 2008). It appears that teachers should adapt research-based practices to match the unique learning needs of their students and make the practice their own (McMaster et al., 2010). Yet they must do so in a way that preserves the integrity of the essential elements of the research-based practice to avoid rendering it ineffective.

These caveats notwithstanding, because of its many safeguards protecting against false-positive and false-negative conclusions regarding what works, scientific research is the best method available for special educators to identify effective instructional practices. By making decisions about how to teach on the basis of collective bodies of peer-reviewed research studies, special educators can identify with confidence practices that are likely to work for their students.

The Research-to-Practice Gap in Special Education

"Educational research could and should be a vital resource to teachers, particularly when they work with diverse learners—students with disabilities, children of poverty, limited-English speaking students. It is not" (Carnine, 1997, p. 513). The research-to-practice gap describes the commonplace occurrence of children and youth being taught with unproven practices while practices supported through research are not implemented. It is a complex phenomenon with many underlying causes that defies simple solutions. Kauffman (1996) suggested that the research-to-practice gap may be particularly extreme in special education, illustrating that an inverse relationship may actually exist between research support and degree of implementation for instructional practices in special education.

Despite reforms and legislation supporting the role of research in education, research findings indicate that the gap between research and practice continues to persist. For example, special educators reported using research-based practices no more often than ineffective practices (Burns & Ysseldyke, 2009; Jones, 2009). Jones also observed that some special education teachers over-reported their use of research-based practices, suggesting that the actual implementation rate of research-based practices may be even lower than reported. To make matters worse, when special educators do implement research-based practices, they often do so with low levels of fidelity (or not as designed; e.g., B. G. Cook & Schirmer, 2006)—potentially rendering the practices ineffective. Furthermore, many special educators report that they do not trust research or researchers (Boardman, Arguelles, Vaughn, Hughes, & Klingner, 2005) and find information from other teachers more trustworthy and usable (Landrum, Cook, Tankersley, & Fitzgerald, 2002, 2007).

The research-to-practice gap has clear and direct implications for the educational outcomes of students with disabilities. Using practices shown to have reliable and positive effects on student outcomes is the most likely way to improve student performance. Using research-based practices should, therefore, be a professional and ethical imperative for educators. This is true for all teachers. But as Dammann and Vaughn (2001) noted, whereas nondisabled students may perform adequately even in the presence of less than optimal instruction, students

with disabilities require that their teachers use the most effective instructional practices to reach their potentials and attain successful school outcomes.

This Textbook and Addressing the Research-to-Practice Gap

Bridging the research-to-practice gap in special education represents a significant challenge. Many issues will have to be addressed, such as improving teachers' attitudes toward research, providing ongoing supports for teachers to adopt and maintain research-based practices, and conducting high-quality research that is relevant to special education teachers (see B. G. Cook, Landrum, Tankersley, & Kauffman, 2003). But perhaps the most fundamental issues for bridging the research-to-practice gap are (a) *identifying* those practices that are research-based in critical areas of special education and (b) *providing the relevant information* (e.g., supporting theory, critical elements of the research-based practices, specific information on the supporting research studies) necessary to guide special educators in deciding whether the practice is right for them and their students and how to implement it. Without these critical first steps of identifying and providing special educators relevant information about research-based practices, the field of special education is unlikely to make significant progress in bridging the gap between research and practice.

Turning to original reports of research is an unsatisfactory alternative for the vast majority of special educators. Most teachers do not have the training to critically analyze technical research reports that often are geared for audiences with advanced training in statistics and research (Greenwood & Abbott, 2001). And even for those educators with advanced training in these areas, their full-time teaching jobs should and typically do occupy their time. It is simply not realistic for teachers to read through, synthesize, and critically analyze entire bodies of research literature for every instructional decision with which they are faced.

Textbooks focused on methods of instruction and assessment seem an ideal place to provide educators with useful information on research-based practices that can be used to bridge the research-to-practice gap. Unfortunately, much of teacher education—both preservice and in-service—is based on expert opinion and the personal experiences of those conducting the training or writing the training materials (e.g., textbooks). For example, textbook authors frequently recommend practices with little justification. Discussion of supporting research, if provided at all, is often too brief and incomplete for educators to make informed decisions about the appropriateness of the recommended practice for their classrooms. For example, Dacy, Nihalani, Cestone, and Robinson (2011) analyzed the content of three teaching methods textbooks and found that when prescriptive recommendations for using practices were supported by citations, authors predominantly cited secondary sources (e.g., books, position papers) rather than provide discussions of original research from which their readers might arrive at meaningful conclusions regarding the effectiveness of the practices.

To address special educators' need for trustworthy, detailed, and teacher-friendly summaries of the research literature regarding what works in special education, the chapters in the complete, four-part text (B. G. Cook & Tankersley, 2013) provide thorough synopses of the research literature supporting research-based practices in core areas of special education: academics, behavior, assessment, and targeted groups of learners. Specifically, in this text on improving the assessment process in special education, chapter authors, who are documented experts on the topics of focus, address how to effectively assess students with disabilities using both informal and formal approaches. The chapters are organized to parallel the broad assessment process in special education.

First, all students are screened to identify students at risk for school failure, and instruction is organized to prevent academic failure (i.e., Response to Intervention, Chapter 2). Curriculum-based measurement is then used to monitor the progress of at-risk students in a reliable and valid manner (Chapter 3). Students whose progress-monitoring data show that they are unresponsive to instruction are referred for evaluation testing to determine if they have a disability (Chapter 4), a process in which parents must be integrally involved (Chapter 5). For students who are identified as having a disability, individualized education programs (IEPs) must be developed appropriately (Chapter 6), and an appropriate placement decision must be made regarding the least restrictive environment (LRE) that meets their needs (Chapter 7). After students with disabilities have IEPs and are placed in the LRE, their performance is assessed using curriculum-based assessment (Chapter 8), and they receive appropriate accommodations on high-stakes assessments (Chapter 9).

Chapter authors discuss and recommend practices based on supporting research, legal mandates, and theoretical and ethical underpinnings. Chapter authors highlight research-based practices related to the assessment procedures where research support exists. However, much of special education assessment is directed by legal mandates (e.g., the Individuals with Disabilities Education Act), ethical imperatives, or both. Chapter authors therefore also provide information on the legal and ethical foundations of recommended assessment practices when appropriate. Using this information, special educators can make informed decisions about how to conduct assessments in ways that are effective, legally defensible, and consistent with the ethical imperatives of the field.

Conclusion

Special educators clearly want to use the most effective practices to enhance the educational outcomes and opportunities of the students they teach. However, given traditional methods for determining what works and the rapid proliferation of information on teaching techniques on the Internet (Landrum & Tankersley, 2004), much of which is misleading, it is increasingly difficult and complicated to know what works, what doesn't, and how to know the difference. Research is the most trustworthy method for determining what works in special education. This text provides readers with a wealth of information on specific research-based assessment practices in special education.

CHAPTER 2

Response to Intervention: *School-Wide Prevention of Academic Difficulties*

Matthew K. Burns and **Sarah Scholin** | *University of Minnesota*

Assessment in special education has fundamentally changed since the inception of the Individuals with Disabilities Education Act (IDEA, originally titled the Education for All Handicapped Children Act) in 1975. Diagnostic assessments dominated the early days of special education under IDEA; educators used the data to identify the extremely high- and low-performing students in order to rank them and to identify disabilities (Reschly, 1996). Assessment in Pre-K–12 schools has evolved, however, from establishing a rank order to raising the foundational skills of all students (Stiggins, 2005), and special education has followed suit. Beginning with the seminal work of Deno (1985), assessment within special education became more instructionally relevant and focused on what to teach in addition to identifying students who need to be taught through special education.

The change in Pre-K–12 assessments from assessment *of* learning to assessment *for* learning (Stiggins, 2005) has resulted in a focus on preventing learning difficulties. Prevention science is the process of identifying potential risk and protective factors in order to eliminate or mitigate major human dysfunction (Coie et al., 1993). Prevention efforts have consistently demonstrated effectiveness in many fields (Botvin, 2004; Hage et al., 2007; Stith et al., 2006), but researchers are only beginning to apply the principles to special education. Academic disabilities are major human dysfunctions that are relevant to special education and could be potential targets of prevention efforts.

School-wide prevention can reduce the number of students identified with disabilities (Burns, Appleton, & Stehouwer, 2005; VanDerHeyden, Witt, & Gilbertson, 2007) through (a) early identification of difficulties with universal screening and (b) providing interventions through tiers of increasing intensity, both of which are consistent with the principles of prevention science (VanDerHeyden & Burns, 2010). However, prevention science also requires coordinated action (Coie et al., 1993), which suggests that efforts must be school-wide in order to be successful and incorporate general, special, and remedial education.

School-wide prevention of academic difficulties is best accomplished with a Response to Intervention (RtI) model in which assessment data are systemically used to make resource allocation decisions to improve student learning (Burns & VanDerHeyden, 2006). In addition to the focus on student learning, RtI can also be applied to the identification of students who have educational disabilities and need special education. The 2004 amendments to IDEA stated that local educational agencies "shall not be required to take into consideration whether a child has a severe discrepancy between achievement and intellectual ability" (Pub. L. No. 108-446 § 614 [b] [6][A]) when diagnosing a specific learning disability. Instead, schools "may use a process that determines if the child responds to scientific, research-based intervention as a part of the evaluation procedures" (Pub. L. No. 108-446 § 614 [b][6][A]; § 614 [b][2 & 3]), which is commonly referred to as *RtI*. The provision for allowing RtI data to be used to make special education identification decisions bridges the two fundamental purposes for assessment in special education by allowing data that are used to improve instruction to also be used to identify students who need special education.

Most school-wide prevention models (e.g., RtI, school-wide positive behavior supports) are essentially extensions of the same construct (Sandomierski, Kincaid, & Algozzine, 2007), which is data-based problem solving as initially described by Deno and Mirkin (1977). As students progress through the three tiers of intervention commonly associated with RtI, practitioners collect data more frequently (e.g., three times per year for Tier 1, but at least weekly for Tier 3) and more precisely (e.g., general indicators of reading skills for Tier 1, measures of specific skills in Tiers 2 and 3) in order to conduct more in-depth problem analyses (Burns & Gibbons, 2008). Following are descriptions of the three tiers of interventions frequently used within RtI, the assessment techniques frequently used at each level, and how the resulting data address specific problem-analysis questions.

Tier 1

The first tier of any school-wide prevention model is quality classroom instruction. It is beyond the scope of this chapter to provide a detailed discussion of quality instructional practices. However, core instruction within an RtI framework should address the recommendations from national research councils for reading (Snow, Burns, & Griffin, 1998) and math (Kilpatrick, Swafford, & Finell, 2001).

In addition to quality core instruction, periodic (e.g., three times per year) screening of all students for academic deficits is also a fundamental aspect of services provided within Tier 1. Measurement in an RtI system relies heavily on curriculum-based measurements of reading (CBM-R) and math (CBM-M) because they result in data that are psychometrically adequate (i.e., reliable and lead to valid decisions) and sensitive to student progress or growth (Gresham, 2002). (For additional information, see Chapter 3 of this volume, where Lembke, Hampton, and Hendricker provide a detailed description of CBM.) Although CBM data are psychometrically sound, other types of data can inform Tier-1 decisions because the primary function of assessment in Tier 1 is to identify individuals or groups of students who need

additional support, as opposed to monitoring student progress over time. Thus, some schools conduct universal academic screenings with highly reliable but less sensitive measures such as the Measures of Academic Progress (Northwest Evaluation Association, 2003) and Star Math (Renaissance Learning, 1998).

Tier 2

Meta-analytic research found that an average of 20% of students were not successful despite quality core curriculum and instruction in Tier 1 (Burns et al., 2005) and required more intensive intervention. The hallmark of Tier-2 interventions is that they are delivered in small homogeneous groups and are often delivered with a standard protocol (i.e., using the same carefully scripted intervention for groups of students with similar needs). Academically, that might involve grouping approximately five students at the elementary level who all require additional assistance in decoding, for example, and delivering a 30-minute phonics-based intervention to the group four or five times each week.

Measurement in Tier 2 must determine whether a student's problem (i.e., low performance) persists but must also indicate specific skills and deficits and must be appropriate for weekly progress monitoring. For example, in Tier 1, school personnel are focused on determining how well the child or classroom reads generally, in order to determine general risk. But in Tier 2, once general risk has been established, educators must determine the specific skill deficits that underlie reading problems in order to improve reading performance (e.g., phonemic awareness, decoding). Moreover, data are collected with Tier-2 interventions once each week or no less than once every other week. These more-frequently collected data are used to monitor progress and to judge the effectiveness of the intervention(s) being implemented.

School-wide prevention efforts for academic difficulties again rely heavily on CBM for Tier-2 decisions because the data can be collected frequently and can monitor student progress. However, data are also needed to identify specific strengths and skills deficits, and CBM does not have strong utility for that purpose (Burns, Dean, & Klar, 2004; L. S. Fuchs, Fuchs, Hosp, & Hamlett, 2003). Decisions made regarding interventions within Tiers 2 and 3 often depend on subskill mastery measurement (Burns & Coolong-Chaffin, 2006) to assess skills in a specific domain. Thus, problem-analysis decisions and instructional planning for Tier-2 interventions may rely on data that explicitly assess skills in different domains such as Star Early Literacy (SEL; Renaissance Learning, 2003) or curriculum-based assessment of instructional design (CBA-ID; Gravois & Gickling, 2008). The former is used to assess individual students' skills in the five areas identified by the National Reading Panel (NRP, 2000) as important aspects of reading instruction (i.e., phonemic awareness, phonics, fluency, vocabulary, and comprehension). The latter assesses the accuracy with which various skills are completed in order to determine skills and instructional material that represent appropriate intervention targets. Both SEL and CBA-ID have been shown to produce data with adequate psychometric properties for instructional decision making (Burns, Tucker, Frame, Foley, & Hauser, 2000; Ysseldyke & McLeod, 2007).

Tier-2 math interventions represent a special situation from an assessment perspective because assessments of general math skills do not inform how well a student can perform a specific skill and because measures of specific skill performance do not indicate overall math proficiency (Hintze, Christ, & Keller, 2002). Thus, a comprehensive assessment system for math at Tier 2 should include evaluations of specific skills (e.g., single-digit by single-digit multiplication, subtraction with regrouping).

Tier 3

On average, 5% of the student population will require intervention intensity greater than that provided in Tier-1 and Tier-2 interventions (Burns et al., 2005). For those students, interventions are highly targeted, derived based on individual student need, and often delivered in one-on-one or two-to-one formats. School problem-solving teams develop the interventions through in-depth problem analyses. Problem-solving teams rely on functional assessments of academic problems such as the five

hypotheses for student failure outlined in Table 2.1 (Daly, Witt, Martens, & Dool, 1997); curriculum-based evaluation (Howell & Nolet, 2000); or the Review, Interview, Observe, Test–Instruction, Curriculum, Environment, and Learner (RIOT-ICEL) matrix (J. L. Hosp, 2008).

Following the progression of increased precision and frequency, teachers (or other trained education personnel, e.g., reading specialists, math tutors, paraprofessionals) collect data in Tier 3 at least once each week, and usually twice weekly, to monitor progress. Progress-monitoring data collected in Tiers 2 and 3 are often produced by general outcome measures (e.g., oral reading fluency, digits correct per minute on a multiskill math probe), but teachers should also monitor progress in the specific skill being taught (e.g., nonsense-word fluency for a phonics intervention, single-digit multiplication probes). However, even more precise data are used to determine the appropriate intervention, and these data often take into account factors such as the accuracy with which a skill is completed and malleable environmental factors that could contribute to the problem such as instruction, curriculum, and learning environment. Sources from which this information can be gleaned include file reviews; interviews of teachers, parents, and students; observations of student performance; and formal and informal assessments/testing. The RIOT-ICEL problem-analysis matrix (J. L. Hosp, 2008) can be used to collect, organize, and analyze this information. Functionally relevant data for academic problems can be generated by examining the five hypotheses for student failure and tested in a brief experimental analysis, which has resulted in improved student outcomes in reading (Burns & Wagner, 2008), math (Carson & Eckert, 2003), and spelling (McComas et al., 1996).

Table 2.1 Five Hypotheses for Student Failure and Relevant Assessment

Hypothesis	Data to Evaluate
The student does not want to do the task.	Collect highly sensitive and specific data (e.g., oral reading fluency of a specific passage or single-skill math measure such as double-digit addition of two numbers) with and without providing an incentive to examine differences in performance.
The student needs more practice.	Collect highly sensitive and specific data before and after implementing an intervention that provide practice without teaching (e.g., repeated reading).
The student needs more instruction.	Collect highly sensitive and specific data before and after providing direct instruction in the skill in a one-on-one tutoring setting.
The student has never had to do the task that way before.	Collect highly sensitive and specific data with a typical task and by completing the task in a different manner (e.g., a different setting, orally versus in writing, and with and without manipulative or visual cues).
The task is too difficult.	Collect highly sensitive and specific data from a typical task and from one that represents an instructional level for that student.

Source: Information from Daly, E. J., III, Witt, J. C., Martens, B. K., & Dool, E. J. (1997). A model for conducting a functional analysis of academic performance problems. *School Psychology Review, 26,* 554–574.

Critical Elements of Response-to-Intervention Efforts

RtI may differ in various states, districts, and schools because each system is unique and because the school-wide prevention effort should address the unique needs of the school in which it is implemented. However, RtI is premised on basic core tenets including data-based decision making through universal screening and progress monitoring, problem analysis, efficient resource allocation, tiered interventions, collaboration across disciplines, and treatments based on student need rather than labels or other arbitrarily determined characteristics to enhance outcomes for all students. Next we describe some of the features and elements of successful school-wide prevention models.

Grade-Level Teams

Many practitioners mistakenly assume that a problem-solving team should drive school-wide prevention efforts, but this approach is highly ineffective. Research has consistently found that on average 20% of students need more support than what is provided in typical core instruction (Burns et al., 2005). Very few schools have the resources necessary to implement effective problem analyses and individualized interventions for 20% of their students. Thus, problem-solving teams are reserved for Tier-3 interventions, which address approximately 5% of the student population.

Grade-level teams, rather than problem-solving teams, should drive the school-wide prevention process at the elementary level, and multidisciplinary professional learning communities (PLCs) often do so at the high school level. Grade-level teams comprise the teachers who teach each grade level, or some other combination of teachers. For example, a school with a small number of teachers at a given grade level could combine teachers to create three grade-level teams (K–1, 2–3, and 4–5). High school models that are driven by a PLC comprise teachers who teach a common group of students and should include English and language arts teachers, as well as appropriate content area teachers. For example, a PLC at a high school could include two Grade-9 English teachers, two Grade-9 Social Studies teachers, one Grade-9 Science teacher, and one Grade-9 Math teacher. We also recommend that the special education teacher, or at least one representative who works with students with disabilities in that given grade, also serve on the grade-level team or PLC.

In middle schools, the instructional system can vary dramatically from school to school. Some middle schools operate with "houses" in which students are assigned to a group of teachers who instruct them in all core areas. The PLC in this scenario would be the teachers assigned to each house. Alternatively, some middle schools function very much like a high school, and the PLC model would mirror the one we described for high schools.

Although the format of the grade-level team and PLC could vary based on the individual school, the process in which they engage remains constant. The primary task of these groups, from a school-wide prevention perspective, is to examine student data and make intervention decisions. There are two kinds of team meetings, one to examine universal screening data that meets three times each year (or how ever often universal screenings are conducted) and one to examine student progress that occurs at least once each month. During the progress-monitoring meeting, the team members examine the growth for each student getting a Tier-2 or Tier-3 intervention to determine whether the intervention is working. Research has not yet developed well-established criteria for comparing student growth data. However, research does support the validity of decisions made with a dual discrepancy (L. S. Fuchs, 2003) in which interventions are deemed as ineffective when a student's (a) postintervention level remains below the grade-level benchmark standard and (b) rate of growth falls at least 1 standard deviation below the average grade-level growth (Burns & Senesac, 2005).

During the triannual meeting to discuss universal screening data, the grade-level team or PLC examines universal screening data for every student in the building. In doing so, the team attempts to answer the following questions: (a) Is there a class-wide problem? (b) Who needs a Tier-2 intervention? (c) Did we miss anyone? Class-wide problems, discussed further in a later section, are the first agenda item in a benchmark assessment team meeting. After determining that no class-wide problems exist, or that they were successfully remediated, the next step is to determine which students need a Tier-2 intervention. Generally speaking, this is accomplished with straight resource allocation. In other words, approximately 20% of students at a given grade level who are most in need of additional support are designated to receive a Tier-2 intervention. For academics, that simply means students at or below the lowest 20th percentile rank for each grade level on the given measure (e.g., the lowest 20 CBM-R scores of 100 third graders).

Although CBM measures represent psychometrically adequate measures of student academic performance, and the lowest 20% is a reasonable cutoff point to indicate problematic performance, this approach is not a foolproof method, and it may fail to identify all students who need support beyond that provided in Tier 1. Accordingly, after determining who needs a Tier-2 intervention, teams should examine students whose data closely approximate the cutoff criterion (i.e., the CBM-R score that represents the 20th percentile rank) and evaluate other sources of data such as classroom performance to be sure that all students who need Tier-2 intervention supports receive them.

Data Management Team

Ideally, teachers who make up the grade-level teams and PLCs would be well versed in how to analyze and interpret assessment data, but this may not be the case in many K–12 schools. We therefore recommend forming a data management team to assist grade-level teams and professional learning communities in consuming the data. The data management team usually comprises two to three members, often including the school psychologist and one or two of the following: general education classroom teacher, Title 1 teacher, reading specialist, behavioral specialist, or special education teacher. The essential attributes of data management team members are that they know how to analyze and interpret data and have a strong understanding of assessment and data-based decision making. Each elementary school usually has one data management team, but more could be created for large schools. High and middle schools often have one data management team for each grade, depending on the size of the school.

As the name implies, the data management teams help facilitate teachers' and teams' use of data. They ensure that data are given to the teachers by a given time of year soon after the benchmark data are collected (e.g., September 30th, January 30th, and May 30th). The data management team presents assessment results arranged so that each teacher has data for each individual student in his classroom and the representative data for the class and grade level. For example, median CBM-R or CBM-M scores would be reported for each classroom within a grade, as would the grade-level average. Median scores are used with smaller data sets of less than 30 pieces of data to prevent undue influence by outlying data.

Identifying Class-Wide Problems

Our experience with schools has shown that teachers are generally excited to provide interventions for struggling learners, and administrators are eager to start systemic interventions to address the needs of groups of students. However, both groups tend to be less enthusiastic about examining their own practice, though without such evaluation the likelihood of interventions being effective diminishes. Many schools have such a large number of struggling students that they cannot possibly implement more intensive Tier-2 interventions for all of them, for two reasons. First, most schools do not have the resources to implement a Tier-2 or -3 intervention with more than 20% to 25% of the students. Second, and perhaps more important, if more than 25% of the students require a Tier-2 intervention, it is a sign that students' needs are not being met adequately by the core instruction at Tier 1, which makes it unlikely that interventions at higher tiers will be effective. For example, in order for students to learn how to read, they need a solid core curriculum that balances instruction in letter sounds, free-choice reading, writing, and word study (NRP, 2000; Snow et al., 1998). Typically, effective Tier-2 and -3 interventions represent highly targeted instruction in one of these core areas (Burns, VanDerHeyden, & Boice, 2008). Thus, a student might receive intensive instruction in letter sounds as a Tier-2 intervention, which might increase ability to sound out words, but without the other aspects of effective reading instruction occurring within the core curriculum, the student will not learn how to read.

The first step in a school-wide prevention model in schools with more than 20% to 25% of students who fall below established benchmarks on universal screeners is to identify class-wide problems, which can then be directly remediated before individual interventions begin (VanDerHeyden & Burns, 2005; VanDerHeyden, Witt, & Naquin, 2003). Class-wide problems are identified for academic domains by comparing the class median on a given measure such as CBM-R to the 25th percentile rank on a national norm (e.g., Hasbrouck & Tindal, 2005). We use the 25th percentile rank because, statistically speaking, the 25th percentile represents the lowest end of the average range for any distribution. Currently no national norms are widely available for math, so we recommend comparing CBM-M data to the instructional level range of 14 to 31 digits correct per minute through third grade, and 24 to 49 digits correct per minute for grades 4 and 5 (Burns, VanDerHeyden, & Jiban, 2006). Class medians that fall below the instructional level range (i.e., below 14 through third grade and below 24 for fourth and fifth grades) suggest that a class-wide problem exists in math. However, little guidance exists for classrooms above the fifth grade.

The core instruction within each classroom is carefully evaluated when a class-wide problem is identified. First, standards for reading (NRP, 2000; Snow et al., 1998) and math (Kilpatrick et al., 2001) instruction are used to evaluate the instruction within the classroom. Grade-level teams and professional learning communities discuss the instructional practices to ensure quality instruction is occurring. Next, a class-wide intervention may be implemented to improve student performance. For example, Peer-Assisted Learning Strategies (PALS; D. Fuchs, Fuchs, Mathes, & Simmons, 1997) is a commonly used class-wide intervention for academic difficulties that has a strong research base (D. Fuchs & Fuchs, 2005; McMaster, Fuchs, Fuchs, & Compton, 2005) and has been shown to be an effective intervention for class-wide problems (McMaster & Wagner, 2007; VanDerHeyden & Burns, 2005).

Implementation Integrity

A strong school-wide prevention model is dependent on quality instruction and research-based interventions. However, the strongest interventions available will not result in improved student performance if they are not correctly implemented. Thus, implementation integrity (i.e., implementing plans and interventions as designed) is another aspect of an effective school-wide model that is not considered frequently enough. Indeed, some have identified implementation integrity as the largest obstacle to overcome in school-wide prevention efforts (Noell & Gansle, 2006; Ysseldyke, 2005). Thus, effective school-wide prevention efforts assess the implementation integrity of the grade-level team's and PLC's data-based decision-making process, the problem-solving team process, and the actual interventions used.

Implementation integrity can be assessed in one of two ways. First, checklists for interventions, and grade-level team or PLC or problem-solving team processes, can be created and the implementation observed to provide feedback (Burns, Wiley, & Viglietta, 2008). Unfortunately, this option may be perceived as threatening by classroom teachers and team members and may be too resource-intensive to be practical. Thus, school personnel could develop a shorter checklist that focuses only on the most critical aspect of an intervention in order to allow for a shorter observation while still providing useful information (Noell & Gansle, 2006); but the observations may not sufficiently represent the entire intervention or team process. Gansle and Noell (2007) recommend using permanent products as well. Most interventions involve creating some product (e.g., flash cards, answer sheets) that can be used to assess whether the intervention occurred. Permanent products with which team processes could be examined include completed summaries of meetings, meeting agendas, or the created list of students within the lowest 20th percentile. A combination of directly observing the critical components of a treatment plan and examining permanent products is likely the most efficient yet valid approach to assess implementation integrity (Gansle & Noell, 2007).

Supplemental (Tier-2) Interventions

Interventions provided at Tier 3 are important to a successful RtI model, but schools often tend to focus on

Tier 3 without first establishing a well-developed Tier 2. Without a well-implemented and effective Tier 2, interventions implemented at Tier 3 have little chance of success because of a lack of resources. Fortunately, research has consistently demonstrated the effectiveness of implementing supplemental interventions. For example, Blachman, Tangel, Bail, Black, and McGraw (1999) implemented supplemental instruction in the alphabetic code with 66 first-grade students and found that these students outperformed the control group in measures of phonological awareness, letter-name and letter-sound knowledge, and multiple measures of word recognition, and further that those differences remained at the end of second grade. Moreover, O'Shaughnessy and Swanson (2000) delivered small-group decoding and word analogy training to high school students during 30-minute sessions three times each week for 6 weeks, which resulted in significantly higher phonological awareness, phonological memory, and word-attack skill in comparison to a control group.

Burns and colleagues (2006) reviewed research regarding Tier-2 interventions and made recommendations based on that review. Research data from several studies found that Tier-2 interventions should be implemented in small groups of approximately five students but should be as large as possible while maintaining effectiveness. This might mean that the Tier-2 groups among young students (i.e., kindergarten) need to be considerably smaller (e.g., 2 or perhaps 3 students), whereas groups could be larger (e.g., 10 students) among middle school and high school students. More important than the size of the group is how they are grouped. Students in each Tier-2 group should have similar deficits so that interventions can be highly targeted. Moreover, the groups should be led by someone qualified to deliver the intervention, which might be a specialist, a classroom teacher, or a paraprofessional with close supervision by a certified teacher or behavior specialist.

It is important to note that Tier-2 interventions are designed to support core instruction, not to supplant it. Thus, all students participating in a Tier-2 intervention should also participate fully in core instruction. For example, if a student receives a Tier-2 intervention for reading 30 minutes each day, then she would also participate in the 90 to 120 minutes of core reading instruction. Keeping in mind that Tier-2 interventions are always in addition to, and never instead of, core instruction, such interventions usually consist of approximately 30 minutes of intervention 3 to 5 times each week, which may again be modified based on individual school requirements or student needs.

No robust, research-based recommendations exist for the length of an academic intervention at Tier 2, but a measurement perspective sheds some light on the subject. Christ (2006) demonstrated that when using slope of growth to determine intervention effectiveness, slopes were not sufficiently reliable until approximately 8 weeks of data were collected, and that was assuming that two data points were collected each week in an acceptably standardized manner. Thus, it seems that 8 weeks' duration is an acceptable target for Tier-2 interventions. Certainly, a grade-level team or PLC could determine that an intervention is effective in somewhat less time than 8 weeks, or they may decide to change the intervention within Tier 2 in less time, but a move to a more intensive intervention (i.e., Tier 3) should not happen until at least 8 weeks of data are collected.

As we have discussed, implementation integrity is critically important for a school-wide prevention model. VanDerHeyden and Burns (2010) provided a checklist, based on the review of research by Burns et al. (2006), with which the implementation of Tier-2 interventions in an RtI model can be evaluated. We provide a similar list in Table 2.2. Practitioners can observe Tier-2 interventions with this checklist and present the resulting data to grade-level teams, PLCs, and school-wide leadership teams as evidence of the degree to which interventions are implemented with fidelity.

Continuum of Intervention Intensity

Although many people use time as an indicator of intensity, other factors must be considered. Interventions implemented in Tier 2 should be more intense than those in Tier 1, and Tier 3 interventions should be more intense than Tier 2. Intervention intensity is best conceptualized as the interaction of dose and intervention duration, with *dose* defined as the number of "properly administered teaching episodes during a single intervention session" (Warren, Fey, & Yoder, 2007, p. 71). Thus, *intensity* can be equated with the dosage (number of times a skill is directly taught) delivered over time, and Tier-2 interventions would consist of more teaching episodes of a highly specific skill than during Tier 1. Moreover, as intervention intensity increases, so should assessment frequency and precision.

Validity

Because RtI can be used as part of the special education identification process for a specific learning disability, the resulting data should demonstrate adequate psychometric properties. Research has consistently demonstrated that data obtained from CBM are reliable and result in valid decisions (Wayman, Wallace, Wiley, Ticha, & Espin, 2007), and other commonly used tools to measure academic progress within RtI also demonstrate sufficient psychometric properties (see the Web site for the National Center on Response to Intervention http://www.rti4success.org/ for a review of specific tools). However, decisions made at various critical points in the RtI process should also be considered when evaluating the technical adequacy of the data from school-wide prevention (Barnett et al., 2006).

Barnett et al. (2006) point out that validity for decisions made within a school-wide prevention model should be evaluated with concepts outlined by Messick (1988, 1995). For example, Barnett et al. state that validity data should be collected at each decision point to

Table 2.2   Characteristics of an Effective Tier-2 Response to Intervention System

Item	Observed	Not Observed
Intervention is implemented by a qualified professional with appropriate supervision as needed.		
The group size is appropriate (e.g., approximately 5 in elementary school, and 8–10 in middle and high school).		
The intervention is implemented 3–5 times each week.		
The intervention is implemented for approximately 15–30 minutes each time.		
The intervention is implemented in addition to core instruction (i.e., does not occur during core instructional time).		
The intervention is targeted but is consistent with core curriculum and instruction.		
The intervention is designed to last at least 8 weeks.		
The intervention is research based.		
Individual student progress is monitored with a reliable source of data.		

Source: Information from Burns, M. K., VanDerHeyden, A. M., & Jiban, C. (2006). Assessing the instructional level for mathematics: A comparison of methods. *School Psychology Review, 35,* 401–418.

evaluate the inferences made from the data. Specifically, particular points within each tier should be examined, which are outlined in Table 2.3. School-wide leadership teams should examine these questions and not just rely on using well-constructed measurement tools. No guidelines have been developed regarding criteria to which data obtained to answer the questions in Table 2.3 should be compared. Needless to say, however, the more times the questions can be answered positively, the more confidence leadership teams can have in their process.

Some previous research can inform the validity conversation regarding school-wide prevention. For example, using a dual discrepancy to determine if a Tier-2 intervention is effective leads to consistent judgments of intervention effectiveness (Burns, Scholin, Kosciolek, & Livingston, 2010), converges with data from standardized measures of reading (Burns & Senesac, 2005; McMaster et al., 2005; Speece & Case, 2001), and reduces ethnic and gender bias in the decision-making

process (Burns & Senesac, 2005). These data support the validity of school-wide prevention services, but the validity of RtI processes can be established fully only by examining their effect on student outcomes (Messick, 1988, 1995).

Effectiveness of School-Wide Prevention of Academic Difficulties

A 2009 survey found that 71% of the respondents indicated that their districts were either starting an RtI initiative or had one in place (Spectrum K12 School Solutions, 2009). Despite this impressive level of implementation, effectiveness research is somewhat limited. Ellis (2005) proposed that in order to evaluate the effectiveness of an innovation, research is needed regarding the effectiveness of implementation not only in a well-controlled

Table 2.3 Questions to Address to Examine the Validity of Decisions Made in a School-Wide Response to Intervention Model

Tier	Questions
Tier 1	• Do core curricula match current scientific standards?
	• Are core curricula being implemented with fidelity?
	• Are instructional methods consistent with current best practices?
	• Are universal screening data reliable?
	• Do universal screening data accurately predict meaningful outcomes?
	• Are grade-level teams and PLCs examining universal screening data to identify class-wide problems and to determine who needs a Tier-2 intervention?
	• Do data support the decision-making rule for identifying who needs a Tier-2 intervention?
Tier 2	• Are Tier-2 interventions being implemented with fidelity?
	• Is student progress being monitored with reliable data?
	• Are Tier-2 interventions directly linked to core curriculum and objectives?
	• Do data support the decision rules for increasing/decreasing intensity?
	• Are the goals and outcomes socially valid (seen as important by teachers and parents)?
Tier 3	• Are interventions in Tier 3 more intense and individualized than in Tier 2?
	• Are problem-solving processes being implemented with fidelity?
	• Are intervention targets selected in a reliable manner?
	• Do data support the decision rules for increasing/decreasing intensity?
	• Are the goals, methods, and outcomes socially valid?
	• Do grade-level teams and PLCs examine both level and trend of progress for students?
	• Do teams document that special services are necessary for further progress due to the degree to which interventions differ from typical routines in terms of resources, time, involvement of professionals beyond the child's teacher, and other factors?

Source: Information from Barnett, D., Elliot, N., Graden, J., Ihlo, T., Macmann, G., Natntais, M., & Prasse, D. (2006). Technical adequacy for response to intervention practices. *Assessment for Effective Intervention, 32,* 20–31.
Note: PLCs = professional learning communities.

setting but also on a wide-scale basis. Innovations that are implemented on a large scale, but that lack well-researched effectiveness, may quickly become educational fads that fail to effect meaningful change.

Considerable research has addressed the effectiveness of school-wide prevention models implemented in applied settings, but essentially none has examined such models in well-controlled settings (VanDerHeyden & Burns, 2010). Burns and colleagues (2005) conducted a meta-analysis of 20 studies that examined the effectiveness of RtI. Some of the studies included in the meta-analysis were evaluations of large-scale implementation (e.g., Ikeda & Gustafson, 2002; McNamara & Hollinger, 2003), and some studied supplemental intervention in a more-controlled trial (e.g., McMaster et al., 2005; Speece & Case, 2001; Torgesen et al., 2001). Large median effect sizes were noted for both large-scale and controlled studies ($d = 1.02$ and 0.86, respectively). A total of 11 studies examined student outcomes (e.g., increased reading scores) and resulted in a median effect size of $d = 0.72$, and 13 studied systemic outcomes (e.g., reductions in students referred to and/or placed into special education) and resulted in a median effect size of $d = 1.28$.

Although most comprehensive evaluations of RtI models use a program evaluation design rather than research designs with strong internal validity, one study examined the effectiveness of an RtI model with a multiple-baseline design. VanDerHeyden and colleagues (2007) implemented an RtI model in five elementary schools across 4 years and saw an immediate reduction in numbers of students referred for evaluation for special education eligibility, as well as those initially placed in special education, after starting RtI. Moreover, approximately 55% of the students referred for a special education eligibility evaluation during the baseline phase were identified with a specific learning disability. However, the proportion of students referred for special education evaluation who were actually identified with a disability increased from 88% to 89% after RtI was modified, indicating a more effective identification model. These data suggested strong systemic effects, but academic outcomes were only anecdotally included.

In addition to research addressing large-scale implementation and supplemental services, research regarding other specific RtI components has found large effects. For example, a core reading curriculum that explicitly taught phonics skills led to better-developed reading skills and fewer students being identified with a specific learning disability in reading (Foorman, Francis, Fletcher, Schatschneider, & Mehta, 1998), and meta-analyses found large effects for formative evaluation ($d = 0.70$, L. S. Fuchs & Fuchs, 1986) and for problem-solving teams ($d = 1.10$, Burns & Symington, 2002).

Limitations of Empirical Research Base

Research regarding school-wide prevention is still ongoing, which makes it difficult to conclusively summarize the state of the current research. Numerous individual studies and meta-analyses support the effectiveness of school-wide RtI approaches, and considerable research addresses various interventions and model components (e.g., Burns et al., 2005; McMaster et al., 2005; McNamara & Hollinger, 2003). Moreover, considerable research has addressed assessment tools within RtI (e.g., VanDerHeyden et al., 2007). In a number of areas, the research has been less clear and future research is needed.

In the early 1980s, Heller, Holtzman, and Messick (1982) recommended RtI as national policy, and by the early 1990s some school districts across the country were using RtI procedures to improve student learning and to make identification decisions regarding specific learning disabilities (Graden, Stollar, & Poth, 2007; Lau et al., 2006). However, relatively little research that meets scientific standards for methodological rigor has addressed RtI models in their entirety. Perhaps the biggest concern that research has yet to adequately address is implementation integrity. Noell and colleagues (Noell, Duhon, Gatti, & Connell, 2002; Noell, Gresham, & Gansle, 2002; Noell et al., 2005) have certainly informed the literature about treatment integrity for individual interventions, and recent research has demonstrated that providing feedback on implementation integrity improved the fidelity of the problem-solving team process (Burns, Peters, & Noell, 2008). However, implementation integrity was identified as a potentially fatal flaw in RtI (Noell & Gansle, 2006).

Researchers have yet to identify ways to ensure implementation integrity within RtI, and many important questions about what should be implemented remain unanswered. For example, the role of parents in RtI seems to be almost completely absent in research. This is especially concerning, given that prevention science is the theoretical basis for RtI, and prevention depends on coordinated services between home, school, and community (VanDerHeyden & Burns, 2010). Moreover, problem analysis is critical to RtI, but the research evaluating the effectiveness of various approaches to analyses such as curriculum-based evaluation is sparse, and the data about math and writing are very limited.

School-wide prevention models have their bases in grassroots movements, and those initiatives outpaced pre-service training. Fortunately, many colleges of education and school psychology programs graduate personnel with the necessary skills (e.g., curriculum-based measurement, data-based decision making, interventions, consultation, problem-solving), but those skills are rarely directly contextualized within school-wide prevention. The field needs a stronger pre-service focus and needs research regarding how to best provide in-service training to current practitioners. Moreover, school effectiveness research has consistently found that the single variable that contributes most directly to effective schools is effective *instructional* leadership by school principals (Levine & Lezotte, 1990), but research regarding administrators' roles within school-wide prevention is yet to occur. Researchers have made several recommendations for school administration regarding RtI (e.g., J. Elliott & Morrison, 2008; Kurns & Tilly, 2008), but even those helpful documents do not fully discuss several important issues such as personnel development and human resource issues.

Due to the increased complexity of high schools, more research is needed on successful implementation of RtI at the secondary level. Specifically, educators need research regarding effective measurement tools for high school students, how to best implement Tier-2 interventions, and how to implement problem-solving teams at the high school level.

Effect on Special Education

Because RtI is directly linked to special education through diagnosis of a specific learning disability, it is important to consider the effect of school-wide prevention on special education. Fortunately, previous research has informed this conversation. Most of the research on RtI focuses on student outcomes, which is appropriate given the focus on enhancing student learning (Burns & VanDerHeyden, 2006). Some have cautioned that RtI would lead to a dramatic increase in the number of children identified with a specific learning disability (J. B. Hale, Naglieri, Kaufman, & Kavale, 2004), but a review of four studies of districts implementing RtI found that an average of 1.26% ($SD = 0.65$) of the student population was referred for a special education eligibility assessment, and an average of 1.68% ($SD = 1.45$) of the population was identified with a special education disability (Burns et al., 2005); it should be noted that these were based on different studies, which is why the percentage of students identified with a disability was slightly higher than the percentage referred for an evaluation. Moreover, the same review found an average percentage of the student population that was referred to the problem-solving team within the RtI model of 5.98% ($SD = 2.97$), which usually occurs within Tier 3 of an RtI model. If approximately 5% of the student population generally is identified with an SLD (Lerner, 2002),

and students with a specific learning disability and those referred to a problem-solving team within Tier 3 both have severe learning difficulties, then schools that used an RtI model in the previous research had approximately the same number of students experiencing significant difficulties as most schools across the country. However, most of the students experiencing significant difficulties in the RtI schools had their needs met without being identified as a student with a disability.

M. M. Gerber (2005) stated that RtI research does little to inform us about the nature of specific learning disabilities, which appears to be true. Perhaps future research regarding the characteristics of students identified with a specific learning disability through an RtI approach will shed light on the nature of these disabilities. However, the current research focuses on outcomes for students and systems, which is appropriate at this point. What we do know is that RtI results in special education decisions that are not biased by gender (Burns & Senesac, 2005). Moreover, research with 13 elementary schools in an urban area found that after 2 years of implementation, schools that implemented an RtI model (Instructional Consultation Teams) experienced significant decreases in the risk of minority students being referred to and placed in special education when compared to 9 control schools (Gravois & Rosenfield, 2006). In fact, the likelihood of a minority student's being identified with a disability was cut in half in the participating schools.

Conclusion

Implementing school-wide prevention can be a long and difficult process, but several excellent examples of successful models exist in the literature (Ervin, Schaughency, Goodman, McGlinchey, & Matthews, 2006; Grimes, Kurns, & Tilly, 2006). Sandler and Sugai (2009) describe the conceptual framework, features, and outcomes of a 10-year initiative to establish a model of Effective Behavior and Instructional Support (EBIS) in a district in Oregon. The district observed increasing fidelity of implementation, increasing numbers of students demonstrating sufficient reading skills, and accurate early identification of children with specific learning disabilities. The EBIS model incorporated prevention of both academic and behavioral difficulties, but it provides an example from which practitioners interested in implementing RtI can learn. The legal justification, theoretical framework, and research base suggest that school districts are wise to move to a school-wide model for preventing academic difficulties.

CHAPTER 3

Data-Based Decision Making in Academics Using Curriculum-Based Measurement

Erica S. Lembke, David Hampton, and **Elise Hendricker** | *University of Missouri*

With the passage of the No Child Left Behind Act (NCLB, U.S. Department of Education, 2001), schools are focusing more on accountability and ensuring that all children are learning and progressing in their education. Schools around the country are collecting data, analyzing student performance, and using research-based practices and instruction that are proven advantageous for student success. To achieve these outcomes, many schools have elected to employ a Response to Intervention (RtI) model (D. Fuchs & Fuchs, 2006; Burns, Appleton, & Stehouwer, 2005) to guide their instruction, intervention, and data-based decision making. Making data-based decisions in an RtI model requires educators to use technically adequate tools for universal screening to determine which students are at risk of later difficulties as well as for monitoring student progress over time to gain reliable information regarding the effectiveness of instructional practices.

This chapter specifically focuses on the use of empirically validated practices to make effective decisions regarding student progress and outcomes. After introducing basic concepts about using simple data to determine who needs help and whether the help they receive is resulting in improved performance, we present research examining technical aspects of progress-monitoring methods and the benefits of their use. In the third section, we illustrate the application of data-based

decision making by showing how a school would employ the procedures we have presented in the first two sections. Finally, we summarize the case for systematically monitoring progress and present needs for future research about curriculum-based measurement (CBM).

What Does Progress Monitoring Contribute to Making Data-Based Decisions?

This section establishes the background on making data-based decisions using progress-monitoring data. It provides a definition and description of progress monitoring; describes measures typically used for monitoring student performance; recounts historical and legal rationale for their use; and concludes by discussing logical and practical reasons that progress monitoring should be used by classroom teachers to inform instructional decisions and increase student achievement.

Progress monitoring is defined as the assessment of student academic performance on a regular basis using standardized, scientifically validated measurement tools (L. S. Fuchs & Fuchs, 2002). Although current teaching practices may include various assessments to monitor student understanding of curriculum and concepts, these assessment tools are often not scientifically validated, a crucial element of progress monitoring. To ensure the technical adequacy of progress monitoring, educators can administer CBM tools that have been scientifically validated and standardized for use across student populations.

CBM is "a simple set of procedures for repeated measurement of student growth toward long-range instructional goals" (Deno, 1985, p. 221). The cornerstones of CBM are threefold. First, it is simple and efficient for teachers to administer, because the measures that are administered (sometimes called *probes*) have standardized directions and most are 1 minute in duration. Second, CBM uses repeated measurement over time with standardized forms; although all probes differ, they are created at the same difficulty level and assess similar skills across time, which allows teachers to derive information that helps them to evaluate the progress of students, classes, schools, and districts over time. Third, and perhaps most important, because CBM tools for progress monitoring are repeated measures, individual student growth and progress can be monitored; teachers therefore can graph CBM results and use the data and graphs to make decisions about instructional programs and teaching methods for students (Deno, Fuchs, Marston, & Shin, 2001).

Uses of Progress Monitoring

CBM tools have been scientifically validated for use and have over 30 years of research support (L. S. Fuchs, 2004). CBM tools have been found to increase student achievement (L. S. Fuchs, Deno, & Mirkin, 1984; Stecker, Fuchs, & Fuchs, 2005), because teachers can identify when instructional changes are needed for individuals or groups of students in the classroom (L. S. Fuchs, Fuchs, & Hamlett, 1993). Graphed data provide an objective view of student performance and facilitate communication among teachers, students, and parents about student progress (M. R. Shinn, Habedank, & Good, 1993). CBM tools also have adequate predictive validity and can predict over time which students are likely to succeed on high-stakes assessments (Good, Simmons, & Kame'enui, 2001). CBM can reliably and validly designate which students are at risk or struggling in academic areas, leading teachers to have confidence in the assessment and easily intervene with these students to alter their academic trajectories.

CBM is used traditionally for two purposes: screening and progress monitoring. *Screening,* or *benchmarking,* refers to an assessment window in the fall, winter, and spring of each school year when all students are given CBM measures within a subject area to assess their current level of performance. These screening measures give teachers, school psychologists, and other educational specialists in the school environment data regarding where each student is performing in comparison to established national norms to determine which students are making effective progress and which students need further intervention strategies. For those students who fall below expected levels of performance, educators can implement progress monitoring using the same CBM measures to monitor academic growth (Brown-Chidsey & Steege, 2005).

Within the school setting, CBM data have many advantages for both students and teachers. Because some commercially available CBM tools have been standardized on thousands of students, progress monitoring can been used to estimate normative rates of student improvement (i.e., Aimsweb.com, dibels.uoregon.edu). This gives teachers an objective, standardized growth rate to determine if students are benefiting from typical classroom instruction (L. S. Fuchs & Fuchs, 2002). When teachers monitor students' performance on a regular basis, the students' performance can be compared either to the performance of a student in the same grade who is average performing or to the students' own past performance. These are the key ways that CBM data help teachers make data-based decisions: The data can be used to identify those students who are not progressing by comparing them with others and can be used to assess growth by comparing scores of the same individual over time. These decisions can be made relatively quickly, rather than waiting for students to fail, which increases the likelihood that interventions can be implemented early in elementary school, which leads to earlier remediation of deficits.

For students who are not benefiting from typical classroom instruction, progress monitoring can help determine their instructional needs or can help monitor the individualized education program (IEP) goals for students who are already in special education. A common source of confusion is the type of information that can be gathered from CBM tools. Because they are quick, general indicators of educational performance, CBM tools do not tell teachers specifically what skills should be taught to certain students. However, CBM tools do indicate reliably when specific children are struggling in a particular academic subject and when the current teaching strategies are not effective for those students and their needs. Teachers can then use various methods, such as follow-up assessments, diagnostic interviews, or error analysis, to make data-based decisions to alter their instructional practices for those students (M. R. Shinn, 1989, 1998).

After monitoring students' progress and objectively determining which students are not making adequate progress, teachers should implement research-based intervention strategies that are both quantitatively and qualitatively different from previous instruction to teach the academic skills. Many struggling students or students with IEPs need more instruction in certain areas, as well as teaching methods that differ from the standard curriculum. During intervention implementation, progress monitoring helps teachers assess the effectiveness of the instruction. This allows teachers to compare the efficacy of different forms of instruction, as well as to design more effective, individualized instructional programs for learners not making adequate progress (L. S. Fuchs & Fuchs, 2002). If it's working, keep doing it. If it's not working, try something else!

Historical, Legal, and Logical Basis for Progress Monitoring

To understand the need and momentum for the use of progress monitoring in the current educational system, it is imperative to examine the historical and legal basis for its use, as well as why it should be used from a logical standpoint. Within the empirical literature, numerous researchers have communicated the need for prevention and early intervention of academic problems (Juel, 1988; Francis, Shaywitz, Stuebing, Shaywitz, & Fletcher, 1996; L. M. Phillips, Norris, Osmond, & Maynard, 2002). Because many programs target children too late in the process, when academic problems have occurred for long periods, the chance of significant change is decreased. In contrast, early intervention programs not only target children when they are young, thus changing their developmental trajectories, but are also cost-effective for society as a whole (Weissberg, Kumpfer, & Seligman, 2003). This window of opportunity between the onset of concerns and later diagnoses of learning disabilities (LD) has forced schools, educators, and researchers to rethink their practices to identify and intervene with at-risk students effectively.

Historically, models of achievement and student progress assumed that students were progressing normally until otherwise noted, often using subjective feelings or instincts of the teacher to make decisions about student progress (Fletcher, Coulter, Reschly, & Vaughn, 2004). This model, often termed "wait to fail," did not provide students with intensive intervention until their academic achievement was significantly below that of their peers. Once this discrepancy occurred, students were diagnosed with LDs and given special education services to remediate their academic skills; however, this model of identification did not result in increased academic skills for these students generally, as many showed few gains and rarely exited special education services (Donovan & Cross, 2002; G. R. Lyon et al., 2001). For example, Chard and Kame'enui (2000) found that students who exhibit delayed reading achievement at the end of third grade show little significant reading

growth into eighth grade and beyond. This knowledge, which highlights the importance of early intervention and prevention, has compelled schools to use valid and reliable screening and progress-monitoring practices to identify problem learners as early as possible.

From a legal perspective, educational legislation such as No Child Left Behind (NCLB) (U.S. Department of Education, 2001) and the Individuals with Disabilities Education Improvement Act (IDEA; U.S. Department of Education, 2004) provides statutes and mandates regarding student achievement and data-based decision making, highlighting the need for and use of progress monitoring in the school setting. Two important mandates of the NCLB legislation are relevant to the use of progress monitoring: First, schools receiving federal funds must employ research-based practices to improve academic outcomes for all students. Second, schools and states must use progress-monitoring tools to ensure that academic programs and curricula are advantageous and effective in meeting the learning needs of students (Brown-Chidsey & Steege, 2005; U.S. Department of Education, 2001). Because monitoring progress with CBM measures is supported by years of research and can be used to monitor student progress toward academic goals, the practice is compatible with the requirements set forth by NCLB, making it a valuable approach employed by many schools around the country.

Within special education law, the 2004 revision of IDEA (IDEIA) defined an alternative approach regarding the procedures schools can use to identify students with LDs. Due to problems with the wait-to-fail model (Fletcher et al., 2004), RtI practices may be used to determine a student's eligibility for special education services (U.S. Department of Education, 2004). In a three-tiered RtI model, in Tier 1, schools must first use a research-based curriculum for all students, ensuring that teaching tools and practices are based on sound empirical research and all students have an opportunity to learn. Using data gathered from CBM screening measures administered to all students, those who are not performing at expected levels would be considered for Tier-2 services, indicating that alternative research-based interventions must supplement the classroom curriculum. Schools must evaluate how students respond to these interventions, with an emphasis placed on data-based decision making for instructional planning and education decision making. Using CBM tools, schools can monitor student progress effectively and determine if Tier-2 interventions are successful. For those students whose CBM data indicate that they have not benefited from the interventions, these data, along with other appropriate evidence, can be used to determine the presence of an LD and the need for intensive special education programming (Brown-Chidsey & Steege, 2005) or, in some cases, more intensive and specific intervention (Tier 3).

Beyond the legal impetus, progress monitoring has many logical, practical uses within the classroom setting. First, progress monitoring using CBM is both efficient and effective for teachers to compare rates of growth over time and has many advantages over other types of assessments. Typical classroom assessment relies on mastery measurement, which focuses on the mastery of single skills throughout the year. These tests are often lengthy to administer and are not administered regularly, as students often take end-of-unit tests or quizzes to determine if they have mastered skills taught within the curriculum. This type of assessment does not offer immediate feedback to the teacher. For example, if students take an end-of-unit test after a month of instruction, and approximately 50% of the class did not master the material, the teacher has not obtained these data until the unit is over. In addition, it is difficult to compare scores and progress over time using these assessments, because different skills are assessed by each assessment. Most importantly, these commonly used assessments are rarely scientifically validated or technically adequate, making it difficult for teachers to understand how trustworthy the test is in assessing student achievement (L. S. Fuchs & Deno, 1991; L. S. Fuchs & Fuchs, 2002). Progress monitoring overcomes many of these deficits: It is efficient and easy for teachers to administer to assess student progress; its reliability and validity have been established; the data can be analyzed to adjust student goals and instructional programs; and the data can be used to assess growth over time, as well as to compare student performance to typically performing peers.

Summary

CBM tools have important uses in general and special education, helping to improve the academic achievement of students at risk of developing academic problems as well as those with identified academic disabilities. Progress monitoring has been developed as a way to improve on historical assessment methods, satisfy educational and legal requirements, and inform teachers regarding student performance to help make instructional decisions based on objective data. CBM tools used for monitoring student progress are reliable and valid. In particular, they have predictive validity. For example, progress-monitoring tools measuring early literacy skills have been found to be predictive of later reading performance, leading teachers to make informed decisions about students at risk of later academic failure (Deno, 2003; Good et al., 2001). Most importantly, research indicates that progress monitoring improves student performance, teaching practices, and instructional decisions (Stecker et al., 2005). When teachers use progress monitoring, they can make better decisions regarding students in

need of different instructional programs and design programs that meet the unique learning needs of students (L. S. Fuchs & Fuchs, 2002).

What Does Research Say About Using CBM in Reading and Mathematics?

As mentioned previously, using CBM for progress monitoring has been well researched for over 30 years. Monitoring progress using CBM demonstrates student growth throughout a school year of instruction in general education classrooms or can be used to evaluate intervention support provided in addition to general education or as part of special education. CBM measures have been developed in academic areas including reading, mathematics, spelling, and written expression, at both the elementary and secondary levels. To date, the preponderance of the research has been done in the areas of reading and mathematics. Although CBM research in reading is extensive, research about CBM of mathematics is gaining significant attention in recent years as federal mandates and statewide assessment requirements have heightened the need for appropriate methods to measure progress over an academic year. Reading and mathematics are the academic areas where students struggle the most, so it makes sense to make them the focal point of this chapter. However, it is important to recognize that, while not the focus of this chapter, much research has been done in other academic areas such as spelling (Deno, Mirkin, Lowry, & Kuehnle, 1980; M. R. Shinn & Marston, 1985; M. R. Shinn, Ysseldyke, Deno, & Tindal, 1986; Tindal, Germann, & Deno, 1983), written expression (Deno, Marston, & Mirkin, 1982; Espin, Wallace, Campbell, Lembke, Long, & Ticha, 2008; Gansle, Noell, VanDerHeyden, Naquin, & Slider, 2002; Marston, 1989; Tindal & Parker, 1991; Espin, De La Paz, Scierka, & Roelofs, 2005), and the content areas such as science and social studies (Espin, Busch, Shin, & Kruschwitz, 2001; Espin, Shin, & Busch, 2005; Tindal & Nolet, 1995).

The technical adequacy of CBM measures for monitoring progress provides teachers and administrators with confidence in measuring students' growth over time by accurately indicating how students, and particularly those students who are academically at risk, are progressing over time. Tindal and Parker (1991) identified four markers that educators can use to assess the technical adequacy of effective assessment procedures. The markers, or criteria, and a brief description of each include (a) consistent administration and reliable scoring methods (teachers use the same directions, time students for the same length of time, and score in the same manner); (b) the ability to discriminate the performance or skill levels of a diverse range of students (the measures provide information about students who are achieving above, on, and below grade level); (c) criterion validity in relation to other validated forms of assessment (the measures compare favorably to other common academic assessments in reading or mathematics); and (d) sensitivity to change (especially growth) in student performance (the measures can be used to monitor growth for even those students who are growing very slowly). Once these technically adequate measures are identified, the most important and useful part of CBM is teacher use of the graphed data to inform changes that might be necessary in instruction. This continued attention to data and use of data-based decision making is what leads to improved student outcomes. In the following sections, we detail examples of research that support progress monitoring in reading and mathematics.

Technical Adequacy in Reading

In this section, we briefly describe some of the CBM progress-monitoring measures that are available in the most prominently researched areas in reading, including oral reading, early literacy measures, and maze. Early research examining CBM validity in reading focused on determining criterion validity of potential CBM measures such as oral reading fluency (ORF; Marston, 1989). Deno, Mirkin, and Chiang (1982) discovered that listening to students read aloud from basal readers for 1 minute was a valid indicator of reading proficiency. Correlation coefficients between ORF and scores on standardized reading measures ranged from 0.73 to 0.91 with the majority of coefficients over 0.80. Since then, other studies have assessed the criterion validity of ORF for both screening and progress monitoring, with coefficients ranging from 0.63 to 0.90 and most above 0.80 (Burke & Hagen-Burke, 2007; L. S. Fuchs, Fuchs, & Maxwell, 1988; L. S. Fuchs, Tindal, & Deno, 1984; Marston, 1982; Tindal, Fuchs, Fuchs, Shinn, Deno, & Germann, 1983). The technical adequacy of CBM measures for first through sixth grade have been well documented in the literature (L. S. Fuchs et al., 1984: L. S. Fuchs & Deno, 1994; M. R. Shinn, Good, Knutson, Tilly, & Collins, 1992; Tindal, 1992).

Given that reading proficiency is critical for academic success, it is important that CBM provide useful information to teachers when they assess progress of their students as they move from pre-literacy skills toward reading competence. M. K. Hosp and Fuchs (2005) examined the relationship between CBM and specific reading progression as a function of grade. They administered CBM reading passages and the Word Attack, Word Identification, and Passage Comprehension subtests of the Woodcock Reading Mastery Test—Revised

(Woodcock, 1987) to 310 participants distributed equally across grades 1 to 4. M. K. Hosp and Fuchs (2005) reported that comparisons across grades for CBM and word reading were highest for grades 1, 2, and 3 compared to fourth grade. The overall results support the notion that CBM assesses different skills across grade levels, and that these skills are aligned with the tenets of instruction that are germane to each grade.

The Dynamic Indicators of Basic Early Literacy (DIBELS; Good & Kaminski, 2007) is also a validated CBM instrument for assessing early literacy. DIBELS is designed for use in early identification of reading difficulties and monitoring progress among elementary students. DIBELS assesses proficiency of a set of early literacy skills identified in the literature as directly related to and foundational for subsequent reading proficiency. Young students' knowledge of letters, phonemic awareness, and sound–symbol relationships in kindergarten have all been identified as important predictors of later literacy proficiency (J. Elliott, Lee, & Tollefson, 2001).

J. Elliott et al. (2001) examined the technical adequacy of four selected DIBELS measures (Letter Naming Fluency, Sound Naming Fluency, Initial Phoneme Ability, and Phoneme Segmentation) for identifying kindergarteners who were at risk for reading difficulties. Seventy-five kindergarteners from four classrooms in three elementary schools in a moderate-sized Midwestern city participated in the study. Elliott and colleagues obtained three types of reliability: inter-rater, test–retest, and alternate form. All reliability coefficients with the exception of Initial Phoneme Ability were 0.80 or higher. Criterion validity received strict scrutiny, which was obtained by correlating "level" estimates (average scores over repeated administration) of the DIBELS measures with (a) the Broad Reading and Skills clusters of the Woodcock Johnson Psycho-Educational Achievement Battery—Revised (WJ-R; Woodcock & Johnson, 1990); (b) the Test of Phonological Awareness (Torgesen & Bryant, 1994); (c) Teacher Rating Questionnaire (Share, Jorm, MacLean, & Matthews, 1984); (d) the Developing Skills Checklist (Clark, 1995); and (e) the Kaufman Brief Intelligence Test (Prewitt, 1992). The DIBELS measures demonstrated the strongest correlations with scores on the Skills Cluster of the WJ-R and the Developing Skills Checklist, with coefficients that ranged from 0.44 to 0.81.

To provide further insight into the relationships between the DIBELS measures and the WJ-R, J. Elliott et al. (2001) conducted hierarchical regression analysis with all analyses statistically significant ($p < 0.01$). Across all analyses, Letter Naming Fluency was the single best predictor of kindergarten achievement scores on the Broad Reading and Skills clusters of the WJ-R and the teacher ratings of student's reading proficiency. This study was particularly important because it examined the technical adequacy of DIBELS measures by increasing the sample size and diversity of participants.

A measure that has been developed and used as a progress-monitoring tool for secondary students is the maze task (L. S. Fuchs & Fuchs, 1992; Espin, Wallace, Lembke, Campbell, & Long, 2010). The maze task is a silent reading task that can be group administered. Students read through a passage in which every seventh word is deleted and replaced with the correct word and three distracters. Students circle the word that they feel makes sense in the sentence. The number that is recorded is the number of correct choices circled in the time limit. At the elementary level, correlations between the maze task and reading comprehension and broad reading scores from standardized tests range from 0.80 to 0.89 (Jenkins & Jewell, 1993; L. S. Fuchs & Fuchs, 1992). At the secondary level, Espin et al. examined the relation between performance on the CBM measures and a state reading test with validity coefficients above 0.70 and reported substantial and significant growth over time for a subset of students ($n = 31$).

Evidence supports the technical adequacy of CBM in reading for monitoring progress of all readers, but especially those who may be at risk of reading failure or struggling with attaining reading proficiency. CBM provides teachers, school psychologists, and administrators with a valuable tool necessary to implement tiered interventions for improving the reading levels of their students. In addition, CBM has been suggested for use in screening and monitoring the progress of students who may have difficulties in mathematics.

Technical Adequacy in Mathematics

With the growing attention that student achievement in mathematics has been receiving, the development of methods for monitoring student progress in mathematics has garnered increased attention among researchers. In a review of the use of CBM in reading and mathematics and subsequent gains in student achievement, Stecker et al. (2005) suggest that, overall, CBM leads to significant gains in student achievement. Achievement is particularly enhanced when CBM data are paired with decision-making rules, skills-focused feedback, and suggestions for instructional changes. Foegen, Jiban, and Deno (2007) reviewed literature regarding progress monitoring in mathematics. Of the studies included in the review, 17 were for elementary mathematics, while four were conducted in early mathematics and four in secondary mathematics. Research on early mathematics was centered exclusively on measures of numeracy and used participants from the general education classroom, a potential benefit when considering validity and reliability of progress monitoring in math for use in an RtI model. Although researchers have found that ORF and scores on standardized reading tests are highly correlated (0.80–0.90; Deno, Mirkin, et al., 1982), Foegen and colleagues (2007) reported that correlations between CBM mathematics measures across grade levels and criterion validity measures are generally moderate (in the 0.50–0.70 range). It is important to note that these coefficients are similar to the coefficients of many commercial achievement tests of mathematics. Commonly used CBM measures in the studies review by Foegen et al. (2007) included number identification, quantity discrimination, computation, concepts and applications, and word-problem–solving measures.

In the area of early numeracy, Lembke and Foegen (2009) conducted a preliminary investigation into the potential of four early numeracy CBM measures [Number Identification (identifying a number between 1 and 100), Quantity Array (naming the numerical amount after looking at a pattern of dots), Missing Number (identifying a missing number from a pattern of 3 numbers and a blank), and Quantity Discrimination (orally saying the larger of two numbers)] for use in screening students who may have difficulties in early math skills. This foundational study assessed over 300 kindergarten and first-grade students in two states to evaluate the technical adequacy of the measures by administering the four measures three times during the school year. Alternate-form reliability coefficients were strong (0.80–0.90), except for Missing Number in kindergarten at all three administrations. Concurrent criterion validity and predictive validity coefficients with standardized early mathematics tests and teacher ratings were obtained and were varied according to the measure and the grade level. The strongest coefficients for both grades for criterion validity were found in Quantity Discrimination (8 of 13 correlations in the moderate, 0.50–0.66, range) and Missing Number (9 of 13 correlations in the moderate to strong, 0.54–0.75, range), with coefficients generally stronger in first grade. Predictive validity coefficients were strongest for Number Identification (3 of 4 coefficients in the 0.58–0.64 range) and Missing Number (3 of 4 coefficients in the 0.67–0.70 range). The findings indicated that Number Identification, Missing Number, and Quantity Discrimination possessed sufficient technical adequacy to be useful tools for teachers to identify young students who struggle with early math content. Quantity Array did not meet the threshold for technical strength and was subsequently dropped from future examinations (Lembke & Foegen, 2009). These results provide an encouraging springboard for continued examination to determine the utility of these measures for use in screening and monitoring the progress of young students in early mathematics skills.

In an extension of the previous study, Lembke, Foegen, Whittaker, and Hampton (2008) examined the technical adequacy of the Number Identification, Missing Number, and Quantity Discrimination measures to monitor the progress of kindergarten and first-grade students over time. Hierarchical Linear Modeling was used at each grade level to determine the ability of the three measures to model growth over time, an important component of determining technical adequacy for use as progress-monitoring tools. All measures produced growth rates that were significant across time for both grade levels, but linear growth was observed only for Number Identification. Growth rates varied from a low of 0.11 items per week increase for Missing Number in grade 1 to 0.34 items per week for Number Identification in kindergarten. Students grew the most on the Number Identification measure. The findings from this study have implications for teachers as they consider which measures might be used for progress monitoring, in that measures such as Missing Number and Quantity Discrimination that have nonlinear growth might produce student graphs that show variable performance or that do not always capture student growth that is being made. More research is needed on the use of these early numeracy measures across weeks, and up-to-date technical reports can be found on progressmonitoring.org.

Although research examining progress monitoring in mathematics using the general education population yields significant information beneficial for future use within the tiered intervention system of RtI, it is still important to consider the utility of monitoring the progress of students with LDs in mathematics. Many students with LDs experience pervasive difficulties mastering even the most basic mathematical concepts (Owens & Fuchs, 2002). E. S. Shapiro, Edwards, and Zigmond (2005) reported findings from a state-wide project that provided weekly progress monitoring for 120 students (104 elementary students and 16 middle school students) in special education classes. All of the participants were monitored in mathematics computation, and 109 were additionally monitored in concepts and applications. Results showed that weekly growth rates of 0.38 digits per week for computation, and 0.38 points for concepts and applications, were obtained by participants, rates of growth that are similar to the growth rates found in general education settings. These results provide additional evidence (see Stecker et al., 2005, for a brief summary of earlier work in mathematics) for considering CBM mathematics measures as an appropriate tool for examining the progress of students who receive services in special education environments.

L. S. Fuchs et al. (2007) examined both screening and progress monitoring using CBM by following 225 students from first grade to the end of second grade.

They assessed Number Identification/Counting (writing the final two numbers in a five-number sequence), Fact Retrieval (addition and subtraction single-digit fact fluency on paper), Computation (solving mixed computation facts with 2 to 3 digits), and Concepts/Applications (solving applied types of problems, e.g., graphs, more/less than, and fractions on paper). Number Identification/Counting and CBM Computation were also administered weekly for 27 weeks in order to test technical adequacy for use in progress monitoring. Results indicated CBM Concepts/Applications was the best predictor of two outcome measures administered in the spring of second grade: the WRAT 3-Arithmetic (Wilkinson, 1993) and Jordan's Story Problems (Jordan & Hanich, 2000). Results also showed that CBM computation demonstrated validity for use in monitoring progress, and Number Identification/Counting did not meet the technical adequacy standards created by the authors.

Monitoring progress in mathematics using (a) computation and (b) concepts and applications measures is an important step to improving student achievement in mathematics (Foegen, Jiban, & Deno, 2007; Stecker et al., 2005), yet students are quickly expected to apply mathematics knowledge on word problems. Word problems require students to integrate their mathematical competence with adequate levels of reading comprehension. Jitendra, Sczesniak, and Deatline-Buchman (2005) examined CBM mathematical word-problem–solving tasks for use as indicators of mathematics proficiency for 77 third graders in the winter and spring of the school year. Specifically, the study assessed the reliability and concurrent and predictive validity of word-problem–solving CBM measures. Results indicated that these CBM measures were technically adequate as indicators of mathematics proficiency of third graders with internal consistency reliability coefficients ranging from 0.76 to 0.83 using the means of two forms and mostly moderate criterion validity coefficients (7 of 8 in the 0.58–0.71 range).

Students in school encounter increasingly complex computation and conceptual tasks as they enter middle and secondary school. Therefore, it is important to identify technically adequate measures to assess student proficiency in the middle school grades. Foegen and Deno (2001) studied the technical adequacy of potential math indicators of growth in the middle school. They gave 100 students four mathematics measures (one involved basic facts, and three involved the concept of estimation) twice in a 1-week period. Results indicated that the measures were reliable: Test–retest reliability coefficients calculated using the mean of two forms ranged from 0.80 to 0.88. Results also indicated that the levels of criterion validity were adequate, with 7 of 8 coefficients in the moderate (0.44–0.63) range with standardized mathematics tests. These measures therefore may be useful as indicators of mathematics competence for children in middle school.

The Effects of CBMs on Students' Outcomes

The evaluation of technical adequacy is an important foundational step in assessing a measurement system's utility for implementation in schools and classrooms. But it is only a part of the equation; one must also consider the benefits for students when using any instructional, assessment, or intervention program for students. All educators and administrators should apply the test of whether a program can demonstrate the ability to improve student outcomes. Monitoring progress using CBM has a large body of evidence to support its ability to improve the outcomes of students in reading and mathematics, but only when teachers use the data to make instructional decisions (Stecker et al., 2005).

The original intent of CBM was to provide educators with technically adequate, easy-to-use data that document student proficiency and growth over a period of time (Stecker et al., 2005). The overriding premise of CBM is that by employing these trustworthy data about student proficiency, a teacher can ultimately improve academic outcomes for students. In their review of literature on the utility of CBM in improving student achievement, Stecker et al. found that CBM produced significant gains in student achievement that were associated with using systematic data-based decision rules, skills analysis checklists, and instructional recommendations for making program modifications.

L. S. Fuchs, Fuchs, and Hamlett (1989) explored the value of CBM in planning effective reading programs and reported that students who were exposed to both assessment using CBM and evaluation of instructional programming performed better than a control group exposed to the assessment program only. In a variation on this research, Fuchs and colleagues (L. S. Fuchs, Fuchs, Hamlett, Phillips, & Bentz, 1994) explored the effectiveness of class-wide decision-making structures within the general education mathematics classroom. They found the students of teachers who used CBM and received instructional recommendations designed to better instructional programming realized greater achievement than peers in the classrooms of teachers who just collected the CBM data. In one of many studies addressing the utility of the use of DIBELS measures to improve student outcomes in early reading skills, Baker and Smith (1999, 2001) found that introducing teachers to using DIBELS data and helping them focus on early decoding competence resulted in improved student

performance on a wide array of measures of basic reading achievement.

Spicuzza et al. (2001) studied whether implementing an instructional management system that included CBM in mathematics would result in positive changes in the classroom environment and, subsequently, improvement in student achievement. They found that implementing progress monitoring can be beneficial to student math achievement, as evidenced by a positive effect on the math achievement growth demonstrated by students on two math achievement assessments. Some of the mathematics studies detailed earlier also provide evidence of the utility of CBM in mathematics as useful tools for improving student outcomes (L. S. Fuchs et al., 2007; E. S. Shapiro et al., 2005). These studies were preceded by work by L. S. Fuchs, Fuchs, Hamlett, and Stecker (1990) that experimentally contrasted teachers' use of CBM with and without skills analysis with teachers in a control group who did not use CBM. The students in the CBM with skills-analysis group performed better on a computation assessment. In another experimental study (Stecker & Fuchs, 2000), students with mild-to-moderate disabilities were matched on mathematics ability and were progress monitored twice weekly. Teachers made instructional decisions for one group of CBM students based on their CBM graphs. Teachers incorporated these changes for the matched partner at the same time. After 20 weeks, all students had grown significantly in mathematics, but those students whose teachers made changes based specifically on the students' CBM graphs grew the most.

Summary

Over the past 30 years, an extensive body of evidence has been amassed that lends support for the validity and reliability of CBM measures as screening and progress-monitoring tools in reading and math. The Research Institute on Progress Monitoring (Espin & Wallace, 2004) identified 141 studies in which technical adequacy and instructional utility were examined. This extensive literature base has served to extend CBM beyond its initial focus on special education progress monitoring to now include universal screening, general education progress monitoring, and LD classification within an RtI framework (L. S. Fuchs, 2004). Further empirical support has been established to link the use of CBM for screening and monitoring progress with improved student outcomes, the primary goal of education at the classroom, school, district, state, and national level. Strengths of the CBM literature are its breadth across time, student type, subject area, and grade level. One specific research need is the use of more sophisticated statistical analysis, although this has been increasing since the early 2000s (e.g., see Hintze, Christ, & Keller, 2002).

Recommended Practices for Using CBM Progress-Monitoring Tools

As detailed in the previous sections, progress monitoring using CBM is an excellent tool to monitor the progress of general education students who are at risk for academic problems or students who already have been found eligible for and are receiving special education services in reading, math, or both. Several elements are critical for teachers to address or put into place as they prepare to implement a system of CBM progress monitoring (Deno, 1985, 2003). These elements include selecting technically adequate measures, organizing materials, scheduling, monitoring reliability of implementation and scoring, graphing data, establishing data-decision rules, making decisions based on a student's graphed data, implementing instructional changes, and continued monitoring. These critical elements for CBM progress monitoring are also summarized in a checklist in Figure 3.1. To illustrate, in the next section, we present the case of a reading specialist, Mrs. Adams, as she and her colleagues work through these elements.

Figure 3.1   Critical elements for implementation of progress monitoring using curriculum-based measurement.

Date Completed	Element	Notes
	1. Select technically adequate measures.	
	2. Complete school-wide screening.	
	3. Select students for progress monitoring using decision-making rules.	
	4. Organize materials.	
	5. Develop a schedule.	
	6. Graph data, including goal setting.	
	7. Monitor reliability of implementation and scoring.	
	8. Make decisions based on a student's graphed data.	
	9. Implement instructional changes.	
	10. Continue monitoring.	

Case Study

Selecting Technically Adequate Measures

It is important to choose measures that are technically adequate. Publishers should provide reports on the reliability and validity of the measures that they are promoting, and teachers who are selecting measures should ask about these important technical features. It is important to know that not just any measures can serve as CBM progress measures. The measures need to have been studied and found to function as reliable indicators of both short- and long-term progress.

Mrs. Adams is working with members of her school team to choose measures for monitoring the progress of the students at risk for reading failure in their school. The team wants to identify measures that have been deemed reliable and valid, but they are also on a tight budget in their district, so they do not have a lot of money to spend. They consult a tools checklist available from the National Center for RtI (rti4success.org) and find measures that fit both of their needs—technically adequate and cost-effective. Because this is the school's first experience with establishing a system of progress monitoring, and because they will monitor reading only, they decide to use the DIBELS measures (Good & Kaminski, 2007). The DIBELS are free for use (if consumers do not purchase the online data management) and also have convincing evidence for use as progress measures on the National Center for RtI's progress-monitoring tools chart. This evidence is provided for reliability and validity of the measures and also for other areas such as reliability of students' slopes over time (the measures demonstrate students' growth consistently over time) and for whether benchmark scores are provided (in this case, for DIBELS, they are). This is a much better method of selecting measures than choosing something that has unknown technical adequacy or developing one's own measures.

School-Wide Screening and Selecting Students for Progress Monitoring

Once the school team has chosen the measures that they will use, the next step is to identify the students who are at risk for or have reading problems and therefore need ongoing progress monitoring. Members of the school problem-solving team (PS team) complete a school-wide benchmarking—meaning that they assess all students in the school using the recommended DIBELS measures for that time of year for that grade. This takes about 10 to 15 minutes per student. These data are entered into an electronic spreadsheet, and students' scores are categorized based on whether they are meeting or not meeting the published and established DIBELS scores for that particular time of year (benchmark scores based on data from all students who have completed the measures at that time of year across the country). Then the PS team meets to examine the data and determine which students are most in need of additional reading help. The students are grouped into tiered levels based on the national norms of the system that the team selected. After looking at the data, PS team members meet with grade-level teams to discuss the data and any students who the teachers feel should or should not be included in progress monitoring and intervention. Because the screening data are reliable and valid, teachers have confidence in the results. However, if teachers have alternative, quantitative classroom data that support placement or nonplacement in intervention, the team also considers those data. If the PS team questions whether a student who is under consideration for intervention needs intervention at this time, the team can schedule a period of progress monitoring before intervention to confirm or disconfirm placement (see Compton, Fuchs, Fuchs, & Bryant, 2006, for one example of a discussion on identifying students for various tiers in an RtI model).

Essentially, the grade-level teams, with assistance from members of the PS team, meet to review screening data and to make determinations about who should receive intervention. These decisions are based primarily on the normative data that group students according to risk status. Mrs. Adams works primarily with students who are at risk for problems but are not in special education. The grade-level and PS teams identify 10 students following screening with whom Mrs. Adams will work during intervention time.

Scheduling, Organizing Materials, Graphing, and Goal Setting

The next steps for teachers implementing the intervention program are logistical in nature—organizing materials and scheduling a time to monitor students' progress. Mrs. Adams works with classroom teachers to schedule times when she will provide reading intervention to the 10 students with whom she works. She wants to meet with the students every day for at least 30 minutes. Because of careful negotiation and planning, the principal at the school has built intervention time into each grade-level schedule, so scheduling is easy. Mrs. Adams's students have very low scores, so the PS team and Mrs. Adams have decided to monitor their progress once per week. Mrs. Adams determines the grade level of the materials that she will use for each child's assessment. For two of the students, this is their grade level, but for the others, Mrs. Adams monitors progress in out-of-grade-level material. She prepares a folder for each student with all of the progress-monitoring probes, as well as a chart to keep track of scores for each student. For the two students being monitored at grade level, their long-range goals are grade-level goals; that is, the target level of ORF is the reading rate typical of students at that grade level. For the students monitored on out-of-grade-level material, Mrs. Adams sets long-range goals according to end-of-year criteria for their instructional levels; this means the target ORF is the reading rate typical for students completing the grade of the materials they are reading.

Regardless of whether students are assessed on materials at or below their grade level, Mrs. Adams adds lines to the graph for each of her students based on her long-range goals for them. To do this she either uses long-range benchmarks that are published as part of the DIBELS system (and are reported for other Web-based systems as well) or she uses a weekly growth rate (i.e., one word growth per week, multiplied by the number of weeks that she will be progress monitoring). The students' median score from the school-wide screening serves as the starting point for the goal line. If the student is being monitored on out-of-grade-level material, three progress-monitoring measures at the student's instructional level are administered, and the starting point is set using the median score from these three measures. The goal line connects this starting level and the long-range benchmark that has been determined for each student.

A sample progress-monitoring graph for one of Mrs. Adams's students, Sonia, is shown in Figure 3.2. Sonia is in fourth grade but is being progress monitored at the third-grade level. Mrs. Adams gives three third-grade passages to Sonia on one day, and her scores are 44, 55, and 66 words read correctly. Mrs. Adams graphs the data and labels it as baseline data. Sonia's median score is 55, so this is the starting point for the goal line for Sonia. The benchmark level for the spring in DIBELS for third grade is a minimum of 110 words read correctly in 1 minute, so Mrs. Adams used 110 as the end point for the goal line.

Figure 3.2 Sample curriculum-based measurement progress-monitoring graph with goal line showing weekly data for Mrs. Adams's student Sonia.

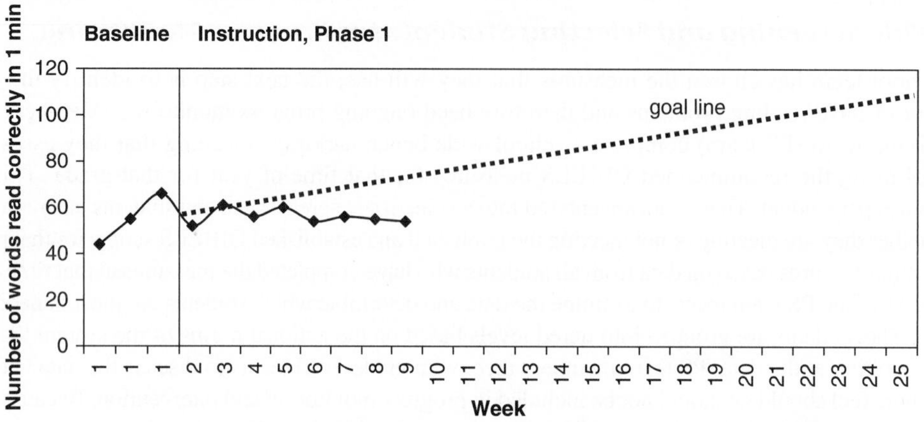

Mrs. Adams decides to assess two students each day. Using this schedule will allow her to have weekly assessments of each of her 10 students. She will score the assessments and enter the data into a computer after the students have left the 30-minute intervention session. The system that the school is using for screening and progress monitoring has a graphing feature, so as Mrs. Adams enters the data, the software creates graphs for each student. Periodically, Mrs. Adams prints these graphs so that she can view them and use the data to make instructional decisions.

Monitoring Reliability of Implementation and Scoring

Before beginning school-wide screening and individual progress monitoring, all school staff members received training on administration of the measures, and they also scored measures as a group to assess the reliability of the scoring. As the year progresses, the PS team recognizes that inconsistencies in administering or scoring the data may have occurred because of lack of review. Members of the team work with each grade level to set up a system of reliability checks; either a grade-level colleague or a PS-team member observes administration and checks scoring as progress monitoring is implemented. A sample administration checklist for CBM ORF is provided in Figure 3.3. As needed, teachers review procedures for administration and scoring at all staff meetings. More detail about scoring procedures for both reading and mathematics measures are provided in administration manuals that are provided with each CBM system (in this case, DIBELS).

Making Decisions Based on a Student's Data

As mentioned previously, the most important aspect of progress monitoring is teacher use of the data, and Mrs. Adams knows that if she wants to see significant growth in her students, she needs to put research-based interventions into place and then assess the effects of those interventions on an ongoing basis. To make the decisions, the teams need to examine data for individual students. Mrs. Adams looks at her students' graphs on a weekly basis and, at least every 6 weeks, she takes student graphs to the appropriate grade-level team meetings for discussion. Using previously established decision-making rules, the teams assess each student's progress. The grade-level team and Mrs. Adams examine the trend of each child's data as compared to the goal line that was set. If the trend line is steeper than the goal line, the teachers consider raising the goal. If the trend line is not as steep as the goal line, they consider changing the intervention they are providing. Decisions are also based on how long the intervention has been in place, with what intensity it has been delivered (student engagement, for instance), whether the intervention is research-based, and with what fidelity the intervention has been implemented. A sample decision-making rubric like the one Mrs. Adams's school uses is included in Figure 3.4. This rubric uses suggested decision-making rules as described in presentations conducted and materials developed by the National Center on Student Progress Monitoring (studentprogress.org), with Lynn and Doug Fuchs as the primary authors. Teams might use the rubric by making determinations about where a student's data fall on each row of the rubric (decision-making rule, class work, behavior, and other). Decisions are listed across the top of the rubric, and the column where the majority of indicators are circled gives teams a suggestion regarding what decision should be made for a student at that time.

When the team examines Sonia's graph and applies the four-point rule (examination of the last four consecutive points in comparison to the goal line), the last four consecutive points are all below the goal line. So in the first row

Figure 3.3   Administration checklist for administration of curriculum-based measurement oral reading fluency aloud.

Administrator _____

Rater _____

Date _____

	Yes	No
1. Presentation of materials		
a. Places student copy in front of the student.	_____	_____
b. Places examiner copy out of view of the student.	_____	_____
2. Reads directions		
a. Reads directions correctly.	_____	_____
b. Demonstrates by pointing when appropriate.	_____	_____
c. Gives appropriate prompts for correct/incorrect examples.	_____	_____
d. Pauses for questions.	_____	_____
3. Timing		
a. Says "begin."	_____	_____
b. Starts/stops timer at the correct times.	_____	_____
c. Times student for 1 minute.	_____	_____
d. Marks student answers on administrator copy.	_____	_____
e. Puts a bracket after the last word said.	_____	_____

Source: Information from Deno, S. L., & Mirkin, P. K. (1977). *Data-based program modification: A manual.* Reston, VA: Council for Exceptional Children.

of the rubric where decision-making rules are applied, the team selects "Trend of data or last four consecutive data points are below the goal line for the past 6 weeks." If the team had access to (or wanted to draw in) a trend line for Sonia's data, they could compare the trend line to the goal line to help make their decision. In the second row, class work is addressed. Mrs. Adams has work samples available, and she had graphed Sonia's scores on weekly reading assignments. Sonia's scores on these classroom assignments clearly are decreasing, so the team circles "Classroom work samples and assessment data indicate that the student is making progress, but not at the expected rate" in the second row of the rubric. In the third row of the rubric, student behavior is addressed. Mrs. Adams feels that Sonia's frustration has been increasingly more evident in class, because she has been delaying starting assignments after they are given, and she has a 70% homework completion rate. This information indicates to the team that on the behavior row of the rubric, they should circle "Inappropriate classroom behaviors are escalating due to frustration with academic performance." Given that two of the three indicators are underneath the decision heading "Student should stay in a tier, and an instructional change should be made," the team determines that at this point, an instructional change needs to be implemented. However, before making the final decision, the team discusses important questions regarding intervention intensity, research base, duration, and fidelity, as detailed in the second part of the rubric.

Implementing Instructional Changes and Continued Monitoring

As the year continues, CBM graphs indicate that several of the progress-monitored students are on track to meet their goals in Mrs. Adams's class, whereas other students are not making adequate progress toward their goal and therefore need changes in their instructional regimens. Based on applying the decision-making rubric to each student's data, Mrs. Adams works with each grade-level team and consults diagnostic data to determine what changes need to be implemented. For Sonia this is just a small refinement of her current intervention plan. This small refinement is made because Sonia's data indicate another change is needed, but Sonia's trend of data is not very far below her graphed goal line. For another student, Mrs. Adams significantly changes the intervention, incorporating a much more explicit and systematic instructional program, because this student's data are far below where the team would expect it to be, given that the student is already receiving intervention. Mrs. Adams uses diagnostic data

Figure 3.4 Decision-making rubric for evaluating student progress and planning intervention.

Decision-making rubric—to be implemented at least every 6 weeks

Three questions to guide discussion on data at problem-solving team meetings:

1. What is the student's goal? Current level?

2. What decision-making rule are we using (four-point; trend; rubric)? Can we apply that now?

3. If a change needs to be made, what do we do?

FIRST, to make a decision on movement/nonmovement between tiers, the following rubric should be applied:

Student should move to a more intensive tier.	Student should stay in a tier, and an instructional change should be made.	Student should stay in a tier with no changes.	Student should be moved to a less intensive tier.
Trend of data or last four consecutive data points are below the goal line for the past 6 weeks, and when the student was checked 6 weeks prior.	Trend of data or last four consecutive data points are below the goal line for the past 6 weeks.	Trend of data or last four consecutive data points are even with the goal line.	Trend of data or last four consecutive data points are above the goal line.
Classroom work samples and assessment data indicate that the student is not making progress in the current curriculum, even after a change has been made.	Classroom work samples and assessment data indicate that the student is making progress, but not at the expected rate.	Classroom work samples and assessment data indicate that the student is making adequate or expected progress.	Classroom work samples and assessment data indicate that the student is making excellent progress and it does not appear that the intervention may be needed.
Inappropriate classroom behaviors are escalating due to frustration with academic performance.	Frustration is evident, although this has not yet manifested in inappropriate classroom behaviors.	Classroom behavior and frustration with academic assignments is status quo or has improved.	Classroom behavior has improved, and frustration is less evident.
Other (i.e. attendance)? Needs to be quantifiable data.	Other (i.e. attendance)? Needs to be quantifiable data.	Other (i.e. attendance)? Needs to be quantifiable data.	Other (i.e. attendance)? Needs to be quantifiable data.

SECOND, if a change needs to be made, the team questions:

1. Has the instruction/intervention been as **intense** as it could be?

    a. Teacher/student ratio, curriculum used, time engaged

2. Has the instruction/intervention been delivered with **fidelity**?

    a. Implementation reports are provided by the teacher, or someone has observed implementation.

3. Is the instruction/intervention **research-based**?

    a. References are provided, or someone has checked on this.

4. Has the **duration** of the instruction been lengthy enough?

    a. Does the team feel that lack of results is due to not having the intervention in place long enough?

Note: This rubric uses suggested decision-making rules as described in presentations conducted and materials developed by the National Center on Student Progress Monitoring (studentprogress.org), with Lynn and Doug Fuchs as the primary authors.

from assessments like running records and teacher-made checklists in her classroom to help determine intervention refinement or selection. Mrs. Adams documents changes on the students' graphs and continues to collect, graph, and examine progress-monitoring data to assess the effects of these changes. When students reach their goals, she sets aside time for a celebration.

Summary

Progress monitoring using CBM is a research-based technique that helps teachers to determine how students are performing compared to national norms or compared to past student performance. Graphed data present a picture of student progress over time and provide teachers with information about whether instruction or intervention is effective for students. Progress monitoring can be conducted in academic areas such as reading and mathematics, and the technical adequacy of measures in both areas has been documented. Measures are available for early elementary, upper elementary, and secondary students, with the largest body of research conducted with elementary students. Progress-monitoring systems have been studied with students who are average achieving or at risk, as well as students who have IEPs.

Teachers who use progress-monitoring systems determine which students in the school are at risk for academic problems through a screening process and then schedule a progress-monitoring routine for those students. The teacher sets a goal for each student and then monitors each student's progress on a frequent basis, graphing and visually examining the data. At least every 6 weeks, the teacher should meet with a grade-level or PS team to share the student's graph and make decisions about future instruction using decision-making rules. Finally, the progress-monitoring regimen should continue as long as the student continues to be deemed at risk. The teacher should continue to examine the graph showing the student's progress on a frequent basis to determine whether instruction needs to be altered or whether it is meeting the student's academic needs.

A weakness of progress monitoring is that sometimes data are misused to target specific instructional areas, rather than to serve as an indicator of overall proficiency in a subject. This might occur, for instance, if a teacher uses ORF to assess student performance solely in oral reading fluency rather than as an indicator of general reading performance. A better course of action would be to assess the student's particular areas of need by conducting follow-up diagnostic assessments when data indicate that a student is not performing well. Another concern arises when teachers use progress-monitoring measures that do not have technical adequacy, including creating their own measures that have unknown technical adequacy. This can result in data that may not be indicative of a student's actual performance or progress. An excellent and easily accessible resource for both screening and progress-monitoring tools are the tools charts available at the National Center for RTI Web site, www.rti4success.org. A technical review committee comprising experts in the field has reviewed CBM screening and progress-monitoring tools and posts results based on the level of evidence available (not convincing to convincing). Finally, a weakness in the progress-monitoring system can result if teachers simply collect data but do not use those data to make instructional decisions. Teachers should engage in ongoing collaboration with their colleagues—either the grade-level or PS team, or both—to appraise progress and apply decision-making rules.

Future research should continue to focus on progress-monitoring measures at the secondary level, including development of measures in all academic areas for high school students, as well as consideration of measures for the content areas. Some work has been completed at the secondary level (for mathematics, see Foegen, 2008, and Foegen, Olson, & Impecoven-Lind, 2008; for writing and reading, see Espin et al., 2008, and Espin, Wallace, Lembke, Campbell, & Long, 2010), but more remains to be done to determine how CBM progress monitoring can be implemented with secondary students. Additional research should also examine measures in other areas outside of reading and mathematics, such as written expression measures for early elementary students, group-administered measures in reading such as maze, and content area measures such as vocabulary matching. More information can be found on current and emerging work in CBM on the Research Institute for Progress Monitoring Web site www.progressmonitoring.org. Continued work needs to focus on teacher supports for implementing progress monitoring, including how to encourage teachers to attend to data and to implement decision-making rules based on data.

Progress monitoring is an important, research-based strategy for teachers that allows them to make more objective, data-based decisions about academic instruction. It is a critical element in an RtI framework and can help both general and special education teachers to more effectively meet the needs of their students. To maximize instruction for students at risk, it is critical that data be examined on a frequent basis so that interventions can be initiated, continued, or changed appropriately. More than 30 years of research suggest that use of CBM data will lead to improved student outcomes.

CHAPTER 4

Best Practices in Assessment for Eligibility Identification

Berttram Chiang | *University of Wisconsin Oshkosh*

Suzanne L. Russ | *Dickinson State University*

Stacey N. Skoning | *University of Wisconsin Oshkosh*

Since its inception in 1975, the Individuals with Disabilities Education Act (IDEA) has specified the types of disabilities that qualify for services, identified the procedures that must be followed to determine eligibility, and required a comprehensive assessment of the referred student to determine whether the child has a disability requiring special education. This seemingly simple process is formidable, however, due to the nuances of the educational system and the complexities of the children who participate in it. Differences in state eligibility criteria relating to the federal definitions and disparate court decisions further complicate the issue. Recent large-scale efforts to increase educational accountability and employ research-based interventions for all students make it more essential to improve the reliability and validity of the special education eligibility determination process. Current practices necessitate broadening the scope of eligibility assessment to include not only disability identification but also a larger prevention and assessment-informed instructional framework.

This chapter explores current eligibility determination processes by clarifying the use of assessment for determining eligibility, extending understanding of the issues underlying the process, and identifying examples of best practices supported by empirical evidence. Three sections serve to meet these purposes: (a) an introductory overview of the historical, legal, and ethical contexts of special education assessment for the purpose of eligibility determination; (b) an overview of the eligibility determination procedures, tools, and individual roles; and (c) a review of empirically supported best practices in eligibility determination for high-incidence disabilities. The chapter concludes with a summary of recommendations for future research and practices.

Historical, Legal, and Ethical Context of Eligibility Determination

The roots of special education eligibility determination can be traced to the Social Security Act of 1956, which stipulated that individuals entitled to services were those "who cannot do work that [they] did before and . . . cannot adjust to other work because of [their] medical condition" (Holdnack & Weiss, 2006, p. 872). This two-part test, examining both the presence of a disorder and its consequential impediment to functionality, became a fundamental tenet for special education eligibility determination. In both the Social Security Act and the later legislation guaranteeing special education services, neither the presence of a disability nor the inability to function in and of itself entitles an individual to benefits; rather, a causal linkage between a documented disability and functional impairment must be established (May, 2009). The two-step approach remains the basis for eligibility determination in special education, despite notable differences in the function and objectives of each law.

This two-pronged approach embodied in IDEA has been preserved throughout the reauthorizations since 1975. The most substantive eligibility determination changes before 2004 included (a) the 1986 reauthorization that extended services to preschoolers with disabilities (Part B) and established new discretionary programs for infants, toddlers, and their families (Part C); (b) the 1990 reauthorization's recognition of Autism and Traumatic Brain Injury as separate disability categories, along with the authorization of states to use significant developmental delay as an additional disability category for children ages 3 through 5; and (c) the 1997 expansion of this category to ages 3 through 9. Additionally, the 1997 reauthorization required greater efforts to ensure that children from culturally and linguistically diverse backgrounds were assessed and identified accurately and appropriately. Without necessitating a major paradigm shift, each of these reauthorizations served to influence the general patterns of referrals and the manner in which eligibility determination procedures were implemented.

Unlike previous reauthorizations, however, IDEA 2004 generated a major shift in the eligibility determination paradigm by stipulating that schools may use a Response-to-Intervention (RtI) framework as part of the eligibility determination process for identification of a learning disability. This framework, which typically involves a three-tiered process "that determines if the child responds to scientific, research-based intervention" (PL 108-446, Sec. 614[b][6][B]), includes funding for interventions to children who are at risk but have not yet been placed in special education. This is a marked departure from all prior legislation, in which funding was designated exclusively for the identification and provision of services for children with disabilities.

The implementation of IDEA has presented legal challenges about a range of issues related to eligibility determination due to the relative imprecision of disability definitions and differences in state interpretation of the federal guidelines. Determining the presence of a disability is sometimes a relatively straightforward process requiring little more than a medical diagnosis. Such cases are often diagnosed at or before birth, and the children have noticeable behavioral or physical characteristics. In the high-incidence areas of specific

learning disabilities (LD), emotional disturbance (ED), and mental retardation[1] (MR), however, this process is fraught with challenges that occasionally lead to legal conflicts between districts and parents. Each of these disability categories can be difficult to diagnose, because they are bounded by nebulous and subjective parameters that vary across states. Legal issues relating to eligibility decisions tend to revolve around the question of whether the condition is within the child or caused by the environment in which the child was raised or educated. Faced with the ambiguous and implicit language of IDEA, the evaluation team must strive to meet ethical standards while exercising its collective professional judgment to apply local norms and reflect "the perception of the school building personnel in terms of the students at the site most in need of, and likely to benefit from, the services available at that site" (MacMillan & Siperstein, 2002, p. 287). The ethical issues considered herein rest in the following areas: (a) early intervention versus delayed classification, (b) meeting educational needs versus necessity to control costs, and (c) the long-term cost of excluding versus the short-term costs of including children who fall on the borderline of a disability category.

Although applicable to all disability areas, early intervention for LD has proven to be particularly controversial. Before the 2004 IDEA reauthorization, common use of the IQ-achievement discrepancy for eligibility decisions delayed treatment by requiring that academic performance be significantly lower than the student's potential ability indicated by intelligence test scores. Thus, young children with LD may not have met the criteria because of a floor effect: the commonly expected academic skills at that level are simply too low to produce a significant discrepancy from IQ. Because more-advanced academic skills are not developed until the upper grades, the children with a disability must lag further and further behind their peers before receiving the necessary special education support. When the discrepancy is finally shown, often not until the upper elementary grades, the optimal period for efficacious support has passed and the child has lost valuable time for special education assistance (Jenkins, Graff, & Miglioretti, 2009).

Many of the eligibility decisions made by states, districts, and individual evaluation teams seek to balance meeting the needs of exceptional students with conserving costs to the district. To do so, they wrestle with a range of potentially competing interests, including federal legislation, state guidelines, district initiatives, and the will and wishes of the parents and teachers. While IDEA defines disability areas in general terms, states

---

[1]Because this chapter focuses on eligibility, we use the term *mental retardation,* as used in legal phrasing, instead of the preferred term of *intellectual disability.*

are given latitude to further expand on and clarify the federal guidelines. Because guidance from the federal government is minimal and clarification by the states is inconsistent, some evaluation teams find themselves at the heart of an ethical dilemma in which they are forced either to "err on the side of missing students who actually should receive services (minimize false negatives) or on the side of making sure students who do not require services do not get them (minimize false positives)" (Lloyd, 2002, p. 431).

IDEA definitions for LD and ED include specific exclusionary clauses. Students cannot be identified as having LD if it is "primarily the result of visual, hearing, or motor disabilities, of mental retardation, of emotional disturbance, or of environmental, cultural, or economic disadvantage" (PL 108-446, Sec. 602[30][C]). In addition, IDEA clearly excludes LD eligibility determination if the determining factor is "lack of appropriate instruction in reading, math, or limited English proficiency (PL 108-446, Sec. 614(b)[5][A], [B], [C]). Students whose conduct problems stem from social maladjustment cannot qualify for ED services "unless it is determined that they have an emotional disturbance" (34 CFR § 300.8(c)(4)(ii)). These exclusions seem sensible: IDEA is designed to serve children whose impairments originate from disabilities, while other programs such as Title I and English as a Second Language (ESL) are generally in place to assist with challenges originating from factors or etiologies not related to disabilities (e.g., lack of appropriate instruction, limited English proficiency). Nevertheless, children who are denied special education services because of the absence of clear etiology may pay a long-term price, because their needs may remain unmet. Therefore, it remains debatable whether such exclusions contribute to the formation of socially unjust educational systems (Artiles, 2003) or to infringement of the five broad ethical standards for psychoeducational assessment: multifaceted, comprehensive, fair, useful, and valid (Jacob & Hartshorne, 2007).

Assessment Procedures for Eligibility Determination

Assessment Tools and Data Sources

The procedure for determining whether a child is eligible for special education includes three key steps: (a) referral—the school district, parents, or the state make a written request for evaluation and obtain parental consent; (b) evaluation—school professionals evaluate the student to determine whether a qualifying disability is present; and (c) eligibility—school professionals and parents meet to determine whether the child is eligible for special education. To make such decisions

judiciously, a comprehensive assessment may include data related to a child's "health, vision, hearing, social and emotional status, general intelligence, academic performance, communicative status, and motor abilities" (34 CFR § 300.304(c)(4)).

With the exception of severe and sensory disability identification, which is usually diagnosed by medical professionals, evaluation teams tend to use a routine battery of individually administered standardized tests as primary assessment tools supplemented by classroom observations and input from parents and teachers. Specific tools and strategies should be selected and weighed in relation to the suspected disability and the child's developmental, linguistic, and cultural background. For example, the Battelle Developmental Inventory (BDI-2; Newborg, 2005) or Developmental Indicators for the Assessment of Learning (DIAL-R; Mardell & Goldenberg, 1998) provides more useful information for assessing a preschool child with potential developmental delays, while rating scales such as the Behavior Assessment System for Children (BASC-2; Reynolds & Kamphaus, 1992) and Child Behavior Checklist (CBCL; Achenbach, 1991) give more relevant information about the presence or absence of characteristics of conduct problems or hyperactivity for a child suspected of ED. The Wechsler Intelligence Scale for Children (WISC-IV; Wechsler, 2004) and Vineland Adaptive Behavior Scales II (Sparrow, Cicchetti, & Balla, 2005) are more likely to be used for assessing intellectual functioning and adaptive behaviors if a child is referred for possible MR, but a nonverbal intelligence test such as the Naglieri Nonverbal Cognitive Test (Naglieri, 1997) can yield more valid information about the cognitive abilities of a child with cultural or language differences. Likewise, systematic observation and parent interviews can be important strategies to assess a child with autism, while collecting repeated curriculum-based probes or administering standardized tests such as the Woodcock-Johnson III Tests of Achievement (WJ III; Woodcock, McGrew, & Mather, 2001) or the Wechsler Individual Achievement Test (WIAT-II; Psychological Corporation, 2002) makes more sense for assessing a child considered for LD.

Roles of Individuals in Eligibility Determination

IDEA requires evaluation to be conducted "by a team of qualified professionals and the parent of the child" (PL 108-446, Sec. 614(b)4(A)). A number of professionals such as the school psychologist, speech and language therapist, audiologist, school nurse, social worker, guidance counselor, occupational therapist, or physical therapist may participate, based on the expertise that is needed. The varied composition of the evaluation team helps to ensure an accurate and comprehensive evaluation of the child and reduce the impact of bias on both the process and decisions.

The respective roles assumed by members of the evaluation team differ on a case-by-case basis. However, three members of this team often play distinctly vital roles that have changed with the IDEA 2004 reauthorization: school psychologists, general education teachers, and parents. Historically, school psychologists spent two thirds of their time in special education eligibility determination and administered over 100 individual intelligence tests annually (Reschly & Wilson, 1995). Because of their expertise in cognitive assessment and behavioral consultation, school psychologists have long played a critical role in the evaluation and special education eligibility determination process. According to a survey of 177 school psychologists by Huebner and Gould (1991), 39% of them served as case managers in their schools. A separate survey of 124 school psychologists in Wisconsin revealed that on average they spent 30% of their working hours conducting assessment, 16% writing reports, and 17% participating in individualized education program (IEP) team meetings (Chiang, Rylance, Bongers, & Russ, 1998). Similarly, in eligibility meetings for students with emotional and behavioral disorders, teachers see school psychologists as playing a dominant role in making final decisions (K. F. Martin, Lloyd, Kauffman, & Coyne, 1995).

With the emergence of RtI as a problem-solving model leading to potential special education identification, however, the roles of school psychologists have shifted. The RtI framework demands that school teams ensure empirically driven best practices in the general education setting (Tier 1) before implementing gradually more individualized interventions in Tiers 2 and 3. Thus, school psychologists no longer serve primarily as psychometricians who interpret test scores in a referral-evaluation-eligibility framework. Instead, they assume a more collaborative role as instructional consultants in selecting technically sound tools, interpreting widely varying data, deriving criteria to identify those not responding to the instruction, and identifying effective interventions (Shinn & McConnell, 1994). In addition to their emerging roles related to instructional consulting, school psychologists also "are well positioned in the schools to advocate, and in some contexts provide leadership for, a proactive and preventive approach to social behavior problems in schools" (Malecki & Demaray, 2007, pp. 161–162). This trend materialized rather dramatically in the Minneapolis Public School District, which reported that school psychologists decreased the proportion of their time spent testing from 58% to 35% after schools switched to a problem-solving model to identify LD and mild mental retardation (MMR) (Marston, Muyskens, Lau, & Canter, 2003). The role of general education teachers, always important because they

are often the first to observe a potential problem, has also shifted somewhat in response to the IDEA 2004 reauthorization. Before the IDEA reauthorization, general educators assumed minimal responsibility in the evaluation process after initiating a referral, being required only to attend the IEP meeting with evidence of the child's present level of performance. Within the RtI framework, general education teachers assumed a much more integrated role. In addition to initiating referrals and describing the child's current level of performance in the general education setting, these teachers are expected to implement research-validated curricular interventions accurately, to monitor student progress by gathering a variety of systematic data, and to collaborate with other building staff to ensure the child's needs are met. Although this integrated role remains predominant in referrals for potential LD, such a shift may begin to influence the role of general educators in other disability areas as well.

Finally, the role of parents in the assessment and eligibility determination process is enhanced still further following the IDEA 2004 reauthorization. Expanding from a time when parent roles were often limited and inconsequential, the reauthorized IDEA continues efforts to make parents genuinely equal partners in the evaluation process. By more actively providing the evaluation team with critical information about family background and the developmental and social history of the child, parents now are often viewed as critical contributors in helping evaluation teams understand the child's performance in terms of general family background and culturally or linguistically relevant differences.

Best Practices in Eligibility Determination for High-Incidence Disabilities

As described earlier, a marked disparity exists in the technical adequacy of special education eligibility determination for the categories of ED, LD, and MR and the medically identifiable categories (e.g., orthopedic impairment, traumatic brain injury, visual impairment, hearing impairment, and severe MR). For high-incidence special education disability areas, however, students' chances of being identified with a disability vary according to the state in which they reside, their minority or linguistic status, the makeup of the evaluation team, the persistence of their parents, and the relative tolerance of the general education teacher.

Emotional Disturbance

Eligibility decisions for students with ED have consistently faced two formidable obstacles: (a) underidentification of children who may benefit from special services (Walker, Nishioka, Zeller, Severson, & Feil, 2000) and (b) disproportionate representation of children with cultural and linguistic diversity (Harris-Murri, King, & Rostenberg, 2006; Landrum, 2000).

Underidentification

For many reasons, the identification of students with ED typically occurs much later than other disabilities. According to the most current available data from the Office of Special Education (2009) 28th Annual Report to Congress, the number of students identified with ED increased incrementally as the student ages—from 7,109 students identified by age 6 years to a peak of more than eight times that number for 15-year-old students (57,267). Further, students with ED waited an average of 2 years for special education services following the onset of difficulties, compared with less than 1 year for other disabilities (Wagner, Kutash, Duchnowski, Epstein, & Sumi, 2005). Because behaviors that are sufficiently problematic to necessitate ED identification in ninth or tenth grade are not likely to have emerged with no prior evidence, it is likely that inadequate attention in earlier grades allowed the behaviors to intensify and become intolerable during adolescence. By delaying interventions, therefore, the most promising years for effective services were lost.

Several factors contribute to the tendency to delay intervention. Landrum (2000) attributed the underidentification phenomenon to parents' reluctance to have their child assigned this stigmatizing and pejorative label of ED and to schools' concerns about funding for relatively costly ED programs. Many school administrators are also reluctant to classify students as ED because of the "constraints it imposes on their ability to discipline students experiencing school-related behavior problems" (Walker et al., 2000, p. 32). Additionally, confusion surrounding the social maladjustment exclusion and the absence of assessment tools that can distinguish ED from social maladjustment further contribute to the tendency toward underidentification (Gresham, 2005).

Disproportionate Representation

Although IDEA reauthorizations placed increased emphasis on culturally appropriate identification procedures, their effect has been only minimally observed in the category of ED. National data of children with ED, in which more than 2,000 carefully sampled parents of elementary- and secondary-aged children were surveyed or interviewed, confirmed the continued existence of significant differences in prevalence rates by gender (males overrepresented), socioeconomic status

(SES; more risk factors associated with low SES), and race (African Americans are overrepresented, while Hispanic students are underrepresented) (Wagner et al., 2005). Both system-based (Harry, Klingner, Sturges, & Moore, 2002) and intergroup differences (J. L. Hosp & Hosp, 2001) have been cited to explain this disparity. For example, teachers in low SES schools and schools with high proportions of African American students may have different classroom management styles and competencies, resulting in increased identification rates in the ED category. It is also possible that the interaction styles of males, students from low SES backgrounds, and African Americans may result in higher levels of ED identification because they are misaligned with the interaction styles of teachers, who are often middle class females. Further, while both poverty and race influence prevalence rates in ED, the interaction between the two remains minimal; problems of racial overrepresentation tend to exist more strongly in affluent than in poor schools (Skiba, Poloni-Staudinger, Gallini, Simmons, & Feggins-Azziz, 2006).

Best Practices in Identification of ED

One process appears to hold the greatest empirical support in identifying students with ED. This multiple gating procedure, known as Systematic Screening for Behavioral Disorders (SSBD), has substantial evidence supporting its efficacy. Further, SSBD has been endorsed by a panel of Stanford Research Institute researchers and project managers in the Office of Special Education Programs as the optimal practice in terms of its standardization, normative characteristics, cost-effectiveness, and successful implementation (Severson, Walker, Hope-Doolittle, Kratochwill, & Gresham, 2007).

Addressing the problem of delayed identification of students with ED, Walker, Severson, and Haring (1985) developed SSBD, which relied on general educators to systematically screen all students for potential ED. SSBD involves three stages, or "gates," through which students must pass in order to be evaluated for ED. In Gate 1, general education teachers rank all students in their class from most to least severe with respect to a list of internalizing (e.g., anxiety, depression) and externalizing (e.g., disruptive, violent behaviors) characteristics. The few students whose characteristics are most severe on either dimension pass to Gate 2, in which teachers complete more detailed measures, such as the Critical Life Events checklist and the Combined Frequency Index for adaptive and maladaptive behaviors, for each of the smaller group of students. The scores on these measures are compared with normative standards, and those whose scores are significantly below the norm pass on to Gate 3. In Gate 3, an outside professional observes and rates the students in natural settings. If both the teacher ratings and the observations are suggestive of a disability, then the child may be referred for special education.

Substantial evidence supports the validity of SSBD. Walker and colleagues (1988) conducted extensive testing of the procedure and tools during the development process. Their initial field tests involved 18 teachers and 454 elementary school children in Oregon, and they conducted subsequent replications using 58 teachers and 1,468 first- through fifth-grade children in Utah (Walker, Severson, Nicholson, et al., 1994). Both the initial testing and replication used two randomly selected students in each classroom to serve as controls during Gates 2 and 3, and students currently identified with ED served as comparison measures when evaluating the efficiency of the process. Their findings revealed that (a) both internalizers (i.e., those who experience symptoms related to anxiety or depression) and externalizers (i.e., those who experience symptoms such as disruptive or violent behaviors) scored significantly higher than controls on the Gate-2 checklists; (b) observational data confirmed the tendency toward internalizing or externalizing responses; (c) the method effectively discriminated among internalizers, externalizers, and non-referred students; and (d) both time and costs were significantly lower for the SSBD procedure than for the traditional process in which students were referred and evaluated based on teacher perceptions.

Use of a systematic screening procedure was also effective for identifying kindergarten students most at risk for later behavioral problems. One well-designed study randomly placed 48 targeted kindergarteners into either a wait-list or a treatment group exposed to the SSBD procedure before receiving comprehensive interventions (Walker, Severson, Feil, Stiller, & Golly, 1998). The group exposed to the SSBD procedures experienced significantly greater behavioral improvement than the control group. In a second longitudinal study using at-risk kindergarten students from Montreal, Canada, Charlebois and Leblanc (1994) employed slightly different measures within a two-gate screening system to determine whether a process employed in early childhood could predict later behavior problems. During Gate 1, all students ($n = 84$) scoring above the 70th percentile on the aggressiveness-hyperactivity-distractibility subscale of the Teachers' Preschool Behavior Questionnaire (Behar & Stringfield, 1974) were identified for further assessment. The more detailed assessment in Gate 2 involved both observations for task-inappropriate behaviors in the classroom and at home and mother and teacher ratings using the CBCL. Based on these children's scores on a Self-Reported Delinquency Questionnaire 5 years later, the predictive efficacy of SSBD procedures for later problems with delinquency and maladaptive behaviors was confirmed.

The efficacy of SSBD with older students was supported by Caldarella, Young, Richardson, Young, and Young (2008) in their study with more than 2,100 students attending middle/junior high schools in Utah. In comparison to school-wide averages, students identified as at risk for ED based on the first two gating procedures of the SSBD tended to be suspended more often and have lower grade-point averages. However, some of the identified students actually were suspended less than average or had higher than average grade-point averages. The potentially false-positive identifications may be attributed to (a) the decreased likelihood that students with internalizing disorders present behaviors necessitating suspensions or (b) the absence of Gate-3 procedures in this study, which have been shown to more accurately pinpoint those with ED (Loeber, Dishion, & Patterson, 1984).

Walker, Severson, and Feil (1995) modified the SSBD items and formats for preschool children and called this downward adaptation the Early Screening Project (ESP). The ESP involves a three-stage process to screen for behavior disorders among preschool children. Teacher ranking constituted the Stage-One screening, teacher rating with normative criteria made up the Stage-Two process, and behavioral observation and parent rating were used as Stage-Three procedures. Feil and Severson (1995) effectively employed a three-stage gating procedure with 3- to 5-year-old children and found that assessment time was reduced up to 16% over other procedures. The ESP was also found to yield no significant racial differences in ED referrals among Oregon's 40 classes of 954 Head Start participants of different ethnic groups (Feil, Walker, Severson, & Ball, 2000), producing a preliminary suggestion that systematic screenings may in fact reduce disproportionality. However, because children attending Head Start come from predominantly lower-socioeconomic classes but racial disproportionality tends to be greater in affluent districts, the impact of ESP on disproportionality requires substantial additional verification.

In summary, determination of an emotional disturbance has been fraught with challenges, resulting in underidentification of children with ED in general, and disproportionate overrepresentation of particular groups (i.e., males, those with low SES, and particular racial or ethnic groups). A more systematic method of identifying and evaluating both internalizing and externalizing behaviors across all children is needed to minimize these outcomes. A multiple-gating approach, as described in this section, may be one way to accomplish this goal.

Mental Retardation

Fewer contentious issues exist in identification of students with MR than the identification of students with

ED or LD, though the criteria are not entirely problem free. Challenges pertain to each aspect of the MR criteria, described by Bergeron, Floyd, and Shands (2008) as "deficits in intellectual functioning, impaired functioning in the daily environment, and onset during the developmental period" (p. 123). Most of the criticisms rest not with the identification of more severe disabilities but rather relate to the larger population of children who would be considered to have MMR. The difficulty with MMR identification is attributed to the fact that characteristics of children with MMR are relatively subtle and often overlap with those children with other disabilities (e.g., LD, attention deficit hyperactivity disorder [ADHD], autism) and those with no disabilities.

Deficits in intellectual functioning are typically assessed through an individually administered intelligence test such as the WISC-IV. Criticisms of the use of IQ tend to relate to (a) the relative importance placed on IQ at the expense of other potentially relevant information (Greenspan, 2006), (b) the absence of agreement on whether subscale rather than full-scale IQ may serve as a more valid measure of intellectual functioning (Bergeron et al., 2008), (c) the use of inconsistent IQ cutoff points that do not consider statistical error of measurement (Scullin, 2006), and (d) the tendency for children from some minority groups to score more poorly and thus be overidentified with MR (Skiba et al., 2006).

Several tools are available to assess deficits in adaptive behaviors, including the Vineland Adaptive Behavior Scales, the AAMR Adaptive Behavior Scale (Lambert, Nihira, & Leland, 1993), the Adaptive Behavior Assessment System—Second Edition (ABAS-II; Harrison & Oakland, 2003), Scales of Independent Behavior—Revised (Bruininks, Woodcock, Weatherman, & Hill, 1996), and the Battelle Development Inventory (BDI-2; Newborg, 2005). General criticisms of such measures include the following: (a) inconsistencies exist across states in terms of which dimensions of adaptive behavior (social, practical, or cognitive) should indicate an impairment (Bergeron et al., 2008; Greenspan, 2006), (b) subtle adaptive behaviors such as gullibility are neglected despite the fact that they create great challenges for those with MMR (Greenspan, 2006), and (c) adaptive behavior measures tend to retain secondary importance relative to IQ scores (Heflinger, Cook, & Thackrey, 1987). IDEA also mandates that deficits in both IQ and adaptive behaviors must be "manifested during the developmental period" (34 CFR § 300.8(c)(6)). This ambiguous age-of-onset definition is complicated by the fact that children with MMR are often misidentified initially as children with LD, ADHD, or other impairments and thus fail to meet the early-onset requirement.

Best Practices in Identification of MR

The framework and tools with which children with MR are identified has varied little in past decades. The relative constancy of MR eligibility determination is somewhat surprising, given that recent IDEA legislation has sought to remedy the overrepresentation of African American students in this category (Allen-Meares, 2008). Given the paucity of best practice assessment models in the literature, the following should be incorporated in MR identification practices:

1. *Balance IQ with adaptive measures:* Because of the challenges addressed with IQ tests, evaluation teams should ensure that both IQ and adaptive measures are considered appropriately. A child who achieves a lower score on an intelligence test but higher adaptive behavior scores should not be more likely to be identified with MR than one who achieves lower adaptive behavior scores but a higher IQ score.

2. *Attend to cultural differences in both IQ and adaptive measures:* Adaptations from standardized procedures "may include removing time restraints, incorporating nonverbal formats, and replacing single procedure and single score instruments with those that are more diverse" (Allen-Meares, 2008, p. 314). For example, a tester can employ language that allows for alternate phrasing or slang terminology or can supplement traditional assessment methods with multidimensional tools such as the Brief Impairment Scale (BIS; Bird et al., 2005). Despite promising efforts a few decades ago, however, little promise has been made in the development of a finely tuned multicultural tool (Allen-Meares, 2008).

3. *Clarify the required domains of adaptive behavior deficits for eligibility criteria:* Because adaptive behavior is typically assessed in terms of social, practical, and conceptual skills, evaluation teams must specify the areas in which a child being assessed for eligibility shows deficits before they identify the child with MR.

4. *Use revised standardized intelligence tests with recent norms in order to avoid the Flynn effect, or systematic increases in IQ scores as norms age (Reschly & Grimes, 2002; Tylenda, Beckett, & Barrett, 2007):* The Flynn effect, in which scores tend to raise by about 3 points per decade due to factors such as better nutrition and increased familiarity with test mechanisms, can lead to inaccurate conclusions if outdated norms are employed.

Specific Learning Disabilities

Since the early 1990s, the dominant method for identifying LD involved a significant discrepancy between intellectual ability as measured by IQ tests and achievement as measured through standardized tests. In 2002, two years before the most recent IDEA reauthorization, 48 of the 50 states relied on significant discrepancy as the primary method of determining eligibility for LD (Reschly & Hosp, 2004). A major shift occurred with the IDEA 2004 reauthorization: states were required to allow other methods for eligibility determination, including an RtI framework. Despite the mandate, however, most states simply added language to their original legislation giving school districts the choice of using significant discrepancy or RtI (Ahearn, 2009). The following paragraphs will examine issues related to the discrepancy approach, issues related to the newly emerging RtI framework, and best practices in LD assessment.

Issues with the Discrepancy Approach

The discrepancy model has received abundant criticism (Donovan & Cross, 2002; Speece, 2002) in recent years. Problems exist in three primary areas: (a) inaccurate or overidentification of students with LD, (b) delayed identification of LD, and (c) low predictive validity.

The first of these challenges, inaccurate or overidentification of students with LD, rests in the overreliance on test scores to determine eligibility at the expense of other potentially important factors. By applying formulas "in a mechanistic, narrow fashion" (Mather & Kaufman, 2006, p. 747), information about attempted interventions, duration of the problem, or the strength of the general education program may be overlooked. Consequently, we may identify children with LD who are disabled by their environment or circumstances (e.g., insufficient support or accommodation) rather than by a true deficit. Because the formulaic nature of the discrepancy model provides a spurious sense of objectivity, it diverts attention from the conditions and potential solutions that could alleviate or prevent the problem.

The second challenge, delayed identification or "wait-to-fail," results from the dubious requirement of obtaining a significant discrepancy between IQ and performance until the child has demonstrated substantial and enduring failure. Because academic learning for younger children is relatively undeveloped, the range of potential achievement is limited. This limited range of achievement, in turn, may mask the seriousness of a performance deficit faced by a child with a potential learning disability. Until the rest of the children have advanced substantially in their learning, the child struggling with LD will simply not be far enough behind to produce a significant discrepancy. Thus, young children with LD will miss out on services during their most formative years, therefore facing mounting failure and frustration while awaiting the actualization of a significant discrepancy.

Finally, the traditional formula has low predictive validity, or accuracy in predicting which students have LD. According to a meta-analysis by Stuebing and colleagues (2002), few differences exist in early indicators of learning problems between struggling readers who are IQ discrepant (IQ and achievement are significantly different) and those who are IQ consistent (IQ and achievement do not differ). If the significant discrepancy formula cannot tease out such differences in young readers, it loses validity as a predictive tool and becomes another factor contributing to unnecessary delay of services.

Issues with the RtI Framework

The inadequacies of the significant discrepancy framework led to the IDEA 2004 mandate that states could no longer require its use in identifying students with LD. RtI has been described most aptly as "a model supported by converging sources of evidence . . . [that] will move the field from an exclusive reliance on eligibility determination into intervention-based practices in the schools for struggling learners" (Gresham, 2007, p. 21). Despite its proven and potential benefits in establishing a closer link between LD identification and treatment, reducing the special education referrals (Ikeda & Gustafson, 2002), and overrepresentation of African American students placed in special education (Marston et al., 2003), the use of RtI to determine eligibility for LD has engendered a number of concerns: (a) timing within the IDEA mandates, (b) paucity of relevant research, (c) ineptitude with decisions regarding students who change schools, and (d) inconsistencies across states.

Timing of special education referrals is clearly stipulated in IDEA: Evaluation must be conducted within 60 days of parental consent. RtI, however, can be a lengthy process that does not fit neatly into such a timeline: Interventions must be planned, implemented, monitored, and modified within each tier of RtI—clearly, a process that could easily exceed the 60-day limit. The issue is further complicated by ambiguity around the beginning and end points of the referral process. Previously, the due process requirements began when the special education referral was initiated. Under RtI, due process requirements may be activated when the concern is first voiced or may be deferred until the student is found nonresponsive to Tier-2 or Tier-3 interventions. This uncertainty, along with a lack of clarity of what might occur if parents act on their right to request a comprehensive evaluation for special education eligibility at any time during the RtI process, suggests that legal clarification will be needed.

Questions persist about the adequacy and appropriateness of using RtI as a diagnostic tool to identify LD based on the limited research in support of such practices (Kavale, Kauffman, Bachmeier, & LeFever, 2008). Current assessment tools for the implementation of RtI are largely limited to the curriculum areas of basic reading and mathematics skills for elementary school students. Because research is scanty and long-term research nonexistent, we risk once again plunging into a new initiative with no sound empirical basis on which to proceed.

Lastly, states and districts apply RtI models inconsistently. Just as the federal government allows states latitude in interpreting its definitions of LD and other disability areas, so is ambiguity present in the new potential uses and practices of RtI. In fact, the inconsistencies may be even greater for RtI as most states simply leave the decision to be made at the district level. Thus, inconsistent application occurs not only among states, but also within individual states or even districts.

Exacerbating the problems of inconsistent application, significant implementation challenges exist in determining eligibility for students who transfer to different schools before the completion of the process. Unlike traditional tests, which use well-publicized standard procedures, protocols, and scores, repeated measures of curriculum-based assessment may vary enormously from one school district to another and thus be nongeneralizable in the public domain. If a student transfers to a different school in the midst of one of the RtI tiers of intervention, interpretation of that student's documents regarding RtI at the transferring school can be a much more daunting task than understanding Woodcock-Johnson achievement battery or WIAT-II scores. Any efforts to continue such an interrupted RtI process at the student's new school requires arduous paperwork and documentation and can be fraught with serious problems of treatment fidelity ("the strategies that monitor and enhance the accuracy and consistency of an intervention to (a) ensure it is implemented as planned and (b) make certain each component is delivered in a comparable manner to all participants over time" [S. W. Smith, Daunic, & Taylor, 2007])—and test validity (the degree to which a test accurately measures what it was designed to measure).

In addition to the aforementioned problems, currently a morass of confusion surrounds nearly every aspect of RtI. Uncertainty exists about the nature of the basic models (Gresham, 2002), the appropriate number of tiers (Reschly, 2005), the optimal duration of intervention for each tier, criteria to identify students who do not respond to interventions (Burns, Jacob, & Wagner, 2008; D. Fuchs & Deshler, 2007), and the nature of interventions applied in each tier. Thus, it is essential to begin the process of developing an RtI model that offers consistency across states as we move forward with

more coherent and uniform large-scale implementations (Burns, Deno, & Jimerson, 2007).

Best Practices in Identification of LD

To illustrate how RtI may address some of the LD-eligibility issues raised in this chapter, the following paragraphs review two programs that employ best practices in eligibility determination: (a) the Minneapolis Public Schools' Problem-Solving Model (PSM; Marston et al., 2003), and (b) Iowa's Heartland Educational Agency Model (Heartland; Tilly, 2003). Both of these frameworks were implemented before the 2004 IDEA reauthorization, paving the way for the broader implementation to come.

The framework employed in Minnesota was initiated through a waiver of typical special education eligibility criteria for LD and MMR. Within this framework, applications of the tiers were clearly outlined. Tier 1 involved 4 to 6 weeks of interventions in the general education classroom, Tier 2 included 6 to 8 weeks of team interventions, and Tier 3 required a comprehensive assessment for possible special education eligibility. Several worksheets were developed to assist classroom teachers in implementing the model, including separate documents for the diverse strategies employed at each tier. A notable feature of the Tier-3 worksheet is the particular attention given to the influences of culture, language, and environment—an often overlooked dimension.

To study the impact of PSM, the district conducted a program evaluation in which they analyzed factors such as identification rates and responsiveness to different plans. Results were promising: (a) identification rates for high-incidence disabilities have remained stable, around 7% between 1994 and 2001; (b) similar students were identified with both PSM and the traditional method (Marston et al., 2003); (c) the number of children referred for Tier 2 more than doubled over the 5-year period; and (d) the number of African American students referred and found eligible for special education declined markedly during the period of PSM implementation.

While the results appear quite promising, the absence of random assignment, the passage of time as additional schools were oriented to PSM, and the absence of information about how schools were selected for participation all minimize the potential claims to causality. Nevertheless, the successful implementation of PSM in a culturally and economically diverse school district provides a beacon for future implementation in similar environments.

The second best-practices model, Heartland (Iowa) has implemented RtI since 1993. Special features of the program include an Instructional Decision Making (IDM) framework for higher-frequency problems (e.g., basic reading or math proficiency concerns) in order to better integrate the problem-solving approach to serve all students. The major concept of IDM includes a core instructional program for all students, a supplemental program for students needing different or additional instruction, and an intensive program for the few students requiring additional support to succeed. Depending on the severity of the problems, different resource levels may be needed to solve low-incidence individual problems at each of the four levels, ranging from Level 1 (consultation between parents and teachers), Level 2 (combination of resources such as Building Assistance Teams), Level 3 (extended consultation team for ongoing support), and Level 4 (special education eligibility or IEP considerations). It has been reported that about 25% of teacher-identified concerns have been satisfactorily resolved at Level 2 or 3 (Ikeda & Gustafson, 2002), and in over 10 years of practice, fewer than 20 IQ or published standardized achievement tests have been administered for over 15,000 initial eligibility evaluations or reevaluations (Ikeda et al., 2007). The RtI process for identifying disability therefore clearly would minimize the need for traditional assessments and instead place more emphasis on systematic prevention efforts before formal referrals for special education.

Conclusion

Assessment for special education identification historically served the primary function of gate keeping in order to determine referred children's eligibility for special education and related services. The general definition provided by IDEA regarding which children are eligible for the disability categories of LD, ED, and MR left ample room for subjective judgment and inconsistent placement decisions. Consequently, "few areas are so thoroughly unsettled, with so few guideposts, as eligibility for special education services under the statute" (Weber, 2009, p. 83). IDEA 2004 generated a major paradigm shift in eligibility determination in order to reduce both false negatives and false positives. Additionally, the shifting philosophy and need to assess for both eligibility and instructional decision-making purposes resulted in a need for collecting and analyzing different kinds of data and a change in the roles of some of those involved in the data collection process. Systematic screening and the use of multiple gates or tiers of assessment support these new developments. However, even these methods are not without their criticisms.

Despite its promising prospect as a viable option for LD identification, infusing culture and linguistic considerations in RtI models has surfaced as one of the greatest challenges in RtI. To answer the crucial question of "what works with whom, by whom, and in what context?" (Klingner & Edwards, 2006, p. 110), educators need to give much greater attention to cultural and language considerations as an integral part of ensuring implementation fidelity. This increased attention is particularly important as educators expand RtI to more students at secondary schools, requiring the use of broader performance measures rather than assessment of specific basic skills such as word recognition or arithmetic computation fluency. Additionally, the culturally responsive use of multiple-gating procedures potentially can reduce the disproportionate minority representation in special education programs for students with ED. In particular, during the problem identification and analysis stages of a problem-solving model, the evaluation team needs to (a) "validate that a referred student was truly exhibiting a problem that merited intervention" (Witt & VanDerHeyden, 2007, p. 347) and (b) direct its attention to a student's response to intervention as well as the intervention's responsiveness to the student (Harris-Murri et al., 2006).

Directions for Future Research

The empirical evidence presented in this chapter described emerging best practices in the field of assessment for eligibility. Outlined next are future eligibility assessment research directions that can inform educational policies and practices in order to positively affect the outcomes for all students.

1. *Develop technology infrastructure:* In moving away from the IQ–achievement discrepancy model, more schools will phase in the implementation of RtI for identification of students with LD. To counter the operational challenges, researchers need to develop and test innovative technology to manage the reams of data generated. Some school districts have already tested and piloted such programs: the interactive Web-based Student Intervention Monitoring System (SIMS), created by Wisconsin's Madison Metropolitan School District (see http://dpi.wi.gov/rti/sims2.html), allows K–12 staff to maintain academic and behavior records and share information about strategies to track and support student progress while considering special education eligibility. Investigations of the effects of incorporating technology into RtI implementation, particularly designed as longitudinal studies, can shed light on the relationship between various RtI parameters (e.g., decision rules, intervention duration) and prevalence rates. Specifically, the data analysis made available through technological

consistency allows for a clearer appraisal of effective and ineffective practices. Other areas of future research that hold the promise of improving the validity and efficiency of eligibility assessment practices include (a) the correlation between RtI progress-monitoring benchmarks (e.g., level, slope, goal) and other student outcome indicators in grade-level standards on the statewide assessment and (b) the roles of professional judgments in problem-solving teams' eligibility decision making (Tilly, Reschly, & Grimes, 1999).

2. *Expand RtI applications:* To advance RtI to district-wide LD and ED identification assessment best practices, we need more controlled studies to validate its diagnostic utility in the social-emotional domain, in academic domains other than basic reading, and for students at the middle and high school levels. As suggested by Kratochwill, Clements, and Kalymon (2007), "a major research agenda in the future must focus on establishing reliability, validity, and utility for a variety of screening measures to be used in the RtI models" (p. 31). Additionally, in the area of eligibility assessment for ED, "continued research on the psychometric integrity and utility of [universal screening instruments such as] . . . SSBD across diverse populations is needed" (Glover & Albers, 2007, p. 131).

3. *Improve discriminative validity:* Another eligibility assessment area that warrants the attention of future research relates to the extent to which students on the mild end of the disability spectrum can be distinguished reliably from one another by the current categorical system and distinguished from other students whose achievement levels are below typical levels and who were found ineligible for any of the aforementioned categories. For instance, the shrinkage of students identified for MR and the simultaneous expansion of the LD category has been well documented and thoroughly analyzed in the existing literature of actual placement committee deliberations (MacMillan & Siperstein, 2002) and in the context of a changing construct of MR and overrepresentation of minority children in the MR category (Donovan & Cross, 2002). It remains an open research question whether the replacement of the IQ–achievement model by the RtI approach will in and of itself produce a more consistent classification and placement system in special education.

4. *Develop early intervention practices:* Given the fact that evaluation of students with ED often involves "reactive school practices in identification" (Donovan & Cross, 2002, p. 266), future research in this area should address the issue of early identification and intervention of emotional and behavior problems with the same rigor and sense of urgency as it did with the "wait-to-fail" model for LD identification. For instance, Nishioka (2001) found that students were often identified with ED 5 or more years after teachers initially documented the presence of behavior problems. The growing number of schools that are embedding positive behavior support within the context of a problem-solving model offer a fertile ground for researchers to identify tools and strategies to provide multi-tiers of proactive interventions for potentially disruptive behavior problems.

A great deal of progress has been made in the practices of special education eligibility assessment since the IDEA reauthorizations in 1997 and 2004. This chapter highlighted the tremendous strides made in the first decade of the 2000s, with school professionals moving away from answering the proverbial question of "to be or not to be" by placing a proper emphasis on preventing students from falling through the cracks of the imperfect classification system. By employing more empirically based decision making regarding eligibility and properly framing the prevention and intervention efforts within the context of general education reform, educators provide reason for great optimism in the future of more effective assessment and services for all students.

CHAPTER 5

Parent Participation in Assessment and in Development of Individualized Education Programs

Katharine G. Shepherd and **Michael F. Giangreco** | *University of Vermont*

Bryan G. Cook | *University of Hawaii*

<p>arent involvement is a key principle of special education with roots in the field's history, laws, practices, and overall goal to meet the needs of all children and youth with disabilities. The U.S. Congress asserted its belief in the importance of parent participation in the passage of the Education for All Handicapped Children Act of 1975 (EHA; Public Law 94-142), and has affirmed the commitment to the importance of parents as educational partners and decision makers in each of its subsequent reauthorizations of the Individuals with Disabilities Education Act (IDEA) (A. Turnbull, Turnbull, Erwin, Soodak, & Shogren, 2011). Although the literature has identified numerous benefits of parent participation in the special education assessment process and generation of individualized education programs (IEP) (S. W. Smith, 1990; H. R. Turnbull, Turnbull, & Wheat, 1982), theoretical analyses and empirical research suggest that the realities of participation generally fall far short of the IDEA vision of parents as partners in planning (Harry, 1992a, 2008; A. Turnbull et al., 2011).

In this chapter, we first review the legal and theoretical justification for parental involvement in their children's schooling generally and in the IEP assessment and development process specifically. Second, we review the literature on observed levels of parental involvement and identified roadblocks to higher levels of parental involvement. We conclude with descriptions of two family-centered practices that are supported by research as increasing parental participation in the IEP process: (a) person-centered planning (PCP) approaches (Claes, Van Hove, Vandevelde, Van Loon, & Schalock, 2010), and (b) Choosing Outcomes and Accommodations for Children (COACH) (Giangreco, Cloninger, & Iverson, 2011). Although we acknowledge that these practices do not meet all of the criteria established for evidence-based practices (see B. G. Cook, Tankersley, & Landrum, 2009), they address many barriers to parent participation, are supported in the research literature, and may be described as "promising practices" with implications for future research and practice.

Parent Involvement and General Education

Although it is beyond the scope of this chapter to give full attention to the general issue of parent involvement in education, it is important to situate the construct of parent participation in assessment and IEP generation within this broader context. In some ways, the history of parent involvement in education as a whole has paralleled that of parent involvement in special education, with responsibility for education shifting from families in an agrarian society (Kaestle, 2001) to schools and professionals by the middle of the 20th century (Cutler, 2000). The increasingly bureaucratic and professionalized nature of schools initially acted as a force that discouraged family involvement in schooling (Henry, 1996). However, by the 1990s, researchers and practitioners began to promote parent involvement as a strategy for improving public schools and increasing student achievement, attendance, and attitudes (J. S. Epstein, 2009; Henderson & Mapp, 2002). Legally, federal statutes have given less attention to parent involvement in general education than special education, with the first mention of the importance of parent involvement appearing in the 2001 reauthorization of the Elementary and Secondary Education Act, also known as the No Child Left Behind Act (NCLB).

Research on the relationship between increased family involvement in general education and improved student outcomes continues to emerge, but to date remains inconclusive. A relatively large body of literature supports a connection between parent involvement and student performance; findings suggest that students whose parents are more engaged with school show higher academic and behavioral achievement (C. Ferguson, 2008; Henderson & Mapp, 2002), improved attendance rates, and higher aspirations for postsecondary education (Jeynes, 2005). At the same time, some researchers have cautioned that the disparate definitions of parent involvement (Mattingly, Prislin, McKenzie, Rodriguez, & Kayzar, 2002) and concerns about study design and effect sizes (White, Taylor, & Moss, 1992) must be considered in drawing conclusions about the impact of involvement on student outcomes.

Historical, Legal, and Theoretical Underpinnings of Parent Participation in Special Educational Planning

Before EHA/IDEA

Historically, the roles of parents of children and adults with disabilities have been viewed in a variety of ways, each of which has influenced expectations for parent participation in educational planning. The eugenics movement of the late 1800s and early 1900s, for example, contributed to a socially constructed notion of individuals with disabilities as deviant and potentially dangerous individuals (A. Turnbull et al., 2011). Societal responses to the perceived "problem" of disability, including institutionalization, typically removed parents from decision-making roles and reinforced the notion that professionals were more knowledgeable and better able to determine the futures of children with disabilities than were their parents. Beliefs about the roles of parents of children with disabilities shifted during the 1940s to 1970s, as a growing number of parents expressed their dissatisfaction and advocated for changes in the residential and educational services available at the time (Yell, Rogers, & Rogers, 1998).

Passage of EHA/IDEA

The efforts of parents, disability advocacy organizations, legislators, and the courts to bring attention to exclusionary and discriminatory practices led to passage of the EHA, now known as the IDEA. IDEA affirmed a new role for parents in the education of their children with disabilities (A. Turnbull et al., 2011), particularly through the requirement for parents to participate in decisions about assessment and educational planning for their children. Further, IDEA articulated the school's responsibility for ensuring parent participation through procedural safeguards and rights, including the right of parents to provide consent to initial evaluations for special education eligibility and placement, revoke consent for services, and pursue their right to due process in the event of disagreements with the school. Bateman (2011) underscored the centrality of the parent participation principle in the IDEA, noting that failure to allow full and equal parent participation can lead to a legal determination that schools have denied a student's right to a free and appropriate public education (FAPE).

Subsequent reauthorizations of IDEA continued to underscore the need for parent participation. Part C of IDEA, enacted in 1986, mandated that services for children from birth to 3 years be delivered through an individualized family services plan (IFSP) that relies heavily on family input to identify the type and extent of special education and related services to be provided to the child (A. Turnbull et al., 2011). IDEA 1990 reaffirmed the importance of parent and student participation by mandating transition planning and the development of goals based on a student's needs, preferences, and interests (Hasazi, Furney, & DeStefano, 1999). The assumption was that although some students would be able to direct the development of their transition plans, parental input would remain critical in many instances.

Theoretical Underpinnings

The definition of parent involvement specified in the IDEA is most connected to sociological theories that emerged in the 1970s and that attributed differences in achievement and social success to differences in opportunity (Foster, Berger, & McLean, 1981). This view proposed that parents who were empowered to take an active role in educational decision making would be more likely to obtain services for their children than parents who were not similarly involved. Moreover, the parent participation principle of the EHA attempted to correct previous practices—such as the exclusion of children with disabilities and discriminatory assessment procedures—by giving parents a role that would hold professionals accountable for implementing IEP services (H. R. Turnbull et al., 1982). The purported benefits of parent participation are also connected to the idea that parents who are active participants in IEP planning will contribute to the development of educational plans with a high likelihood of success (S. W. Smith, 1990). The IEP planning process has been characterized as a constructive way for parents to gain knowledge of the school setting, for teachers to gain knowledge of the students and their home environments, and for the IEP team to create a mutual understanding that will lead to mutually agreed-upon goals.

Observed Levels of Parental Involvement and Observed Roadblocks

Early Studies of Parent Participation

The IDEA legal provisions for parent participation did not translate into immediate changes in educational practices or the actual roles of parents. In the first 15 years following passage of the EHA, researchers focused on examining the roles of parents in the IEP process and identifying factors that appeared to promote or inhibit their participation (Foster et al., 1981). For the most part, these studies reported that during IEP meetings, parents engaged in less verbal participation than educators, asked fewer questions, and demonstrated behaviors that were assumed to indicate their agreement with professional judgments (Cone, Delawyer, & Wolfe, 1985; S. Goldstein, Strickland, Turnbull, & Curry, 1980; Lusthaus, Lusthaus, & Gibbs, 1981; Vacc et al., 1985; Vaughn, Bos, Harrell, & Lasky, 1988). A finding that was initially perplexing was that most parents reported overall satisfaction with the planning process, contradicting the assumption that they would be dissatisfied with IEP meetings in which professionals maintained control over planning and decision making.

Studies focused on teachers' perceptions and behaviors indicated that many educators in fact defined "appropriate" parent roles in a passive rather than an active sense. Analyses of teacher self-reports indicated that the majority felt it was more appropriate for parents to gather and present information than to participate in educational decision making (Yoshida, Fenton, Kaufman, & Maxwell, 1978) and believed that parents should be allowed to waive their right to participation and place educational decision making solely in the hands of professionals (P. L. Gerber, Banbury, & Miller, 1986). Studies of IEP meetings identified additional barriers to parent participation, including teachers' use of unexplained and technical educational jargon in the reporting of test results and insufficient allocation of time for IEP meetings (Hughes & Ruhl, 1987), as well as presentation of completed or nearly completed IEPs that lacked parental input (P. L. Gerber et al., 1986; S. Goldstein et al., 1980).

Reconceptualizing Parent Participation

As the 1980s drew to a close, early characterizations of parents as passive participants who were generally satisfied with the IEP process were called into question. For example, because most participants in the studies were Caucasian mothers from middle class backgrounds, findings could not be generalized to other populations (A. Turnbull & Turnbull, 1990). Moreover, the 1980s witnessed a paradigm shift in which proponents of parent participation and early intervention began to focus on family systems theory and family support models that conceptualized families as social systems with unique characteristics and needs (Blue-Banning, Summers, Frankland, Nelson, & Beegle, 2004). These models posited that professionals should focus their work on identifying families' needs and choices, encouraging family control in decision making, and creating effective and collaborative partnerships that extended beyond the IEP planning context. Family-centered approaches also encouraged parents to establish their own expectations for involvement, acknowledging that some families want to play greater roles in their children's educational programs than others (Bruder, 2000; MacMillan & Turnbull, 1983).

The literature also reflects a shift in language during the 1980s. Whereas the IDEA continued to refer to "parent" participation, researchers and practitioners began to refer to the participation of "families" (Blue-Banning et al., 2004). This change was indicative of the fact that although the IEP process continued to focus on the legal authority of one or more parents, expanded definitions of participation reflected a need to collaborate with the individuals in a student's broader family constellation, both within and outside of the IEP and IFSP processes.

Reconceptualizing Barriers to Parent Involvement

As the research on parent participation moved away from a singular focus on behavior during IEP meetings, it evolved to include a deeper exploration of cultural and contextual barriers to meaningful participation and the development of collaborative relationships between parents and professionals.

Culture and Context

In the 1980s and 1990s, researchers began to explore issues of diversity and their relationship to parent participation in the IEP process (Greene, 1996; E. W. Lynch & Stein, 1983; Sileo, Sileo, & Prater, 1996; Sontag & Schacht, 1994). These studies generally described parents from diverse backgrounds as playing passive roles in the IEP process, but the studies provided alternate explanations for previous deficit views of this dynamic and identified issues of power and differences in cultural values and beliefs that were often subtle but defined many of the relationships between professionals and parents (Harry, 1992a, 1992b, 2008; Geenan, Powers, & Lopez-Vasquez, 2001; Rao, 2000; Sileo et al., 1996).

The literature has identified ways in which definitions of and responses to disability are culturally situated, which, if not understood, may serve as a barrier to effective school and family collaboration (Harry, Allen, & McLaughlin, 1995). For example, Western perspectives of disability as an individual phenomenon with medical, biological, and physical origins and a need for remediation (Kalyanpur & Harry, 1999) are quite different from cultural and religious beliefs that may define disability from a more spiritual perspective (Lamory, 2002). Qualitative studies conducted with Latino mothers of children with developmental disabilities (D. G. Skinner, Correa, Skinner, & Bailey, 2001) and families of children with autism (Jegatheesan, Miller, & Fowler, 2010) identified spiritual and religious lenses on disability that are not generally acknowledged by white, middle class educators and may result in misunderstandings and frustration in the IEP process (Harry, 2008). Additionally, Sileo et al. (1996) noted the ways in which ideals such as efficiency, independence, self-determination, and equity are valued by Americans of European descent but may clash with the values held by families whose cultures prize family associations and the extended family structure.

Relationships, Collaboration, and Language

Barriers related to language have been identified among parents from diverse linguistic backgrounds, as well as among parents who are fluent in English but do not understand the vocabulary and terms used in the IEP process

(Dabkowski, 2004). Parents also report feeling excluded based on subtle messages and nonverbal communication conveyed by professionals. Parents find it difficult to participate when they lack information regarding special education processes, terminology, and parental rights (Lytle & Bordin, 2001), and when they encounter IEPs that have been written before meetings (Spann, Kohler, & Soenksen, 2003). They continue to report that the IEP process is characterized by a lack of trust, poor communication, and failure to develop positive, collaborative relationships that could support effective planning and service delivery (Rao, 2000; Whitbread, Bruder, Fleming, & Park, 2007). This appears to be the case for families of children of all ages, including young children receiving early intervention services (McWilliam, Tocci, & Harbin, 1998) as well as older students preparing for the transition from school to adult life (McNair & Rusch, 1991; Salembier & Furney, 1997).

Strategies for Enhancing Involvement

One set of strategies proposed to enhance parent participation in the IEP process focuses on defining indicators of effective family and professional partnerships and developing related skills among professionals and parents. Blue-Banning et al. (2004) suggested that the field conduct research to operationalize the construct of positive partnerships among families and professionals. They and others maintained that a commonly accepted set of definitions would allow the development of measures that could be used in conducting empirical studies of parent participation, promoting accountability among professionals, and identifying a clear set of competencies and skills that could be addressed through pre-service education. Strategies proposed for enhancing skill development include expanding the pre-service curriculum for educators to include a focus on the development of skills in collaboration, problem solving, and cultural perceptions of difference (Hoover-Dempsey, Walker, Jones, & Reed, 2002); providing joint training and opportunities for dialogue among parents and professionals (Whitbread et al., 2007); fostering self-reflection and awareness among educators regarding cultural sensitivity and cultural reciprocity (Harry, 2008; Kalyanpur & Harry, 1999); and providing information and support to parents regarding special education processes and research-based practices (A. Turnbull et al., 2010).

A second set of strategies focuses on implementing specific approaches for conducting IEP and other planning meetings in a manner that emphasizes families' expertise and creates an environment conducive to building trust, respect, communication, and positive and collaborative relationships (Furney & Salembier, 2000; Geenan et al., 2001). These include PCP approaches

(Claes et al., 2010) and the COACH process (Giangreco et al., 2011), which are discussed in more detail in a subsequent section.

Effectiveness of Strategies for Increasing Parent Participation

Although the literature provides many suggestions for increasing parent participation and positive school and family partnerships, relatively little research has been conducted on the effectiveness of specific strategies. In addition to the empirical literature examining PCP and COACH, reviewed in the following section, Boone (1992) explored the use of a parent-training strategy designed to increase parent participation in transition planning for students with disabilities but found no significant differences between the degree and levels of active participation of parents receiving and not receiving the intervention. Whitbread et al. (2007) concluded that a joint training strategy involving parents of children with disabilities and school professionals improved participants' skills in collaboration, but the authors acknowledged a need to follow-up on long-term effectiveness.

Studies of the relationship between strategies to improve parent participation and student outcomes are even rarer. Poponi (2009) conducted an extensive review of the literature on family involvement in both the IEP and broader school contexts, identifying only one study that measured the relationship between increased parent participation and improved student performance. In this study, McConaughy, Kay, and Fitzgerald (1999) compared outcomes between students in kindergarten whose parents were included in regularly scheduled multidisciplinary team meetings and students whose parents were not included, finding significantly greater reductions in the exhibition of children's problematic behaviors for the first group, as rated by teachers and parents. Poponi's retrospective review of 270 records of students with disabilities found significant differences in students' grades based on their parents' attendance or nonattendance at IEP meetings. This study represents a step toward linking increased parent participation with improved outcomes for students with disabilities; however, it examined participation as a function of attendance, rather than through broader constructs such as active participation, collaboration among families and professionals, or other factors.

Examples of Family-Centered Practices

We turn now to a description of two family-centered practices that are supported by research and show promise for increasing parental participation in the IEP

process: (a) PCP approaches (Claes et al., 2010) and (b) COACH (Giangreco et al., 2011). Both processes are typically conducted before the IEP meeting and focus on creating a planning context that enhances the development of partnerships between professionals and families and encourages family and individual choice and decision making around the identification of educational goals and services.

Person-Centered Planning

In reaction to traditional planning meetings that tended to be dominated by professionals, PCP has emerged as a viable alternative (Keyes & Owens-Johnson, 2003) "that is focused entirely on the interests of an individual with disabilities and keeps them first" (Rasheed, Fore, & Miller, 2006, p. 48). Rasheed et al. noted that although no clearly accepted definition of PCP exists, it can be described generally as a reflective, strength-based planning process attended by and focused on an individual with disabilities and a variety of people close to the individual (typically including parents), which results in a vision of the future for the individual with disabilities (based on his or her preferences) and plans for achieving that vision. As summarized in Figure 5.1, Flannery, Newton, Horner, Slovic, Blumberg, and Ard (2000) delineated nine critical attributes of PCP.

PCP has become a popular planning approach used for individuals (a) with a variety of disabilities, most commonly those with developmental and intellectual disabilities; (b) at varying ages, from young children into adulthood; and (c) in a variety of settings (e.g., school,

Figure 5.1 Nine critical attributes of person centered planning.

1. The individual is present at the meeting(s).
2. The individual participates in the process.
3. The individual (and family/advocates, if appropriate) determines who will be present at the meeting.
4. The people participating in the planning know the individual well.
5. The planning is based on the individual's interests, preferences, and strengths.
6. The planning is based on the individual's vision of the future.
7. The process results in an action plan.
8. The action plan includes a clear process for monitoring implementation of the plan.
9. The process is flexible and informal.

Source: Information from Flannery, K. B., Newton, S., Horner, R. H., Slovic, R., Blumberg, R., & Ard, W. R. (2000). The impact of person centered planning on the content and organization of individual supports. *Career Development of Exceptional Individuals, 23,* 123–137.

home community). Although PCP may involve a variety of processes for eliciting input from participants to envision and plan for the future of an individual with disabilities, PCP often uses an established tool for this purpose, including Essential Lifestyle Planning (ELP; Smull & Sanderson, 2005), Lifestyle Planning (J. O'Brien & Lyle, 1987), the McGill Action Planning System (MAPS; Forest & Lusthaus, 1987; Vandercook, York, & Forest, 1989), Personal Futures Planning (Mount & Zwernik, 1988), and Planning Alternative Tomorrows with Hope (PATH; Pearpoint, O'Brien, & Forest, 1993).

Historical and Theoretical Underpinnings of Person-Centered Planning

As summarized by C. L. O'Brien and O'Brien (2000), PCP evolved out of communities of practice devoted to the principles of normalization in the 1970s and 1980s. The normalization movement posited that all people, including those with intellectual disabilities, should be perceived and treated as developing, full-fledged human beings (Wolfensberger, 1972). The principles of normalization were used to deconstruct the services, supports, and planning provided to individuals with intellectual disabilities. Perceptions of individuals with disabilities as inferior or even subhuman historically led to segregation (e.g., institutionalization) and inadequate provision of services and supports, which in turn perpetuated negative attitudes and low expectations. PCP originated in reaction to these conditions and in the context of social and political activism associated with the 1970s for improving and normalizing the opportunities of individuals with disabilities (e.g., advocacy for and passage of the Rehabilitation Act of 1973 and the EHA in 1975).

The principles of self-determination were a logical outgrowth of the normalization movement that also provided the conceptual foundation for PCP. Wehmeyer (1996) defined *self-determination* as "acting as the primary causal agent in one's life and making choices and decisions regarding one's quality of life free from undue external influence or interference" (p. 22). Traditionally, professionals have made the critical decisions in the lives of many individuals with disabilities. Self-determination holds that individuals should make their own decisions, regardless of their disability status. PCP bases planning and supports on the hopes and desires of individuals with disabilities with the assistance and input from those closest to them (e.g., family), rather than solely on the basis of professionals' recommendations.

Description of PCP Implementation

Describing the implementation of PCP can be challenging because *person-centered planning* is an umbrella term encompassing a variety of practices meant to be applied flexibly. In this section, we describe the procedures used in an experimental study supporting the effectiveness of PCP for improving parental participation in developing IEPs (Miner & Bates, 1997). Miner and Bates used procedures adapted largely from the Personal Futures Planning model (Mount & Zwernick, 1988). Activities included (a) developing a personal profile, (b) describing a desirable future, and (c) planning for attaining goals. To conduct these activities, the student and family met with a trained facilitator at a location of the family's choosing.

To generate a personal profile, the student and family first developed a circle of support by naming people in the student's life at four levels (represented by four circles): (a) closest and most important people (e.g., family members, close friends), (b) people close to (but not closest to) the student, (c) people in the student's life (e.g., via church, sports teams, clubs), and (d) people paid to be involved in the student's life (e.g., teachers, doctors). The student and family next developed a community presence map, listing community settings the student used. These two processes and the resulting documents provided a frame of reference in subsequent discussions about how the student could "be assisted in developing greater choice and autonomy in community participation" (p. 107). The final steps in the personal profile development involved listing things that work and do not work for the student (e.g., identifying student preferences) and listing the students' gifts and capacities (e.g., "What do people who like the student say about her or him?"). Primary members identified in the circle of support were invited to subsequent planning sessions.

In the next step, describing a desirable future, the planning team answered questions from the facilitator regarding future living situations, community participation, employment, and recreation and leisure. The facilitator stressed that the vision for the student's future being developed should not be based on the perceived limits of the student's disability. In the final step, planning for attaining goals, participants identified three to five activities that could immediately move the student closer to goal attainment. The meeting ended by summarizing the student's future goals, activities identified for moving toward those goals, the needed services and supports for those activities, and the individuals responsible. The facilitator also encouraged the team to meet periodically to review progress and to identify new activities needed to attain the student's vision.

A detailed lesson plan starter—including an objective, setting and materials, content taught, teaching procedures, and method of evaluation—on the PCP procedures used by Miner and Bates (1997) that were shown to result in improved parental participation in the IEP process is available on the National Secondary Transition Technical Assistance Center's Web site (NSTTAC, n.d.). A number of online resources provide further information on implementing PCP (e.g., Inclusive Solutions, n.d.; Interactive Collaborative Autism Network, n.d.).

Research on PCP and Parental Participation in the IEP Process

Research on PCP has examined its effect on outcomes such as social networks, community involvement, choice making, knowledge, reduction of problem behaviors, and process issues (e.g., participation of parents) (see Claes et al., 2010, for a review of this literature). In this chapter, we specifically review research related to PCP and the participation of parents in the IEP process.

Experimental research.   In Miner and Bates's (1997) experimental study of PCP, 22 adolescents with intellectual disabilities and their families were matched by program placement, IQ, anticipated year of school exit, and communication skills. One student/family from each pair was randomly assigned to either the experimental (7 males, 4 females) or control group (5 males, 6 females); ethnicity of participants was not described. PCP activities took place at sites selected by each family. All but one opted to meet at their homes; one meeting was conducted at a high school. Procedures were adapted primarily from the Personal Futures Planning model (as detailed in the previous section). The PCP meetings took place with experimental group families approximately 2 weeks before IEP meetings. Materials and results from the PCP meetings were reviewed with and provided to the families by the facilitator approximately 2 days before their IEP meetings. The control group did not receive any support before IEP meetings but were provided opportunities to engage in PCP after their meetings were completed.

An observer recorded who was speaking at all of the IEP meetings using a momentary time sampling approach with 15-second intervals. Two trained observers collected data at six of the 22 (27%) IEP meetings to collect inter-rater reliability data. Mean inter-rater agreement for speakers was 90%. Implementation fidelity was not assessed, although the same experienced, trained special educator facilitated all PCP meetings. Participants completed satisfaction surveys directly after each IEP meeting and again 2 months after the IEP meeting.

Parents were observed speaking at 26% of intervals ($SD = 11.2$) in the experimental group, compared to 14% ($SD = 10.9$) in the control group, a statistically significant difference. Parents in both the experimental and control groups expressed high levels of satisfaction with the IEP meeting related to preparation, input, satisfaction with goals, and likelihood of goal achievement (all means > 4 on a 1 [highly dissatisfied] to 5 [highly

satisfied] scale). Differences between groups were not statistically significant.

On the follow-up survey (2 months after the IEP meetings), participants compared the recently completed IEP meeting with the previous year's IEP meeting on a 1 (much less favorable) to 5 (much more favorable) scale. Although statistical analyses were not conducted, when matched pairs were compared, parents in the experimental group ($M = 4.11$, $SD = 0.59$) gave higher ratings than parents in the control group ($M = 3.47$, $SD = 0.33$) for 10 of the 11 pairs (SDs calculated from data provided in article). Because these data were provided in the article, we were able to conduct a t-test, which indicated that parents in the experimental group provided significantly higher ratings than those in the control group ($p < 0.01$), with an effect size (Cohen's d) of 1.29. When asked to rate the value of the PCP activities, six parents in the experimental group rated them as extremely valuable, three as valuable, and two as neutral.

Within-group comparison research.   Flannery et al. (2000) conducted an evaluation of PCP on a single group of students with disabilities and their families that included examination of parental participation in the IEP-planning process. The study involved 10 students (7 female, 3 male) ages 19 to 21 and their parents. The students were categorized as having intellectual disabilities ($n = 3$), specific learning disability (SLD; $n = 3$), speech and language impairment, hearing impairment, other health impairment and SLD, and orthopedic impairment and SLD. The families had all taken part in PCP meetings facilitated by educators who were trained as part of the Oregon Transition Systems Change Project.

Using a 1 to 4 Likert scale (from "strongly agree" to "strongly disagree"), parents and students indicated statistically significantly higher satisfaction with IEP meetings and planning occurring after PCP training in comparison to before PCP training on these items related to their participation:

- "I was allowed to talk about my hopes and dreams" ($p < 0.05$).

- "At the meeting, I was allowed to contribute to the discussion of the goals, actions, or next steps included on my plan" ($p < 0.05$).

Flannery et al. (2000) also reported that educators rated the structure for family and student involvement ($p < 0.001$), family involvement ($p < 0.001$), and their understanding of the family's goals and desires ($p < 0.001$) as significantly higher at the post-PCP meeting in comparison to the pre-PCP meeting. Moreover, parents and students ($p < 0.05$), as well as educators ($p < 0.001$), indicated a significantly higher level of overall satisfaction with the planning at the post-PCP meetings in comparison to the pre-PCP meetings.

Qualitative research. Childre and Chambers (2005) studied six students and their families. The students were 10 to 15 years old, with moderate intellectual disabilities (*n* = 2) and orthopedic impairments (*n* = 4); three were African American and three Caucasian. Using established person-centered tools, the researchers developed a new approach to PCP that explicitly emphasized the link to IEP meetings, which they referred to as Student-Centered Individualized Education Planning (SCIEP). The SCIEP uses written forms to guide and document person-centered techniques. Before IEP meetings, families completed three forms: the Relationship Circle, Dreams, and Goals. Students completed two forms: Strengths and Preferences, and Goals and Dreams. A trained special educator facilitated the IEP meetings by incorporating the information on these forms and the perspectives of individuals attending the IEP meeting onto seven forms, which were used to help design the students' IEPs: Relationship Circle, Community Survey (to identify places in the community frequented by the family in order to develop community-based curricula), Now (i.e., present level of functioning), What Works (factors that promote student success), Dreams, Goals, and Who and When (describes team members' responsibilities).

In interviews conducted after the SCIEP process, families reported they generally enjoyed the SCIEP process and found it productive and worthwhile. Specifically related to their involvement in the IEP meetings, parents noted,

> The process encouraged communication, brainstorming, and problem solving between families and professionals. These meetings were characterized by their shift from simple exchange of information between team members toward true collaboration. "Everybody, each one, put in their input and discussed it to the fullest." (p. 226)

Case studies. The positive effect of PCP on parental participation in the IEP process is also supported by reports from case studies. For example, in a case study of PCP in two culturally distinct communities (one primarily Caucasian, one primarily Latino), Trainor (2007) reported that, "PCP increased the amount and quality of participation of both youth and families" (p. 98) in both communities. Furthermore, the bilingual special education teacher who facilitated PCP meetings in the Latino community noted that, "when you do a PCP, they become the experts. The parents are the ones telling you, the kid is the one telling you, and, if you think about it, that's the way a normal IEP should be, but it's not" (p. 97).

In another case study, Salembier and Furney (1994) described a PCP process based on a modified MAPS procedure that was used to write the transition section of the IEP for Peter, a 10th-grade student with a nonspecified disability, over 2 years. Peter's special education teacher observed that PCP

> really helped his parents take a more active role in planning. By the time of the second MAP, they were more vocal and clearer about Peter's future goals and needs. They now have a feeling that they are partners with the school in making things happen for Peter. (Salembier & Furney, 1994, p. 16)

Finally, Chambers and Childre (2005) provided a case study of PCP on a first-grade student. The authors described and applied the "true directions" model of PCP, which uses the SCIEP tools and forms described previously. The authors reported that the child's parents and grandparents were both active and influential participants in their child's IEP.

Summary of research. The effectiveness of PCP for improving parental participation in the IEP process is supported by a small number of research studies, including one experimental study with a randomly assigned control group (Miner & Bates, 1997). However, this is the only experimental study we identified on the topic. Accordingly, educators should be cautious in drawing the conclusion that PCP causes improved parental participation in the IEP process until subsequent experimental research replicates these findings. More research also seems warranted related to the impact of different models of PCP. Additionally, component analyses will be important to identify which components of PCP are essential for attaining desired outcomes. Although some initial research (e.g., Trainor, 2007) and theoretical analysis (e.g., Callicott, 2003) have indicated that PCP can be successfully adapted for students and families who are culturally and linguistically diverse, further research is also warranted regarding its application for improving parental participation among diverse populations. Furthermore, given the important role of the facilitator in the PCP process, future researchers should examine facilitator skills and attributes that may be associated with levels of parental participation. Although limited in number and scope of studies, research supporting PCP as a tool for improving parental participation in the IEP process has been conducted by multiple investigators in different settings, and findings suggest that students, families, and educators express satisfaction with PCP (e.g., Flannery et al., 2000; Miner & Bates, 1997).

Choosing Outcomes and Accommodations for Children

Overview of COACH

Now in its ninth version since 1985, COACH is an assessment and planning process designed to assist school personnel in working collaboratively with families to develop IEPs for students with intensive special education needs (Giangreco et al., 2011). A secondary aim of COACH is to assist families in becoming better consumers of educational services and partners in the educational process. COACH is designed primarily to plan for students, ages 3 through 21, with low-incidence disabilities whose curricular content needs extend beyond the typical general education curriculum corresponding to their chronological age. In other words, some of the most important things these students need to learn (e.g., foundational communication, socialization, and academic access skills) have already been mastered by most other students their age and therefore are not reflected in typical general education curricula.

COACH is divided into two parts (Part A, Determining a Student's Educational Program, and Part B, Strategies and Processes to Implement a COACH-Generated Educational Program), including six major steps (see Figure 5.2), and also includes strategies for implementing COACH-generated plans in inclusive classrooms (e.g., scheduling matrix, tools for planning

instruction). Information presented here focuses on the first three steps of Part A of COACH because they include family participation. The Family Interview (Step 1) is the heart of COACH—it provides a unique combination of features to assist families in selecting a small set of the highest-priority learning outcomes for their child. To ensure students have sufficiently broad curricular opportunities, Additional Learning Outcomes (Step 2) assists in identifying a set of learning outcomes from both those listed in COACH and the general education curriculum. General Supports (Step 3) assists in identifying supports to be provided to or for students with disabilities across six categories so they can pursue the learning outcomes identified in Steps 1 and 2.

Conceptual Basis for COACH

COACH is rooted in a set of foundational principles that potential consumers of COACH should consider, so their team, including the family, can make an informed

Figure 5.2 Parts and steps of Choosing Outcomes and Accommodations for Children (COACH).

Part A: Determining a Student's Educational Program

Preparation Checklist

Step 1: Family Interview

Introducing the Family Interview

Step 1.1: Valued Life Outcomes

Step 1.2: Selecting Curriculum Areas to Explore During the Family Interview

(a) Communication, (b) Socialization, (c) Personal Management, (d) Access Academics, (e) Applied Academics, (f) Recreation, (g) School, (h) Community, (i) Vocational

Step 1.3: Rating Learning Outcomes in Selected Curriculum Areas

Step 1.4: Prioritizing Learning Outcomes in Selected Curriculum Areas

Step 1.5: Cross-Prioritization

Step 2: Additional Learning Outcomes

Step 2.1: Additional Learning Outcomes from COACH

Step 2.2: Additional Learning Outcomes from General Education

(a) Language Arts, (b) Math, (c) Science, (d) Social Studies, (e) Physical Education/Health, (f) Foreign Language, (g) Art, (h) Music, (i) Other

Step 3: General Supports

(a) Physical Needs, (b) Personal Needs, (c) Sensory Needs, (d) Teaching Others About the Student, (e) Providing Access and Opportunities, (f) Other General Supports

Part B: Translating the Family-Identified Priorities into Goals and Objectives

Step 4: Annual Goals

Step 5: Short-Term Objectives

Step 6: Program-at-a-Glance

Source: Information from Giangreco, M. F., Cloninger, C. J., & Iverson, V. S. (2011). *Choosing outcomes and accommodations for children (COACH): A guide to educational planning for students with disabilities* (3rd ed.). Baltimore: Brookes.

Figure 5.3   Principles forming the basis of Choosing Outcomes and Accommodations for Children (COACH).

1. All students are capable of learning and deserve a meaningful curriculum.

2. Quality instruction requires ongoing access to inclusive environments.

3. Pursuing valued life outcomes informs the selection of curricular content.

   - Safety and health (physical and emotional)

   - A home—now and in the future

   - Meaningful relationships

   - Control over personal choices (suited to the student's age and culture)

   - Meaningful activities in various and valued places

4. Family involvement is a cornerstone of educational planning.

   - Families know certain aspects of their children better than anyone else.

   - Families have the greatest vested interest in seeing their children learn.

   - Families should be approached in culturally sensitive ways.

   - The family is likely to be the only group of adults involved with a child's educational program throughout his entire school career.

   - Families have the ability to positively influence the quality of educational services provided in their community.

5. Collaborative teamwork is essential to quality education.

6. Coordination of services ensures that necessary supports are appropriately provided.

Source: Information from Giangreco, M. F., Cloninger, C. J., & Iverson, V. S. (2011). *Choosing outcomes and accommodations for children (COACH): A guide to educational planning for students with disabilities* (3rd ed.). Baltimore: Brookes.

decision about whether to use it (see Figure 5.3). Although each step of COACH includes a statement of purpose, forms, explicit directions for use, and helpful hints, it is purposely not standardized. Part of its family-centered approach encourages thoughtful individualization to match variations across the wide range of families schools serve. To maintain the internal integrity of the tool if adapting any aspects of COACH, facilitators are advised to do so in ways that are congruent with its underlying principles.

Some Unique Elements of COACH

Although it shares some similarities with other assessment approaches (e.g., checklists of observable behaviors across multiple curricular domains, scoring based on parent reporting), COACH also embodies elements that distinguish it from other tools and deliberately links the collection of certain types of assessment data (e.g., parent perspectives) with curricular and instructional planning. This section describes a few embedded aspects unique to COACH that have been designed to contribute to its effectiveness.

Posture of listening.   Many well-intended parent–professional interactions are dominated by professionals sharing data (often deficit based) they have collected, followed by telling parents what they think is important.

COACH reverses this common and potentially problematic practice, first during the Family Interview by having professionals assume the roles of question asker and listener, with the goal of better understanding what the family thinks is important. An explicitly designed set and sequence of questions, field tested and adjusted over many years, provides a facilitated process culminating in the selection of a small set of high-priority learning outcomes by the student's family. As COACH proceeds through Steps 2 (Additional Learning Outcomes) and 3 (General Supports), it continues to provide a facilitated forum for professionals and parents to listen to each other and establish shared expectations about a student's educational program components. Having shared goals and a productive dynamic that acknowledges the respective expertise of professionals and families is foundational to collaborative teamwork and constructive home–school relationships.

Valued life outcomes.   An initial substep within the Family Interview, valued life outcomes (Step 1.1), sets the context for selecting curricular content by asking families a series of carefully crafted questions about the current and desired future status of five valued life outcomes for their child (see Figure 5.2). These questions are purposely worded in broad terms so families can attach their own personal meaning. Step 1.1 ends with the family being asked to rate their level of concern/importance about each of the valued life outcomes. This substep provides valuable information to school personnel in planning an appropriate educational program responsive to a vision for the student identified by the family and emphasizes improving quality of life indicators for individuals with disabilities (Dennis, Williams, Giangreco, & Cloninger, 1993).

Creative problem solving.   Professionals with good intentions often seek input from families but with inadequate attention to the methods used. Open-ended questions such as, "What would you like to see on Sam's IEP this year?" or "What are your priorities for Cara?" might work for some families, but all too often such broad queries result in parents' deferring to professionals or making selections that do not adequately reflect their perspectives. This can occur because families are faced with trying to make priority selections based on hundreds of potential options without any strategies to help generate, organize, sort, and select from among a vast array of possibilities.

COACH relies on selected elements of the Osborn-Parnes Creative Problem-Solving Process (CPS) (Parnes, 1988), an approach with a history of documented effectiveness (Parnes, 1992), to gather meaningful input from families and facilitate the selection of priorities for their child. Although COACH does not employ a classic application of the CPS process, it embeds some of its key features, a few of which are presented here. The first three steps in COACH (Part A) offer multiple opportunities to alternate between divergent and convergent thinking to facilitate the selection of desired elements of the students' educational program. The divergent aspects encourage problem solvers to explore and generate possibilities by posing various types of fact-finding questions in an atmosphere of deferred judgment. Convergent aspects encourage analysis of the divergently generated possibilities and fact finding to focus on a smaller set of options, moving toward ultimate selections. The opportunities to alternate between the divergent and convergent aspects of COACH are purposely separated and repeated because generating ideas and attempting to evaluate them at the same time can inhibit informed decision making.

Research Base for COACH

Research on COACH summarized here is separated into two categories: (a) studies that directly informed the development of new or revised elements of COACH, and (b) studies about COACH (e.g., its use and impact). Step 1.1 (Valued Life Outcomes) was developed as a direct result of a qualitative study of 28 Vermont families

whose children, ages 3 to 20, had sensory and multiple disabilities (Giangreco, Cloninger, Mueller, Yuan, & Ashworth, 1991). Based on semi-structured interviews, this study sought to better understand parents' perspectives about the impact of educational and related services on the lives of their children. The findings (a) highlighted the importance of connecting the selection of individualized curriculum content to quality of life indicators; (b) resulted in the articulation of the underlying principles of COACH; and (c) offered explicit categories of what parents identified as a "good life" (p. 18) for their children, which are reflected in the Step 1.1 questions and are embedded elsewhere in COACH.

A qualitative document analysis of 46 IEPs of students in grades K–12 with multiple disabilities in nine states (Giangreco, Dennis, Edelman, & Cloninger, 1994) identified a series of problematic characteristics of IEP goals and objectives. Some of these included IEP goals that were so vague (e.g., "Peter will improve communication skills," p. 290) that they were virtually meaningless to an educational team. Other IEP goals (a) lacked observable behaviors, (b) were selected based on what was valued independently by various professionals, or (c) were written with excessive related-services jargon. Many of the IEP documents analyzed were 20 to 30 pages long (one was 49 pages), with dozens of annual goals, rendering them quite improbable to deliver. The numerous negative findings from this study informed alternatives reflected throughout the principles of COACH and practices found in virtually all the steps of COACH (e.g., observable learning outcomes, selection of a small set of parent-selected priorities, and clear distinction between learning outcomes and general supports).

A descriptive, quantitative study followed changes in educational team membership for 18 students with sensory and multiple disabilities in four states over 4 years (Giangreco, Edelman, Nelson, Young, & Kiefer-O'Donnell, 1999). The findings revealed substantial team membership changeover from year to year, including 384 different team members, and identified families as the only constant for all 18 students across all 4 years. Data from this study further strengthened the principles of COACH, particularly those related to the importance of family involvement, and are reflected in practical aspects of facilitating COACH (e.g., COACH participants, team membership and roles, language used in Introducing the Family Interview).

Six studies have been conducted specifically about COACH. A national expert validation of COACH included two descriptive, quantitative studies (Giangreco, Cloninger, Dennis, & Edelman, 1993). The first study included 78 participants from 27 states who met specified criteria from two respondent categories: (a) national and state experts (e.g., university faculty, national technical assistance providers), and (b) field-based experts (e.g., parents, special educators, related services providers). Using a survey instrument, each participant reviewed COACH and rated it as highly congruent with a set of 20 exemplary practices it purports to embody across six categories: (a) family-centered practices, (b) collaborative planning, (c) social responsibility, (d) curriculum planning, (e) individualized instruction, and (f) family–school collaboration. The second study within the national validation (Giangreco et al., 1993) sought to extend the initial qualitative research on parents' perspectives (Giangreco et al., 1991) by exploring how a larger set of parents from geographically diverse states would perceive the valued life outcomes in COACH. From four states, a group of 44 parents of children with sensory and multiple disabilities, ages 5 to 20, validated that the valued life outcomes included in COACH were highly consistent with what they perceived as a "good life" for their children with disabilities.

A mixed-methods study about the use and impact of COACH was based on 30 students, ages 5 to 21, in eight states (Giangreco, Edelman, Dennis, & Cloninger, 1995). Researchers relied on interviews, observations, and document analysis, with data collected from 78 educational team members (e.g., special educators, parents, teachers). In part, the findings documented how COACH contributed to parent–professional relationships (e.g., better collaboration, improved perceptions of families by professionals, more parental involvement in decision making). Specifically related to parental participation, the findings reported the elements and structure of COACH (a) increased parent participation in educational planning, opened dialogue on previously undiscussed topics, and shifted educational decision-making control toward families; (b) provided opportunities that resulted in professionals' viewing parents more favorably; (c) encouraged parents to think about potential priorities in ways that they would not have considered before; (d) helped parents organize and communicate their ideas; and (e) ultimately helped parents identify relevant priorities that contributed to positive changes in valued life outcomes for their children. As one parent stated, "Of everything we've tried, and we've tried lots of different approaches over the years with Sandra of coming up with IEP goals, this just gave us so much assistance in really getting what we wanted for her and helping us crystallize what we really did want" (p. 126). Two single-case studies, one based on a preschool student with Down syndrome (Giangreco, Whiteford, Whiteford, & Doyle, 1998) and the other based on a high school student with deaf-blindness and intellectual disabilities (Edelman, Knutson, Osborn, & Giangreco, 1995), reiterated the positive impact of using COACH on parent participation, educational teams, and students with disabilities.

Lastly, a qualitative, cross-cultural review of COACH was conducted. Fourteen individuals from a wide range of minority cultures in the United States, who met specific selection criteria, reviewed COACH and then participated in interviews about it (Dennis & Giangreco, 1996). The findings presented issues pertaining to cultural sensitivity in family interviewing while avoiding stereotyping and generalizations. Findings from the study were incorporated in the principles of COACH and are embedded in a variety of specific directions, forms, and helpful hints in COACH (e.g., considerations for seating arrangements, use of translators, asking parents whether they want to be asked categories of questions in Step 1.1).

The evidence base for COACH has four main limitations: (a) only a small number of studies about COACH ($n = 6$) have been conducted; (b) all of the studies are descriptive in nature (i.e., no experimental or quasi-experimental studies have yet been published; (c) existing research is dated, and no recent research on COACH is available or known to be forthcoming; and (d) the studies highlighted were conducted by the developers of COACH or close associates. One descriptive study by researchers not involved in developing the program identified COACH as a useful practice to facilitate choosing and planning what to teach students with moderate and severe disabilities in inclusive classrooms (Jackson, Ryndak, & Billingsly, 2000). Although the research base is modest and nonexperimental, few other planning tools report evidence. Because it is designed to be a nonstandardized planning tool with assessment elements, rather than a standardized assessment, and because its potential impact might reasonably be thought of as two or three steps removed from direct student outcomes, COACH is not very amenable to evaluations that use research designs that seek to experimentally verify its impact on student outcomes. The nonstandardized nature of the tool and its directions, which include parents' making informed decisions to use it, presents a self-selection bias that could further hamper experimental comparisons. Despite the modest data available on the impact of COACH, it continues to be used by consumers in the field with some regularity. Future research by nondevelopers of the tool would be a welcome contribution to the literature.

Conclusion

The IDEA identifies a central, specific, and active role for parents in their children's education and IEPs, reflecting the ethical, theoretical, and empirical support for parent involvement in the education of students with disabilities (A. Turnbull et al., 2011). However, research has identified numerous barriers to meaningful parent participation, including differences in culture and context, failure to develop positive relationships, a lack of emphasis on families' wishes regarding their child's future, and challenges related to language and communication. This chapter includes a description of two practices, PCP and COACH, which are identified as promising practices for enhancing parent participation in the IEP process on the basis of their research support. The preceding reviews of the literature suggest that although much has been learned, there is a continued need to identify and conduct research on practices to enhance parents' roles as educational decision makers in the IEP process.

Although PCP and COACH appear promising, we recommend developing the research base on these and other practices for improving parent participation in the IEP process in a number of ways. First, although PCP and COACH are implemented with some frequency in schools, they are hardly commonplace. We recommend that researchers investigate what training and supports are associated with educators using PCP, COACH, and other approaches to enhance parent participation effectively and pervasively throughout schools, districts, or communities. Furthermore, the majority of the studies conducted on parental participation to date have relied on qualitative case studies and interviews, surveys, and observations to collect information. Many of these studies have been critical to expanding our understanding of parents' perspectives on the IEP process and the cultural, linguistic, and relational barriers to participation (Harry, 2008). At the same time, the dearth of experimental studies makes it difficult for parents and educators to draw firm conclusions about the effectiveness of specific strategies. As such, we recommend that researchers conduct more intervention research, including single-subject research studies (e.g., multiple baseline across participants), to examine the effectiveness of specific strategies for improving parent participation in the IEP process.

Future research should also examine the impact of new developments in the educational landscape on parental participation. For example, the context of parental participation in their children's education has changed with the advent of the Internet and social media. Future research should investigate whether parents are accessing information about their legal rights and research-based interventions for their children through these sources, whether they are using that information in planning meetings, and whether online communication tools can be incorporated into existing approaches to increase parent participation in the IEP process to make them even more effective.

CHAPTER 6

Individualized Education Programs:
Legal Requirements and Research Findings

Christine A. Christle and **Mitchell L. Yell** | *University of South Carolina*

According to Yell and Crockett (2011), before the mid 1970s, students' with disabilities access to public education was limited in two major ways. First, many students were completely excluded from public schools. Second, many students with disabilities were admitted to school but did not receive an education that was appropriate to their needs. These students were often "left to fend for themselves in classrooms designed for education of their nonhandicapped peers" (*Board of Education v. Rowley*, 1982, p. 191). Because of these challenges faced by students with disabilities, the U.S. Congress passed legislation to ensure the educational rights of all students with disabilities. In 1975, the Education for All Handicapped Children Act (EHA) was enacted to guarantee that eligible students with disabilities received an education suited to their unique needs. When the EHA was reauthorized in 1990, the name of the law was changed to the Individuals with Disabilities Education Act (IDEA). Note that every 5 or 6 years Congress reauthorizes, and usually amends, the IDEA. These amendments often make significant changes to the law. In this chapter when we address specific changes made in the amendments, we will refer to the specific year in which the law was changed (e.g., IDEA 2004). When we are not referring to these specific changes, we will use the actual name of the law: IDEA.

With EHA and IDEA, Congress granted every eligible student with a disability the right to receive a free appropriate public education (FAPE). Congress believed that the goal of providing a FAPE was best ensured by individualizing a student's education. Toward that end, Congress ensured that students with disabilities would receive an individualized and appropriate education through the use of individualized education programs (IEPs). The purpose of the IEP process was to develop an *individualized* and *appropriate* education program for students with disabilities, which Congress viewed as crucial in achieving the primary goals of the EHA (Zettel & Ballard, 1982). In the IEP process, school-based teams (a) conduct assessments of students' unique educational needs, (b) develop measurable annual goals based on the assessment, (c) determine the special education and related services that will be provided to the student, and (d) establish evaluation and measurement criteria by which a student's progress toward his goals will be monitored. The IEP, therefore, is of critical importance to educators, parents, and students. It is the process by which school-based teams determine the content of a student's program of special education and a written document that is the blueprint of the student's FAPE. Because of the legal and educational importance of the IEP, it is imperative that school-based teams develop IEPs that are both educationally meaningful and legally correct.

Our purpose in this chapter is to (a) review the legal requirements for developing, implementing, and evaluating IEPs; (b) describe the process for developing educationally meaningful and legally sound IEPs; (c) examine the research that has been conducted on IEPs; and (d) provide recommendations for district and school administrators, pre-service teacher educators, and school-based teams charged with fulfilling the IEP requirement. We begin with a brief examination of the IDEA.

Legal Requirements

The IDEA set forth a process by which school-based teams must develop IEPs. A challenge faced by IEP teams is that properly crafted IEPs must address two sets of requirements: procedural and substantive. These requirements guide the development and implementation of a student's FAPE (Drasgow, Yell, & Robinson, 2001). It is critical that practitioners and researchers understand the distinction between procedural and substantive compliance with the IEP requirements of the IDEA. We next examine each set of requirements.

Procedural Requirements

Procedural requirements of the IEP refer to those aspects of the IDEA that compel schools to follow the strictures of the law when developing an IEP. These procedures include the process by which the team develops a student's program of special education and the document itself. The IDEA requires that (a) IEP meetings must be scheduled at a mutually agreeable time and place, (b) the IEP team must consist of mandated team members (see Figure 6.1), and (c) certain components must be included in the IEP (see Figure 6.2).

Figure 6.1   Required participants in the IEP meeting.

- The student's parents
- A student's special education teacher
- A general education teacher who teaches the student
- A representative of the local educational agency
- A professional who can interpret the instructional implications of the evaluation results (one of the preceding members can serve here because members can serve more than one role)
- The student, if appropriate
- Other specialists (e.g., school psychologist, school nurse, representatives of community agencies) can be invited at the discretion of the school and parents but may require parental consent. Additional members must have knowledge or special expertise regarding the student.

Figure 6.2   Required components of the IEP.

A statement of

- Present Level of Academic Achievement and Functional Performance (PLAAFP)
- Measurable annual goals
- Method for collecting and reporting student progress
- Special education and related services
- Extent to which student will not participate in general education classroom
- Student's participation in state-wide or district-wide assessments
- Projected date for beginning services, anticipated frequency, location, and duration
- Transition services (IDEA requires this at age 16, but many states require transition services at a younger age.)

Adherence to these requirements is necessary because major procedural errors on the part of a school district may render an IEP inappropriate in the eyes of a hearing officer or court (Bateman & Linden, 2006; Huefner, 2000; Yell & Drasgow, 2000). According to the IDEA of 2004 (hereafter, IDEA 2004), serious procedural errors include those that (a) impede a student's right to a FAPE, (b) interfere with the opportunity for parents of a student with a disability to participate in the special education decision-making process, or (c) cause a deprivation of educational benefits (IDEA 20 U.S.C. § 1415(f)(1)(B)(i)(3)(E)(ii)(I-III)). The most serious procedural error that IEP teams can make is to fail to involve a student's parents in a meaningful collaboration when developing an IEP. In fact, this error may be the most likely to result in a hearing officer or judge invalidating an IEP. According to Bateman (2011), the IDEA makes parent participation central in all decisions regarding their child's program, and when full and equal parent participation is abridged or denied, a denial of FAPE is likely to be found. Indeed, the U.S. Court of Appeals for the Ninth Circuit ruled that interference with parental participation in IEP development undermines the very essence of the IDEA (*Amanda J. v. Clark County School District,* 2001). Figure 6.3 depicts common procedural errors that IEP teams make (Lake, 2010; Yell, 2009).

Substantive Requirements

Crafting educationally meaningful and legally correct IEPs requires more than following procedures; it demands attention to the development of special education programs that lead to meaningful educational benefit for students. As the President's Commission on Excellence in Special Education (2001) noted, educators unfortunately

Figure 6.3   Common procedural errors in IEP development.

- Failing to notify parents of their procedural rights.
- Failing to obtain informed parental consent when it is required (e.g., to conduct an initial evaluation of a student to determine eligibility, to provide special education services for the first time, to conduct a reevaluation of a student, to excuse an IEP team member from an IEP meeting in which the member's areas or service is being discussed).
- Predetermining a student's placement or IEP services.
- Improperly excusing IEP members from attending IEP meetings (i.e., without parental permission).
- Improper IEP team membership.
- Failing to ensure the availability of a continuum of alternative placements.
- Failing to consider the five special factors (i.e., behavior, limited English proficiency, blind/visually impaired, deaf/hard of hearing, and assistive technology) when developing an IEP of a student when these factors are relevant.
- Making decisions based on the availability of services.
- Making decisions based solely on costs.
- Failing to consider the results of an independent educational evaluation.
- Failing to allow a student's parents meaningful participation in the IEP process.

Figure 6.4   Common substantive errors in IEP development.

- Failing to conduct a full and individualized evaluation of a student that provides the IEP team members with important information that leads to programming decisions.
- Failing to address all of a student's academic and functional needs in the Present Levels of Academic Achievement and Functional Performance (PLAAFP) statements.
- Failing to link a student's needs from the PLAAFP statements to the student's annual goals and special education services.
- Writing annual goals that are not measurable.
- Failing to measure a student's progress toward her annual goals.
- Failing to provide services to meet all of a student's needs from the PLAAFP statements.
- Failing to properly address transition services when necessary.
- Failing to include positive behavior supports and interventions in a student's IEP when necessary.
- Failing to provide the services written in a student's IEP.

often place "process above results, and bureaucratic compliance above student achievement, excellence, and outcomes" (p. 3). Procedurally correct IEPs will not meet legal standards if a student's IEP does not result in her achieving meaningful educational benefit.

According to Drasgow et al. (2001), the crucial determinant in hearings or cases involving the substantive standard of the IDEA is whether the student makes educational progress. Regrettably, school personnel often seem to have a difficult time with the substantive requirements for developing and implementing IEPs. In fact, compliance with the mandate that students show educational progress probably occurs less often than compliance with any other IDEA-related obligation (Bateman & Linden, 2006). IDEA 2004 increases the emphasis on meaningful programming by requiring that IEPs include (a) special education services that are based on peer-reviewed research, (b) measurable annual goals, and (c) progress-monitoring systems. In fact, IDEA 2004 now requires that when hearing officers rule on cases involving IEPs, they base their decisions on "substantive grounds based on a determination of whether a child received a free appropriate public education" (IDEA, 20 U.S.C. § 1415(f)(3)(E)(I)). Whereas the procedural

requirements retain importance, this section of IDEA 2004 requires hearing officers to base their rulings on whether a student makes meaningful academic and functional progress in their special education program. In summary, to provide an appropriate education to a student with disabilities, school professionals and the student's parents must develop an IEP that meets the requirements of the law and provides meaningful educational benefit. To do so requires careful attention to both the procedural and the substantive requirements of the IDEA. Figure 6.4 depicts common substantive errors that IEP teams make (Lake, 2010; Yell, 2009).

Developing Educationally Meaningful and Legally Sound IEPs

The IEP, as both a process and a document, is tremendously important in the special education process. In fact, the document is the embodiment of FAPE, which school districts are required to provide to every student in special education. Because of the crucial nature and legal basis of the IEP, one might assume that special education teachers are prepared to meet both the procedural and substantive requirements of the IDEA when they take part in developing IEPs. Unfortunately, this is frequently not the case. Too often the pre-service and in-service education programs for special education teachers stress the procedural requirements of IEPs and do not include professional development in substantive development of IEPs (Yell, 2009). The problem with such a focus is that an IEP team may develop a procedurally impeccable IEP that is substantively worthless. That is, just because an IEP has passed the procedural litmus test does not mean that the IEP will confer meaningful educational benefit. To ensure that students' IEPs meet the substantive requirement of the IDEA, it is crucial that IEP teams understand the importance of assessment, research-based special educational programming, and progress monitoring.

Assessment

The purpose of the special education assessment/evaluation in the IEP development process is to determine the student's unique educational needs on which the IEP will be based. Thus, the assessment is the keystone of the IEP process. The information gathered from the assessment is, in essence, the baseline information from which annual goals are written, special education services are determined, and educational progress is measured. The importance of the assessment process was directly addressed by a U.S. District Court Judge when he ruled that a school district had denied a student a FAPE because the student's IEP was based on an inadequate assessment. In his opinion, the judge wrote:

> This deficiency goes to the heart of the IEP; the child's level of academic achievement and functional performance is the foundation on which the IEP must be built. Without a clear identification of [the child's] present levels, the IEP cannot set measurable goals, evaluate the child's progress and determine which educational and related services are needed. (*Kirby v. Cabell County Board of Education,* 2006, p. 694)

The assessment results are included in the Present Level of Academic Achievement and Functional Performance (PLAAFP) section of an IEP. When IEP teams develop PLAAFP statements, they must (a) describe the effects of a student's disability on his performance in all areas that are affected by his disability (e.g., reading, mathematics, behavior), (b) write the statement in objective and measurable terms that are easily understood by all members of the team, and (c) describe how a student's disability affects his involvement and progress in the general curriculum. Moreover, the IEP team must ensure that a direct relationship exists between the PLAAFP and the other components of the IEP (e.g., annual goals, special education services, progress-monitoring system). For example, if the PLAAFP statement

describes a reading problem, the IEP must provide an annual goal for reading, a special education service that will address the reading problem, and a data-based method for measuring a student's progress toward her reading goal.

Special Education Programming

Following delineation of the PLAAFP and a discussion of a student's educational needs, team members develop and delineate a student's special education program on the IEP. The special education program consists of (a) measurable annual goals and (b) special education services.

Measurable Annual Goals

The purpose of the annual goals is to measure the progress a student makes in his special education program. The Individuals with Disabilities Education Act Amendments of 1997 (hereafter, IDEA 1997) added the requirements that annual goals must be written in measurable terms and that IEPs must also include a statement about how educators will measure a student's progress toward the goals. Unfortunately, goals are too often not aligned with the PLAAFP statement and frequently lack measurable outcomes, which would very likely invalidate an IEP in the eyes of a hearing officer or judge (Bateman & Linden, 2006). Neither the IDEA nor the regulations implementing the IDEA indicate the specific form that goals are to take, beyond requiring that they be measurable. One method that can be used to ensure that IEP goals are measurable is to use the model first proposed by Mager in 1962. Mager suggested that measurable goals, which he referred to as *instructional objectives,* needed to have three components. These components were (a) a target behavior, (b) the conditions under which the goal was to be measured, and (c) a criterion for acceptable performance. Figure 6.5 depicts a goal with these three components.

Figure 6.5 Measurable annual goal.

> **Goal:**
>
> In 32 weeks when presented with a passage from the second-grade reading textbook, Stacy will read aloud 48 words in 1 minute with no more than two errors.
>
> - *Target Behavior:* Reading aloud.
> - *Conditions:* In 32 weeks when presented with a passage from the second-grade reading textbook.
> - *Criteria for Acceptable Performance:* 48 words in 1 minute with no more than two errors.

Special Education Services

The services to which students with disabilities with IEPs are entitled include special education services, related services, supplementary services, accommodations, and program modifications. These services represent the educational "strategies that will be most effective in realizing (the student's) goals" (IDEA Regulations, Appendix A). Essentially, the services provided are an IEP team's response to effectively addressing a student's unique educational needs. The special education services, therefore, must be aligned with the PLAAFP and the measurable annual goals in an IEP.

Perhaps the most significant change in IDEA 2004 was the requirement that special education services must be based on peer-reviewed research to the extent practicable (IDEA Regulations, 34 C.F.R. § 300.320(a)(4)). The U.S. Department of Education defines *extent practicable* as "to the extent it is possible," given the availability of peer-reviewed research (*Analysis of Comments and Changes,* 2006). Congress included this peer-review requirement because of the belief that special education had not been achieving the goals of the IDEA because of low expectations for students and an "insufficient focus on applying replicable research on proven methods of teaching and learning" (IDEA, 20 U.S.C. § 1401(c)(4)). Additionally, the U.S. Department of Education defined peer-reviewed research as "research that is reviewed by qualified independent reviewers to ensure that the quality of the information meets the standards of the field before the research is published" (71 *Fed. Reg.* 46664 (Aug. 14, 2006)).

The peer-reviewed research requirement applies to the selection and provision of (a) special education services; (b) related services (e.g., counseling services, occupational therapy, physical therapy, psychological services, speech-language services); and (c) aids, services, and supports provided in regular education settings (Etscheidt & Curran, 2010). The legislative history of IDEA 2004 and the peer-reviewed research requirement reveal that the intent of this section of the law was to ensure that IEP teams' selection of educational approaches reflect sound practices that have been validated empirically whenever possible (Etscheidt & Curran, 2010).

Progress Monitoring

All IEPs must include objectively measurable annual goals. An equally critical requirement is that a student's progress toward these goals must actually be measured. In fact, failing to measure a student's progress most likely would result in a hearing officer's or judge's invalidating an IEP and determining that FAPE had been denied if the IEP were challenged in a due process hearing or court case (Bateman & Linden, 2006). If IEP members do not establish the means to measure a student's progress toward the IEP's goals, then those goals become meaningless and useless (Bateman, 2007a).

Every student's IEP must include a description of how and when a student's progress will be measured. Moreover, a student's progress must be reported to her parents as often as the parents of nondisabled children receive progress reports or report cards, usually every 6 to 9 weeks. An important consideration in determining how progress will be monitored is that the measures must be objective and meaningful. That is, subjective or anecdotal data (e.g., a teacher's general impressions) are not sufficient. If the data show that the student is not progressing, something in her program must be changed. Yell and Stecker (2003) asserted that IEP teams must continuously collect meaningful data to document student progress and, thus, to demonstrate the effectiveness of the special education program. Students' IEP teams can meet these requirements of the IDEA by using appropriate data-collection procedures and using the data to guide instructional decision making. For example, to monitor student progress in reading, a team could collect reading-fluency data using curriculum-based measurement (see Deno, 2003); or if data were being collected on student behaviors, a team could systematically observe and graph the frequency of the occurrence of those behaviors (Kazdin, 2010).

The IEP requirement of the IDEA is the method by which local education agencies (LEAs) provide a FAPE to all students in special education. Unfortunately, the procedural and substantive requirements of IEPs have been challenging to school districts. Clearly, many IEP team members have basic misunderstandings of both the IEP process and IEP document (Simon, 2006). In fact, in interviews and surveys, researchers have found that some special education teachers regard IEPs as paperwork exercises for legal purposes (Yell & Stecker, 2003) and find IEP meetings burdensome (E. C. Lynch & Beare, 1990; Nickles, Cronis, Justen, & Smith, 1992; S. W. Smith, 1990b), rather than understanding the crucial nature of the process and document. We have addressed these challenges in this section by briefly outlining the legal requirements in developing, implementing, and evaluating IEPs, as well as the process for developing educationally meaningful and legally sound IEPs.

Researchers have also examined the issues involved in both the IEP document and the IEP meeting with regard to compliance issues. In fact, J. Gallagher and Desimone (1995) identified a number of problems with IEPs in their review of the literature. They described two major problem areas that emerged from 15 years of IEP research: satisfying content requirements of the IEP document (i.e., procedural issues), and developing and implementing effective IEPs (i.e., substantive issues). Next, we provide a representative sample of the literature about potential problems and recommended practices regarding compliance issues with the IEP document. We follow this with an examination of examples from the literature describing problems and recommended practices in developing and implementing IEPs.

Research on IEP Compliance Issues

The literature on IEPs is vast, especially before 1997, and we have chosen to review a sample of studies from 1990 to the present to illustrate the findings of this literature base. For a more comprehensive review of the literature on IEPs before 1990, see S. W. Smith (1990b); Rodger (1995); and McLaughlin and Warren (1995). See Sopko (2003) for a synthesis of literature on IEPs from 1997 to 2002. In this section, we examine two major areas of IEP research: (a) studies that focus on the extent to which practitioners have written and implemented the required components in the IEP document and (b) studies

involving training practitioners in the development and implementation of the IEP requirement. The research on compliance issues can inform practice by highlighting the need for careful consideration of components that must be included in the IEP document. This research also emphasizes the need for effective practitioner training in writing and implementing educationally meaningful and legally sound IEPs.

Research on IEP Components and Implementation

In this section we provide a sample of studies that represents the literature on the adequacy of IEPs, specifically in relation to IEP goals, IEP accommodations, and IEP transition plans. Table 6.1 provides a summary of findings from these studies.

Research Involving IEP Goals

Although Congress intended for the IEP to be the vehicle to ensure that students with disabilities receive an individualized and appropriate education (Yell & Stecker, 2003),

Table 6.1 Studies Examining IEP Components

Variables Examined	Reference
IEP Goals	
Appropriateness of goals and objectives for students with EBD and MID categories and relationship of IEP goals to classroom instruction.	E. C. Lynch & Beare, 1990
Types of goals for students with EBD and LD and congruence of goals with present levels of performance.	S. W. Smith, 1990a
Appropriateness of goals and objectives for the EBD, LD, and MID categories.	Nickles et al., 1992
Types of goals for students with EBD and congruence of goals with present levels of performance.	M. Epstein et al., 1992
Relationship of IEP goals for students with MID to classroom instruction.	Krom & Prater, 1993
Quality of IEP goals for students with deaf-blindness.	Giangreco et al., 1994
Quality of IEP goals and objectives for students in early childhood special education programs.	Michnowicz et al., 1995
Congruence of IEP goals with diagnosed reading disabilities in basic skills.	Catone & Brady, 2005
IEP Accommodations	
Validity of testing accommodation for students with learning disabilities.	L. S. Fuchs & Fuchs, 2001
Relationship between instructional and assessment accommodations.	Ysseldyke et al., 2001
Definitional, legal, and validity issues involved in decisions on testing accommodations.	S. N. Elliott et al., 2002
Relationship between accommodation assignments, teachers' recommendations, and students' performance data.	Ketterlin-Geller, Alonzo, et al., 2007
IEP Transition Plans	
Quality of transition plans related to federally mandated content.	Shearin et al., 1999
Quality of the transition plans and relationship of transition goals to transition programming.	K. M. Powers et al., 2005

Note: EBD = emotional and behavioral disorder; IEP = individualized education program; LD = learning disability; MID = mild intellectual disability.

it did not offer specific details on how to write the IEP document, particularly IEP goals. It has indeed been a challenge for practitioners to develop IEP goals that are appropriately aligned to students' needs, are measurable, can be understood by IEP team members, and can be effectively implemented in classroom settings. Various studies specifically examined the relationship between IEP goals and present levels of performance, the appropriateness and quality of IEP goals for various students, and the relationship between IEP goals and classroom instruction.

The following three studies represent the research addressing the relationship between IEP goals and present levels of performance. These studies all examined archival data and employed correlational research designs. S. W. Smith (1990a) examined 120 IEPs of fourth-, fifth-, and sixth-grade male students with emotional and behavioral disorders (EBDs) and learning disabilities (LDs) to assess (a) procedural compliance, (b) substantive content, and (c) congruence (i.e., the match between present levels of performance and annual goals). M. Epstein, Patton, Polloway, and Foley (1992) assessed the IEPs of 107 junior high students with EBD to determine the relationship between the students' current behavioral problems listed on their IEPs with their annual goals. Catone and Brady (2005) examined the congruence of the annual goals of 54 high school students who had diagnosed reading disabilities in decoding and word recognition to the listed needs and present levels on their IEPs. The overall finding of these studies revealed substantial problems regarding congruence, most notably, a mismatch between listed areas of need, present levels of performance, and annual goals.

We identified four descriptive studies examining archival data that typify the research on the appropriateness and quality of IEP goals for various students. E. C. Lynch and Beare (1990) examined the IEPs of 48 students identified as having either an EBD or an educable mental handicap (i.e., mild intellectual disability). They found that nearly all of the IEP goals were academic—to the exclusion of social skills, vocational skills, or other functional living skills. They also found that goals and objectives were vague and lacked criteria for successful performance and evaluation. Nickles et al. (1992) examined the categories of objectives in the IEPs of 150 students with EBD, LD, and mild intellectual disabilities. The researchers found a number of deficiencies in the IEP goals and objectives, such as few social/behavioral objectives for the students with EBD, and an insufficient number of goals in basic living skills for the students with intellectual disabilities. Giangreco, Dennis, Edelman, and Cloninger (1994) analyzed the IEP goals for 46 students with deaf-blindness in kindergarten through 12th grade who attended general education classes either full- or part-time. The researchers

identified three major problems with the IEP goals: (a) goals were broad, inconsistent, and inadequately matched to the general education context; (b) goals addressed staff behavior (e.g., repositioning students) rather than student learning outcomes; and (c) goals described broad curricular categories rather than student learning outcomes. And finally, Michnowicz, McConnell, Peterson, and Odom (1995) examined the IEPs of 163 children in early childhood special education programs. The researchers found that most of the goals and objectives were not measurable and that the majority of the IEPs were so vague that students' progress could not be monitored. They also found that nearly half of the IEPs did not include goals for social interactions, even when assessment data showed a need for social interaction interventions with preschool children with disabilities.

Three descriptive studies represent the research addressing the relationship between IEP goals and classroom instruction. In their study of 48 students with EBD and mild intellectual disability, E. C. Lynch and Beare (1990) also examined the relationship between IEP goals and instruction by observing the students in their general and special education classrooms. During the observations, the researchers saw little relationship between IEP goals and instruction. Krom and Prater (1993) compared the IEP goals of 21 intermediate-aged students with mild intellectual disability to the teachers' self-reported subjects and content they taught. The researchers found wide discrepancies between the written IEP goals and the content teachers reported teaching. Giangreco et al. (1994), in their study of students with deaf-blindness, also observed 20 students during their classes and concluded that daily instruction in the general education settings did not incorporate students' IEP goals.

These research studies demonstrate that teachers need instruction, practice, and support in cultivating skills for developing and implementing IEPs, particularly in writing goals. The researchers recommended that teacher preparation programs and professional development programs explore strategies to help practitioners develop quality IEPs. They suggested stressing the importance of the relationship between IEP goals and daily instruction, as well as evaluating the IEP as an instructional tool.

Research Involving IEP Accommodations

IEP teams are entrusted with the difficult task of selecting valid accommodations for individual students before their participation in state proficiency testing (i.e., high-stakes testing). Accommodations are intended to level the playing field for students with disabilities, yet the very nature of individualizing accommodations seems to contradict the purpose of testing standardization that allows for score comparisons across groups. Several researchers have examined issues involved in determining appropriate accommodations for students with disabilities who are required to participate in high-stakes testing. Some of the problems identified in documenting accommodations on students' IEPs include: (a) determining which accommodations are appropriate and valid for individual students, (b) recommending accommodations too frequently, (c) inconsistency between instructional and assessment accommodations, and (d) confusion between accommodations and modifications. Modifications exceed accommodations and refer to changes in the content of curricula or assessments that represent meaningful differences from that given to other students (e.g., excluding certain items from an assessment). Modifications are generally not allowed for state proficiency testing (Ysseldyke, Thurlow, Bielinski, House, Moody, & Haigh, 2001).

The following three studies addressed issues of determining appropriate accommodations for students with disabilities who are required to participate in high-stakes testing. L. S. Fuchs and Fuchs (2001) discussed two controlled experimental studies, one focused on reading (L. S. Fuchs, Fuchs, Eaton, Hamlett, Binkley, et al., 2000) and one focused on math (L. S. Fuchs, Fuchs, Eaton, Hamlett, & Karns, 2000), in which the researchers examined testing accommodations for students with LD. Their studies involved approximately 200 students with LD and 200 without LD in fourth and fifth grades from several schools. L. S. Fuchs and Fuchs (2001) concluded from the results of these studies that teachers granted many more reading and math accommodations to students than were warranted. They further suggested that teachers seemed to base their decisions for accommodations on student demographics, recommending accommodations more frequently for students who were African American, qualified for free/reduced-price lunch, had been retained, had lower IQ scores, and read at lower levels.

Ysseldyke et al. (2001) conducted a descriptive study in which they examined the relationship between instructional and assessment accommodations in the IEPs of 280 students with various disabilities in grades 1 through 8. The researchers found that overall students' instructional accommodations matched their testing accommodations (84%). Some of the problems raters identified on these IEPs for instructional or testing accommodations included (a) lack of documentation, (b) providing more or fewer accommodations than appeared justified, and (c) confusion about terminology (i.e., listing an accommodation as a modification).

Ketterlin-Geller, Alonzo, Braun-Monegan, and Tindal (2007) used a correlational research design to examine the IEPs of 38 third-grade students to assess the consistency of accommodations assigned, teachers'

recommendations, and students' performance data. Ketterlin-Geller, Alonzo, et al. concluded that teachers recommended more accommodations than were designated on the students' IEPs, and that teachers recommended more accommodations than needed, when considering student performance data.

These examples of research studies involving IEP accommodations provide an outline of the issues that practitioners need to address. For example, it appears that IEP team members use subjective judgment to make accommodation decisions. These decisions often lead to unjustifiable accommodations that were not distinctly beneficial to students with disabilities (i.e., leveled the playing field). S. N. Elliott, McKevitt, and Kettler (2002) illustrated this in a summary of four experimental studies examining statistical effects of accommodations on test scores of students with and without disabilities. Results from these studies revealed that teachers recommended accommodations that did not significantly and differentially affect test scores for students with or without disabilities. For example, they found that extended time made no significant difference for students with or without disabilities on a math assessment, and that a read-aloud accommodation gave a boost to both groups.

S. N. Elliott et al. (2002) recommended that practitioners who select testing accommodations need knowledge of (a) the student's abilities, disabilities, and instructional accommodations; (b) state and district testing guidelines; (c) the test's item content and format; (d) tests' validity and how test scores can be invalidated; and (e) any previous accommodations successfully used with the student. IEP teams need support and guidance in fulfilling the difficult task of selecting valid accommodations for individual students with disabilities. Specifically, IEP teams need support and guidance to provide accommodations that address the student's disability, are consistent with instructional accommodations and previously successful testing accommodations, do not invalidate the test, do not contradict testing guidelines, and are consistent with the test's items and content.

Research Involving IEP Transition Plans

Poor outcomes for students exiting from special education have served as an impetus for federal initiatives to improve transition planning. IDEA requires that IEPs include transition goals, services, and plans for students who are 16 years of age, and for younger youth if determined appropriate by the IEP team. Specifically, transition plans must consider the following postschool outcomes: (a) postsecondary education, (b) vocational training, (c) integrated employment, (d) continuing and adult education, (e) adult services, and (f) independent living or community participation. A number of researchers have examined the extent to which transition planning in students' IEPs incorporates the IDEA mandates and effective transition practices.

The following two descriptive studies represent the research addressing the quality of transition plans. Shearin, Roessler, and Schriner (1999) evaluated transition plans in the IEPs of 68 high school students identified as having either LD or intellectual disability. Their results revealed the following inadequacies in transition planning within these IEPs: (a) transition goals addressing future living arrangements, postsecondary education, and employment were vague or missing (e.g., of the 68 documents examined, 43% did not address employment and 78% did not address postsecondary education); (b) few plans referred to self-advocacy and family planning; and (c) few plans specified adult service agencies (e.g., 7% referred to vocational rehabilitation). K. M. Powers et al. (2005) examined 399 IEPs for students aged 16 to 22 with learning, physical, intellectual, and emotional disabilities. The researchers found that transition plans were missing for 24% of the sample and that the overall quality of the plans was low. For example, students' current work experiences were inconsistent with employment goals for 27% of the sample. The authors reported that (a) the transition plans did not provide sufficient detail; (b) the participation of transition specialists and vocational rehabilitation personnel in the IEP process was low; and (c) few IEPs referenced self-determination education, even though self-determination skills have been found to support students' current success and postschool outcomes. The researchers also found that the IEPs of students with developmental disabilities included the lowest-quality transition plans.

These research studies involving IEP transition goals highlight the need for training for practitioners who must write and implement transition goals. Some IEP teams appear to lack basic information about the requirements of IDEA relative to transition goals and objectives, especially regarding access to adult service agencies, and the range of curricular and employment opportunities available for students.

This sample of the literature on compliance issues suggests the need for careful consideration of components that are included in the IEP document. Studies revealed that IEPs often lacked required components and that misconnections or no connections occurred among the components (e.g., Catone & Brady, 2005; Nickles et al., 1992). Additional findings indicated that many IEPs contained inappropriate goals and that goals did not match classroom instruction (e.g., Krom & Prater, 1993; E. C. Lynch & Beare, 1990). Accommodations included in IEPs for students taking state-wide assessments seemed to lack individuality, and practitioners often made subjective decisions based on

student demographics (e.g., L. S. Fuchs & Fuchs, 2001). Researchers questioned the validity of such accommodations when scores improved for both students with and without disabilities, or did not improve for either group (S. N. Elliott et al., 2002). Researchers also found that the quality of transition plans included in IEPs was problematic, with goals either missing or too vague to be meaningful (e.g., K. M. Powers et al., 2005). These studies point to a critical need for practitioner training, guidance, and support. Teacher-preparation programs as well as state and district administrators need to explore strategies to ensure that those who are responsible for the important tasks of developing and implementing IEPs have the knowledge and skills necessary.

Research on Training Practitioners to Develop and Implement the IEP

In the previous section, we focused specifically on required components within the IEP document; now we review intervention studies focusing on the development and implementation of the IEP. Unfortunately, few studies have specifically examined training practitioners to develop and implement IEPs. Nevertheless, the following examples from the literature (see Table 6.2) address training practitioners on writing IEP goals and transition plans, determining and documenting accommodations in the IEP, implementing IEP goals in the classroom, and student participation in the IEP process.

Research on Training Practitioners to Write IEP Goals and Transition Plans

As described previously, investigations of IEP goals and transition plans written by educational personnel often do not meet recommended practice guidelines. Strategies are needed to close this gap between recommended practice and actual practice. In theory, well-developed IEP goals lead to effective instruction, and well-written transition plans lead to positive student outcomes and successful postschool experiences. Researchers have demonstrated that teachers need instruction, practice, and support in cultivating skills for developing and implementing IEPs, particularly in writing goals (e.g., M. Epstein et al., 1992; Nickles et al., 1992). Although states and districts have reported providing an array of training efforts for educators on developing and implementing IEPs, the literature is lacking in studies designed to assess the impact of such training (J. Gallagher & Desimone, 1995). Following are two examples of intervention studies on training practitioners to write goals.

Pretti-Frontczak and Bricker (2000) conducted a quasi-experimental study that involved using a training

Table 6.2 Studies Examining Development and Implementation of IEPs

Variables Examined	Reference
Writing IEP Goals	
Writing IEP goals and objectives using a CBA.	Pretti-Frontczak & Bricker, 2000
Writing IEP Assessment and Participation Accommodations	
Increasing the quality and extent of participation and accommodation documentation on the IEP.	Shriner & DeStefano, 2003
Writing IEP Transition Plans	
Improving the quality of transition components in students' IEPs.	Finn & Kohler, 2009
Implementing IEP Goals	
Embedding instruction of IEP goals for students with disabilities in inclusive classrooms.	Horn et al., 2000
Perceptions of the IEP Requirement	
Comparing perceptions of IEP meeting participants.	Menlove, Hudson, & Suter, 2001
Comparing teachers' and parents' perceptions of the IEP requirement.	J. E. Martin, Marshall, & Sale, 2004; Simon, 2006
Involving Students in their IEP Process	
Using an IEP lesson package to increase student participation in their annual IEP meeting.	Allen et al., 2001
Increasing student participation in IEP conferences.	Hammer, 2004
Review of intervention studies to involve students in their IEP process.	Test et al., 2004
Increasing student participation in IEP meetings.	J. E. Martin, Van Dycke, Christensen, Greene, Gardner, & Lovett, 2006

package to help practitioners write IEP goals. The researchers arranged training for 86 participants from five states. They implemented a training package over 2 days that included information on writing IEP goals and objectives, as well as using a curriculum-based assessment and an evaluation measure. Results indicated statistically significant improvement in IEPs from pre- to post-training. Although this study lacked a control group and did not examine student outcomes, writing quality IEPs is an important first step in the process of achieving desired outcomes for students with disabilities.

In another example of training practitioners to improve the quality of transition planning, Finn and Kohler (2009) conducted a quasi-experimental study in which they analyzed the data from one state on their implementation of the Transition Outcomes Project using the Transition Requirements Checklist (O'Leary & Doty, 2001). The researchers analyzed the content of 166 students' IEPs to determine whether the IEPs complied with the transition requirements of the IDEA at two points: before a 3-day training provided by state transition leaders and 2 years following completion of the training. Mixed results revealed that the content of some students' IEPs showed improvement, whereas others did not. In some cases, compliance of transition items in the IEP did not improve at all, and in other cases compliance declined.

Research on Training Practitioners to Document Accommodations in IEPs

In the previous section on research involving the IEP document, we reviewed several studies that addressed documenting accommodations on students' IEPs and determining which accommodations are appropriate and valid for individual students. Those researchers recommended training IEP teams in this area; however, research on training practitioners to select appropriate accommodations is limited. We identified one study that involved this type of training. To improve decisions regarding state-wide assessments, Shriner and DeStefano (2003) conducted a quasi-experimental intervention study in three school districts in which they provided 8 to 10 hours of training in (a) IDEA requirements regarding participation in state proficiency testing and accommodations in that testing, (b) revising current IEP forms and processes to facilitate and document participation and accommodation decisions, (c) state learning standards, and (d) assessing and documenting students' participation in the general curriculum and their instructional and classroom assessment accommodations. The researchers found that following training, the IEPs in all three districts were more complete in documenting assessment accommodations planned for state testing, and the IEPs reflected planned increases in student participation in state-wide testing.

Research on Training Practitioners to Implement IEP Goals

Teachers' implementation of IEP goals and the resulting student outcomes make up perhaps the most important area researchers should be addressing. Unfortunately, this is another area where a major gap exists in the literature. J. Gallagher and Desimone (1995) found that many teachers viewed the IEP as an administrative rather than instructional task, and once written, they often did not use the IEP for instruction. The authors suggested that when IEP teams neglect progress monitoring of IEP goals, they are not meeting the original intent of the IEP. Indeed, in Hill's (2006) review of federal and state IEP-related court decisions from the years 2000 to 2006, more than 50% of the cases involved procedural violations of the IEP process. This affirms the need to examine the extent to which teachers are implementing the IEP and monitoring progress toward meeting those goals.

The following study is an example of an intervention aimed at helping teachers implement IEP goals and monitor progress. Horn, Lieber, Li, Sandall, and Schwartz (2000) conducted three case studies in which they examined a three-step procedure to assist early childhood inclusive teachers in developing strategies for embedding instruction of targeted IEP goals and objectives for students with disabilities into daily activities. The researchers (a) gave teachers examples of embedding IEP goals and objectives into daily activities, (b) clarified and discussed each student's IEP goals and objectives with the teachers, and (c) guided teachers in designing their own strategies for embedding the goals and objectives into daily activities. In each case, the teachers increased instruction of the targeted IEP goals, and each of the children demonstrated improvement on these targeted goals. This type of study offers important implications for the field in demonstrating that, with varying degrees of support, inclusive teachers can provide instruction on students' IEP goals within existing classroom activities; and when they do, student outcomes on their IEP goals are positive.

Research on Training Students to Participate in the IEP Process

The IDEA requires that educators must invite a student to her IEP meeting when postsecondary goals and transition services are being considered (IDEA regulations, 34 CFR 300.321(b)(1)). In addition, promoting students' self-advocacy and self-determination skills are important goals in special education programs (Wehmeyer, 2005). Thus, involving students in their IEP process should be common practice. Nevertheless, this practice does not appear to be widespread. Teachers have expressed

a need and desire for training in how to teach students self-advocacy and self-determination skills as well as a need for information on related curricula (Test et al., 2004). Several researchers have examined interventions designed to increase students' involvement in their IEP process. Test and colleagues conducted a review of this literature from 1972 to 2002 (2004). They found that the use of published curricula (e.g., IPLAN by Van Reusen & Bos, 1990; The Self-Directed IEP by J. E. Martin, Marshall, Maxson, & Jerman, 1997; Next S.T.E.P. by Halpern et al., 1997) as well as person-centered planning (see Miner & Bates, 1997; Timmons & Whitney-Thomas, 1998) effectively increased student participation in their IEP meetings. The results also indicated that providing direct instruction to the student before the meeting as well as the meeting facilitator's behavior during the meeting (e.g., directing questions to students, avoiding jargon, using understandable language), enhanced student performance. We selected the following three studies as examples of training students and teachers to promote student participation in the IEP process.

Allen, Smith, Test, Flowers, and Wood (2001) conducted a single-subject, multiple-baseline research study in which they taught four students aged 15 to 21 with moderate intellectual disabilities the skills needed to manage their own IEP meetings. The researchers modified a multimedia package called The Self-Directed IEP (J. E. Martin et al., 1997), which included a Teacher's Manual, Student Workbook, and two videos. After completing the units, students demonstrated increased participation in mock IEP meetings and in their actual IEP meetings. J. E. Martin, Van Dycke, Greene, et al. (2006) conducted a randomized group experiment to assess the effectiveness of the Self-Directed IEP strategy. The researchers collected and analyzed data from 764 IEP team members participating in 130 middle and high school transition IEP meetings. Students were randomly assigned to the intervention and control groups, with 65 students with various disabilities in each group. The findings revealed that students who were taught the Self-Directed IEP strategies significantly outperformed the control group on the following measures: (a) attendance at IEP meetings; (b) active participation in their IEP meetings; (c) engagement in IEP leadership behaviors; (d) expression of their interests, skills, and limits across transition areas; and (e) recall of IEP goals after the meetings ended. In addition, their postschool vision section on the IEP document included more comprehensive postschool transition statements. Finally, Hammer (2004) conducted a single-subject, multiple-baseline research study in which she used the Self-Advocacy Strategy (Lancaster & Lancaster, 2003) to increase participation in IEP meetings of three students aged 12 to 13. The students learned the IPLAN strategy, which includes the following steps: (a) **I**nventory your strengths, areas to improve or learn, goals, and choices for learning or accommodations; (b) **P**rovide your inventory information; (c) **L**isten and respond; (d) **A**sk questions; and (e) **N**ame your goals. Teachers then role-played IEP meetings with the students. Results indicated that after training using the IPLAN strategy, the three students were more involved with writing goals and participating in their IEP meetings. For example, all three students verbalized relevant statements about their strengths and areas for improvement.

This sample of the literature on compliance issues suggests the need for careful consideration in developing and implementing the IEP. Studies revealed that with training, teachers can improve the quality of written IEP goals, the documentation of mandated transition components on IEPs, the documentation of assessment accommodations, and the implementation of IEP goals within existing classroom activities. Additional findings revealed positive effects of specifically training and instructing students in how to write goals and participate in their IEP meetings.

Summary of Empirical Literature

In this section, we presented examples from the literature involving the IEP requirement. We reviewed several research studies that addressed compliance issues involving components of the IEP document. Researchers found various inadequacies when examining the IEP document, specifically with IEP goals, accommodations, and transition plans. We also reviewed several research studies that addressed the IEP process. The problems found with the process mirrored those found with the content in the IEP document, such as writing and implementing the IEP, as well as students' participating in the IEP meeting. Researchers discovered that specific training improved the writing and implementing of IEPs and students' participation in their IEP meetings.

These research findings make it clear that practitioners are having difficulty fulfilling the mandated IEP requirement of the IDEA. J. Gallagher and Desimone (1995) asserted that the difference between policy development and policy implementation is often vast. Policy makers' mandated requirements often are well intended and based on good theory, yet short on practicality at the local level. For example, policy makers may assume that a team of professionals from different disciplines can collaborate well as a transdisciplinary IEP team. In reality, it is difficult to coordinate schedules and share information among the various professionals to accomplish this (J. Gallagher & Desimone, 1995). A theme that has emerged from the empirical literature to date is the need to narrow this gap between policy and practice.

Most of the empirical literature on implementing the IEP requirement has focused on the content of the IEP document, with a few studies addressing interventions on training practitioners in how to write IEPs. These studies were informative and demonstrated the value of specific training on developing components in the IEP document. Researchers also demonstrated the positive effects of training on student participation in their IEP meetings. Unfortunately, research on the implementation of IEPs and the link between IEPs and student outcomes is scarce. Assessing the implementation and impact of IEPs on student outcomes is critical, and thus future research should address the following issues: (a) the extent to which teachers currently implement IEP goals in classroom settings; (b) the extent to which students master IEP goals; (c) the effect of pre-service training on new teachers' development of IEPs, and implementation of IEP goals, accommodations, and transition plans; (d) the effect of professional development training on teachers' development of IEPs, and implementation of IEP goals, accommodations, and transition plans; and (e) the effect of accommodations on student outcomes during instruction and testing.

Finally, to conduct investigations of the IEP process, researchers need a reliable and valid tool to evaluate the procedural and substantive quality of IEPs. Such a tool could be used as a dependent variable in research to improve the IEP. At least one such instrument, the IEP Quality Indicator Scale (IQUIS), was developed by Yell, Dragsow, and Oh (2008) to analyze IEPs in a study of a web-based IEP tutorial (Shriner, Carty, Trach, Weber, & Yell, 2008). The development of a reliable and valid IEP evaluation instrument is important to research in this area.

Recommendations for Practice

Researchers have repeatedly suggested the need for training at the practitioner level and have recommended that teacher-preparation programs and school district professional development programs provide the needed training in implementing the IEP requirement of the IDEA (Bateman & Linden, 2006; Catone & Brady, 2005; Etscheidt & Curran, 2010; M. Epstein et al., 1992; Huefner, 2000; Nickles et al., 1992; S. W. Smith, 1990b; Yell, 2009). Both teacher-preparation programs and school districts can use the information from the empirical literature to develop training programs that address the observed weaknesses in fulfilling the IEP requirement. Based on the legal requirements and research findings, we suggest recommendations for practice that emphasize a general need for training, guidance, and support for practitioners and students in various aspects of the IEP requirement. Readers should note that we distinguish between *pre-service training* in those skill areas that teachers should possess on leaving their preparation programs and *in-service training,* which refers to professional development opportunities conducted by school districts and state educational agencies to ensure that teachers become fluent in newly developed research-based procedures.

Pre-service teacher trainers should ensure that special education teachers leave their programs with the skills to plan, develop, implement, and evaluate IEPs that lead to meaningful and legally sound educational programs for the students they teach. Pre-service training should specifically address the following five areas: (a) conducting meaningful assessments; (b) developing appropriate, measurable goals; (c) using research-based practices; (d) monitoring the progress of students toward achieving their goals; and (e) collaborating with parents and professionals in IEP development.

First, special education teachers must have the skills to plan, conduct, and interpret meaningful assessments. Whereas assessment begins with eligibility determination, it is crucial that special education teachers understand that a meaningful assessment must also contribute useful and functional information that leads directly to educational programming (Bateman & Linden, 2006; Deno, 2003; Yell, 2009).

Second, teachers need to be able to write goals that are measurable, linked to student deficits, reflect skills needed to access the general education curriculum, and include measurement procedures for monitoring and evaluating performance (Bateman, 2007a; Yell, 2009). The annual goals are statements of what the IEP team believes a student can reasonably be expected to accomplish in 1 year with effective research-based educational programming. For students who are of transition age, IEP teams and students themselves must be able to collaborate with various service agencies to develop meaningful and measurable transition goals that lead to a full range of life, curricular, and employment opportunities.

Third, teachers must be able to develop special education services that are based on the peer-reviewed research (Etscheidt & Curran, 2010; Yell, 2009). Thus, special education teachers must be knowledgeable about peer-reviewed research and be able to integrate effective, evidence-based practices into students' program to facilitate advancement toward their goals. Table 6.3 includes examples of Web sites where teachers and administrators can access and identify empirically validated practices and procedures.

Fourth, special education teachers must understand how to collect and analyze progress-monitoring data (Bateman & Linden, 2006; Deno, 2003; Yell, 2009). The IDEA requires that all IEPs include statements of how students' progress toward their annual goals will be measured and how students' parents will be informed of their children's progress. This will require that the IEP team adopt an effective, data-based method of monitoring students' progress. The most appropriate data collection systems are those that rely on quantitative data in which target behaviors can be measured, graphed, and visually inspected (e.g., curriculum-based measurement, direct observation) to monitor students' progress toward achieving their goals (Yell, 2006). Anecdotal data and subjective judgments are not appropriate for monitoring progress and should not be the basis of a teacher's data collection procedures.

Finally, pre-service programs should also prepare their students in collaborating with parents and other professionals on multidisciplinary teams, working together in IEP meetings, and involving students in their IEPs.

Table 6.3   Web Sites on Research-Based Practices

Web Site	URL
Council for Exceptional Children	http://www.cec.sped.org/AM/Template.cfm?Section=Evidence_based_Practice&Template=/TaggedPage/TaggedPageDisplay.cfm&TPLID=24&ContentID=4710
National Center on Response to Intervention	http://www.rti4success.org/tools_charts/instruction.php
National Dissemination Center for Children with Disabilities (NICHCY)	http://www.nichcy.org/Research/EvidenceForEducation/Pages/Default.aspx
National Dropout Prevention Center for Students with Disabilities	http://www.ndpc-sd.org/knowledge/practice_guides.php
National Professional Development Center on Autism Spectrum Disorders	http://autismpdc.fpg.unc.edu/content/evidence-based-practices
National Secondary Transition Technical Assistance Center	http://www.nsttac.org/ebp/ebp_main.aspx
Office of Special Education Programs, Technical Assistance Center on Positive Behavioral Interventions and Supports	http://www.pbis.org/
What Works Clearinghouse	http://ies.ed.gov/ncee/wwc/

School district administrators are responsible for implementing appropriate professional development opportunities for their teachers. Because of the constant expansion of the knowledge base in special education, professional development activities should focus on keeping teachers fluent in the latest peer-reviewed research findings. Professional development activities should also target general educators and help to clarify their roles in the IEP process and how to implement IEP goals and monitor progress. In addition, district and school administrators should develop a system of accountability in which they follow up on team members' performance in developing IEPs and evaluating student performance. They should promote collaboration and communication among IEP team members and provide continued training and opportunities for writing measurable goals, linking goals to instruction, and monitoring student progress. For specific information on how to link assessment, IEP goal development, intervention, and evaluation, see Grisham-Brown, Pretti-Frontczak, Hemmeter, and Ridgley (2002) and Pretti-Frontczak and Bricker (2004).

Practitioners, including all IEP team members, face numerous challenges in attempting to fulfill the IEP requirement of the IDEA. Although professional development and teacher-preparation programs should provide the needed training in implementation of the IEP requirement, practitioners must put the training into practice. In addition to the recommendations provided here, IEP team members should focus on (a) providing specially designed instruction based on assessment data; (b) developing IEP goals for academic and functional areas that are relevant, measurable, and individually meaningful; (c) implementing educational programs that are based on peer-reviewed research; and (d) monitoring student progress toward their IEP goals frequently and systematically using appropriate data collection systems. Additionally, teachers must maintain good communication and effective working relationships with parents and elicit feedback from IEP team members to constantly improve the IEP process.

Practitioners and researchers need to understand the distinction between procedural and substantive compliance with the IEP requirements of the IDEA. Too often, school district personnel assume that procedurally compliant IEPs will result in substantive compliance (i.e., improved education and services and better outcomes for students) with the IDEA. This is clearly not the case. In fact, a procedurally compliant IEP can be substantively useless if the IEP does not provide meaningful educational benefit to a student (Yell, 2009). If IEPs are to meet the promise envisioned when the EHA was passed in 1975, school personnel must understand that the IEP is more than a document; it is in actuality the process by which a student's FAPE is developed and delivered.

CHAPTER 7

Using Assessments to Determine Placement in the Least Restrictive Environment for Students with Disabilities

Frederick J. Brigham | *George Mason University*

Jean B. Crockett | *The University of Florida*

Special education decisions should be deliberative. The actions taken should be based on clear thinking and rooted in data that address the specific issues of concern. In many cases, special education decisions, particularly those involving placement, are made without adequate data to support clear thought and reasoned actions. Actions that are independent of thought and data are unlikely to result in actual benefits for the individuals with disabilities they are intended to help.

Some educators point to recent revisions in federal and state regulations, claiming they are no longer required to conduct many assessments that were a part of special education deliberations in the past; others question the utility of assessment tools in making placement decisions; and others suggest that placement is a moot point because *all* students with disabilities should be taught in general education settings. We contend that these beliefs are incorrect, and in this chapter we examine the ways that regulations continue to require timely and meaningful assessments to make individual placement decisions based on individual needs. We also examine issues surrounding various forms of assessment data in pursuit of the union of data, thought, and action in placement.

Special education in the United States is carried out under requirements of the Individuals with Disabilities Education Act (IDEA), the federal law that ensures each student with a disability receives a free appropriate public education (FAPE) in the least restrictive environment (LRE) for that student. The tool for carrying out these requirements is the student's individualized education program (IEP). At first glance, the meanings of FAPE and LRE appear straightforward and easily understandable. The amount of contention surrounding these concepts, however, suggests that *if* their meaning was ever clear to lawmakers, it is no longer clear to decision makers concerned with determinations of special education eligibility, appropriate services, and the settings or placements in which those services might be provided.

The topic we address is broad, and generalizations that apply uniformly across disability types, various purposes of schooling, and age groups are rare. For this reason, the *I* in IEP stands for *individualized* (not *interchangeable*). Therefore, we limit our focus to academic curricular issues for students of school age with high-incidence disabilities (i.e., specific learning disabilities, emotional or behavioral disorders, and mild intellectual disabilities). We also limit our discussion to students with adequate proficiency in English.

Contextual Bases for Making Instructional Placement Decisions

The contextual background with which one approaches deliberations about instructional placement decisions can greatly influence the questions to be raised and the way that answers should be framed. We consider three contextual referents for educational placement decisions: (a) the legal context, (b) the empirical context, and (c) the conceptual context.

Legal Context

Volumes have been written about behavior issues and the procedural requirements for serving students with frequently occurring disabilities. However, comparatively little attention has been directed toward these students' academic achievement when making instructional placement decisions. Given the alignment of the IDEA with the provisions of the Elementary and Secondary Education Act (currently authorized as the No Child Left Behind Act [NCLB]), the dominant legislation governing American public education, it is surprising that so little attention and research is directed to this topic. NCLB makes clear that the purpose of schooling is academic achievement. The alignment of IDEA with NCLB by extension makes clear that special education similarly targets academic achievement.

The IDEA requires school officials "to ensure that all children with disabilities have available to them a free appropriate public education [FAPE] that emphasizes special education and related services designed to meet their unique needs, and prepare them for further education, employment and independent living" (20 U.S.C. § 1400(d)(1)(A)). School officials must also ensure that students with disabilities are educated in settings alongside classmates without disabilities, to the maximum extent appropriate to the individual learning needs of the students with disabilities.

Placement decisions—or decisions about the instructional settings where an individual student might receive an appropriate education—are governed by the LRE provisions of the federal regulations to the IDEA (34 C.F.R §§ 300.114-120). The LRE requirements set out factors to consider in educating students with and without disabilities together to the maximum extent appropriate (20 U.S.C. § 1412(a)(5)). The law presumes that all students will be taught in general classes, but this presumption is rebutted by convincing evidence that an appropriate placement cannot be delivered in the general education classroom, or that an alternative placement would provide the student with a more appropriate education. As a result, school district officials are required to make a full continuum of alternative placements available, ranging from inclusion in general education classes to special classes, separate schools, residential facilities, hospitals, and home settings.

Under the IDEA, the LRE is not a specific location but the outcome of a decision-making process that places greater weight on the standard of FAPE than on the actual place where instruction occurs. Decisions about where an individual student can be taught appropriately must be made by the team that develops the student's IEP—a group of people that includes parents and others who are knowledgeable about the student, the placement options, and the meaning of the assessment data. Placement decisions for special education students must be reviewed annually, must be based on the IEP, and must give consideration to potentially harmful effects on the child and the quality of the required services (Crockett, 2008). Unless an IEP requires otherwise to achieve FAPE, students should attend a school as close to home as possible or the school they would attend if they did not have a disability.

IEPs and Appropriate Services

Not all disputes about an appropriate education involve concerns about placement, but all disputes about placement in the LRE are determined by the appropriateness of a student's IEP (Crockett, 2008). The meaning of an appropriate education under the IDEA was defined by the Supreme Court in the case of *Board of Education v. Rowley* (1982). Amy Rowley was a girl with a hearing impairment who was denied the services of a sign language interpreter. Her family sued, stating that such services would allow her to reach her optimal level of performance. The court held that the law does not require optimal services, but rather, appropriate services. According to the opinion, when students are attaining passing marks and moving easily from grade to grade, the services provided are appropriate. Since then, the meaning of FAPE has hinged on the provision of an IEP that addresses a student's unique educational needs; in recent years, this has meant considering those needs in the context of standards-based reforms.

IEPs and LRE

To date, the Supreme Court has decided no LRE cases, and consequently, no U.S. standard exists for making instructional placement decisions in students' IEPs. Analytical frameworks for determining LRE were used in several important cases in lower courts from 1984 to 1997, including the Roncker Portability Test, the Daniel Two-Part Test, the Rachel H. Four Part Test, and the Hartman Three-Part Test; these frameworks continue to guide legal determinations of LRE in different parts of the country (see Rozalski, Stewart, & Miller, 2010; Yell, 2006).

Questions to Guide Placements in the LRE

The type of services required for an individual student, as well as the intensity of those services, should be guided by systematic assessment of the student's needs, and his response to the instructional program. The following questions address components embodied in the LRE frameworks, and answers to them rely on the assessment of student-centered data collected throughout the LRE determination process (Yell, 2006). Questions one through three are particularly amenable to assessment information, and we shall return to them later in the chapter.

1. *Has the school taken steps to maintain the child in the general education class?* What supplementary aides and services were used? What interventions were attempted? How many interventions were tried?

2. *What are the benefits of placement in a general education setting with supplementary aids and services versus the benefits of placement in a special education setting for this child?* What are the academic benefits? What are the nonacademic benefits such as social communication and interactions?

3. *What are the effects on the education of other students?* If the student is disruptive, is the education of other students adversely affected? Does the student require an inordinate amount of attention from the teacher and, as a result, adversely affect the education of others?

4. *If a student requires an alternative setting, are appropriate opportunities for integration available?* In what academic settings is the student integrated with nondisabled students? In what nonacademic settings is the child integrated with nondisabled students?

5. *Is the full continuum of alternative services made available across the school system from which to choose an appropriate placement?* (Yell, 2006, p. 326)

Each set of questions about a student's educational placement depends on the union of careful thought, data, and concerted action that begins with assessment of the individual child and considers the interaction of instruction with the environment where teaching and learning is to occur. Instruction that (a) focuses on different content from the general curriculum, (b) incorporates intensive remedial activities to develop skills already mastered by other students of the same age or grade, (c) progresses at a different pace from the general education program, or (d) employs systematic teaching of cognitive strategies not needed by other students may require specialized settings for the delivery of appropriate services.

Empirical Context for Placement Decisions

Placement decisions are governed by law and should be guided by empirical research (Bateman, 2007b). Empirical evidence is lacking, however, to support the notion that the needs of *all* children can be met in the same environment, even when inclusive classroom strategies such as differentiated instruction (see Tomlinson, 2003) and Universal Design for Learning (see Rose & Meyer, 2006) are used (M. M. Brigham, Brigham, & Lloyd, 2002). The positive response of *some,* or possibly *many,* or even *most* students in no way establishes that *all* students will respond positively, or need *only* these approaches to derive FAPE.

The impact of instructional placements on a student's academic performance remains a debatable point (e.g., Carr-George, Vannest, Willson, & Davis, 2009; Zigmond, Kloo, & Volonino, 2009). Elbaum, Vaughn, Hughes, Moody, and Schumm (2000), however, provided meta-analytic evidence that placement in various instructional groupings can substantially alter students' performance. Multiple-grouping strategies, such as small-group instruction and individual tutoring, resulted in tangible gains in reading compared to whole class or heterogeneous instructional grouping for students with high-incidence disabilities. This evidence suggests that placement for reading instruction in whole-class, individual, or smaller groups makes a difference in the rate at which struggling students acquire skills and progress to higher levels of mastery. These data suggest that more supportive, or restrictive, placements must be maintained for *some* children and that a diversity of educational placements based on instructional need should be celebrated and maintained.

Where a student receives instruction is only one component of a defensible educational plan (Crockett, 2008). Special education settings that afford (a) low expectations and reduced assignments, (b) weak accommodations that undermine employability in the postschool world, and (c) assessments that misrepresent performance levels so that educators and students have a false sense of accomplishment threaten the provision of FAPE in the LRE and should be avoided (Chandler, 2009). Conversely, general education settings in which instruction (a) moves at a faster pace than can be mastered by a given student with a disability (Engelmann, 1997), (b) yields few meaningful opportunities for success (Hallenbeck & Kauffman, 1995), and (c) focuses on skills or conceptual learning that differ from the student's needs (H. L. Swanson, Hoskyn, & Lee, 1999) should also be avoided. Inclusive placements can be difficult to justify as "least restrictive" when conditions impede a student's successful performance.

The default placement for students is the general education classroom, and most special education students have previously demonstrated inadequate response to basic instruction. In cases where FAPE requires instructional elements that extend beyond general education with the supports of supplementary aids and services, other placements must be considered. If an alternative placement makes FAPE possible, that placement is the LRE. From a conceptual perspective, typical placements where a student is failing to make academic and/or social progress despite appropriate supports could be considered more restrictive (in terms of achievement) than are highly specialized settings.

Conceptual Context of Placement Considerations

When the Education for All Handicapped Children Act, the forerunner of IDEA, was enacted in 1975, many individuals with disabilities were excluded from public education, and many others were afforded inappropriate educational programs (Yell, Rogers, & Rogers, 1998). School systems were required to provide educational services to each student but were not required to have every service available within the local district. Children whose needs could not be met appropriately were often sent to neighboring districts, multidistrict service centers, or residential centers at the district's expense. The prevailing sentiment was that highly specialized programs would often be impractical or impossible to create locally, and so children were sent to existing programs within a broad geographical region. Under such circumstances, the place (i.e., physical location) of the program was a highly salient feature.

Over time, specialized aspects of such programs were scrutinized and sometimes found wanting (Goldman, 1994; Merulla & McKinnon, 1982; Taylor, 1988). Early efforts to develop effective treatments for students with learning problems focused on interventions aimed at training or repairing the student's cognitive makeup presumed to be different or damaged relative to most other individuals (e.g., perceptual motor training). Such treatments, it was thought, would enable more typical interactions with the world than would otherwise have been afforded to the student. Interventions, in other words, attempted to change individuals in fundamental ways. Over time such approaches to intervention have largely been abandoned.

Kavale and Forness (2000) emphasized the conceptual changes in educating students with disabilities by suggesting that interventions designed to change the individual focus on the SPECIAL in special education: *SPECIAL education* engaged in remedial practices unique to the individual and different from the educational programs provided to most students. In contrast, the alternative was referred to as special EDUCATION. From this perspective, *special EDUCATION* means adapting and modifying the instruction provided to most students so that it is more accessible and beneficial for students with disabilities. The outcomes reported for *special EDUCATION* greatly exceeded those reported for *SPECIAL education* (Kavale & Forness, 2000), and the 2004 reauthorization of IDEA codified that special education programs were to reflect the goals and content of general education programs (Gordon, 2006).

Changing the focus of instruction to address the same elements as general education seemed to undercut the need for different placements, because the content and ostensibly the pace of instruction in pursuit of adequate yearly progress goals would be similar for most students. However, data regarding homogeneous placement of heterogeneous groups of students (i.e., full inclusion) remains inconsistent at best (Kavale, 2002). Although the goals may be similar, the methods and supports necessary to attain them may be very different for students with disabilities compared with their peers without disabilities (Weiss & Lloyd, 2001).

An optimal environment or level of support for one individual might be detrimental to another, and "an everyday setting that inclines one individual to feel and function well can push another in the opposite direction" (W. Gallagher, 1993, p. 18). In short, even though people may be working toward the same or similar goals, their educational background, personal characteristics, rates of progress, and instructional needs may respond to instructional approaches that are better carried out in different educational placements than a general education setting.

Summary

The IDEA requires special education students to be educated in environments that provide them with the opportunity to participate and progress in the general curriculum alongside classmates who are not disabled to the maximum extent appropriate to their learning needs. When a student cannot be taught appropriately in a typical setting, a continuum of placement options must be made available so that instruction can be delivered in what is determined by the IEP team to be the least restrictive alternative to the typical class. Decisions about alternative placements are contentious in many cases, but they are also crucial to supporting a student's FAPE. In the next section, we describe some of the assessment tools available for determining placement in the LRE for students with disabilities.

Tools in the Workshop

Skilled artisans have workshops equipped with a variety of tools. The key to excellence in a craft is not so much the possession of a single tool that works all the time, but in appropriately applying a combination of different tools to do the job at hand. Good assessment decisions work the same way. Better tools increase the chances that results will be meaningful, and using the appropriate combination of tools vastly increases the chances of making beneficial decisions. Therefore, we discuss various assessments available to educators responsible for making placement decisions. Our list is not exhaustive, but the categories are illustrative of the kinds of tools available to IEP teams making these important decisions.

Formal, Standardized Tests

The term *standardized* simply means that a test is administered to each individual under the same (standardized) conditions; however, "standardized tests have been the objects of scorn primarily because critics do not understand what they are designed to do and why they are important" (Kauffman & Konold, 2007, p. 81). Standardized tests can provide a constant backdrop of behavioral expectations so that differences in scores can be attributed primarily to an individual's performance and not to differences in testing procedures.

Large-Scale State Assessments

Large-scale assessments are most often associated with state-administered competency measures for accountability and, in many states, graduation requirements (Cortiella, 2006). All students, even students with disabilities, *must* participate in state educational accountability systems in some way. Students might participate in general assessments with or without

accommodations, or in an alternative assessment. Regardless of the manner in which students participate in assessments, the yielded data can help to guide placement decisions.

Passing scores on large-scale assessments.   If a student is passing large-scale tests without special education support, then the student has little need for additional special education supports (see *Alvin Independent School Dist. v. A.D. ex rel. Patricia F*, 2007). For a student who is already receiving special education services, passing scores on state assessments could be a suggestion that the placement and intensity of services currently provided are appropriate, at least relative to the test domain and conditions. Passing scores on state tests could also indicate that the services being provided are beyond those *needed* by the student. However, passing scores are not an automatic indicator that levels of service should be reduced, or that students can be served successfully in less-restrictive environments. It does not necessarily follow that a student who performs well with support can do so independently in a general education classroom.

Failing scores on large-scale assessments.   It is unrealistic to expect that *all* students (even students with appropriate IEPs) will attain passing grades in an era of standards intended "to (a) focus the general education curriculum on a core of important and challenging content and (b) ensure that *every* student in a state or district receives instruction on the *same* challenging content" [emphasis in original] (Nolet, 2005, pp. 6–7). Students may not perform well, even when they use familiar accommodations (Thurlow & Thompson, 2004). Having standards means some will fall short of them; having high standards means a greater percentage of people will fall short of the mark.

Failing scores on a state test do not automatically indicate an inappropriate educational program or placement; however, failing state tests is certainly a prompt to examine the appropriateness of the educational program, including the adequacy of the placement. Identifying the reasons for poor performance can provide relevant information for making decisions regarding instructional needs and corresponding placement options.

False negatives.   Two major causes of false negatives (erroneous failing scores) must be considered before using large-scale assessments in guiding FAPE and LRE placement decisions. First, failure on a state test should be unrelated to extraneous factors such as anxiety or being ill on the day of the test. In such cases, the information yielded by the test is invalid and of no use for making placement or any other kind of decision beyond the decision to discount the data. Second, a student with a disability may fail a large-scale test because required testing accommodations were unavailable. Providing appropriate accommodations is a complicated enterprise. Many teachers insert multiple accommodations into the IEP, hoping that at least one of them will help the student (Thurlow, 2000). Further, accommodations are often assigned based on subjective beliefs unrelated to the individual student's disability characteristics (L. S. Fuchs & Fuchs, 2001). Confusion about the nature and purposes of accommodations appears to be more common than unusual.

The Dynamic Assessment of Test Accommodations (L. S. Fuchs, Fuchs, Eaton, & Hamlett, 2003) is one instrument that can provide guidance in selecting accommodations. However, schools may be unlikely to expend the added time and expense to administer such a personalized instrument in the absence of substantial pressure from state and federal agencies for districts to ensure the appropriateness of accommodations (Della Toffalo & Milke, 2008). Nevertheless, the appropriateness of assessment accommodations for the student and the test should be examined before concluding that the failing grade indicates lack of FAPE or inadequate placements.

Failing scores and FAPE.   Failing scores on a state test could be an accurate measure of student accomplishment, and therefore a valid indicator rather than a false negative. In such cases, the failure could indicate lack of FAPE. One way to *undermine* FAPE is to insist on placement options that prevent the specialized instruction specified in the IEP to be delivered with sufficient frequency or intensity for the student to derive adequate benefit. For example, co-teaching is currently a recommended strategy for many students with high-incidence disabilities. In co-teaching, "the student with disabilities and his/her special education teacher are both integrated into the general education classroom, and the two teachers share instructional responsibilities" (Zigmond & Magiera, 2001, p. 1). In many cases, an arrangement such as co-teaching is profitable for the student, but in other cases, the arrangement provides a seat in the classroom but yields little meaningful progress (Weiss & Lloyd, 2001). When co-teaching provides an inadequate level of service, the student may be *immersed* in the general education curriculum but fail to *master* challenging content. Failing to pass the state proficiency test may suggest that the access to the general education curriculum is not meaningful, and educators need to consider something different.

When students with IEPs fail state examinations, their IEP teams should examine the IEP to determine whether (a) the supports specified on the IEP are adequate and (b) whether those supports can reasonably be carried out in an effective manner within the current placement. If the IEP team determines that additional supports are needed and that they cannot be carried out in the present environment, educators have good reason to consider a different placement. Given the default preference for general education placements, such considerations often suggest the need for more specialized (more-restrictive) environments. Although efforts to make students with disabilities successful in general education settings are clearly worthwhile, educators should not be so enamored of the goal of inclusion that they exchange a seat in a general education classroom for meaningful instruction in another setting.

Individually Administered Tests

Individually administered achievement tests have long been the workhorses of special education eligibility decisions and, therefore, may be helpful in placement decisions. Two examples of such measures include the Kaufman Test of Educational Achievement II (Kaufman & Kaufman, 2004) and the Woodcock-Johnson—III, Tests of Achievement (Woodcock, McGrew, & Mather, 2001).

Individual measures have the distinct advantage of offering greater probability of valid administration than is possible in tests administered to groups; however, they also have the disadvantage of being abstractions of a generalized curriculum, representing performance across the entire nation rather than being tied to local or state standards. Additionally, norm-referenced achievement tests sample the curriculum at a sparse level with as few as one or two items representing an entire school year's growth. The high reliability of these measures is obtained at the cost of sensitivity to small increments of progress (Galagan, 1985). Therefore, these kinds of tests can be problematic if one wishes to measure small increments of progress across time.

Problems in interpretation.   Unlike state tests that are evaluated binomially (pass or fail), individual tests do not typically carry a bright-line marker for adequate scores. No universally accepted set of cut points is available for determining when scores rise from the low range to the "good-enough" range, and then to the high range. Traditional statistical analysis suggests that the average range is determined by the first standard deviation on either side of the mean, but some tests and school district policies set narrower constructions of typical performance.

Even though bright-line tests on such instruments are unwise, some ways of interpreting scores may be helpful in making placement decisions. One of the more common uses of achievement tests is to determine adequacy of progress in comparison to performance predictions from IQ tests. In general, students who perform at a similar level (e.g., standard scores that are similar to each other) on the IQ and achievement tests are often said to be performing at a level commensurate with their ability. How close the scores need to be to each other remains an open and debatable issue. Additionally, some scholars question the utility of IQ tests relative to special education placement decisions (e.g., Kortteinen, Närhi, & Ahonen, 2009; MacMillan & Forness, 1998). Nevertheless, IQ tests are commonly used, and achievement measures that reflect the IQ scores are one suggestion that educational placements may be adequate and yielding appropriate achievement benefits.

Another method of using achievement test scores to demonstrate adequacy of placement is in consideration of scores from repeated administrations of the instrument over time. Norm-referenced tests yield measures of relative standing, so individuals who are making progress that is notably faster than the norm group will attain increasingly high scores from administration to repeated administration. Individuals who keep pace with the norm group will maintain scores of approximately the same level with each administration of the test. Individuals who make notably less progress than their peers will, however, attain scores that are lower from initial to repeated administrations of the measure. Using this method requires educators to be sensitive to the variation in scores that can be attributed to random error. All high-quality assessments provide indicators of the measurement error (standard error of measurement [SEM]) for the test across different scales and characteristics such as the age of the individual test taker. Any gain or decrease in performance must be outside of the estimated measurement error to be meaningful. Scores that vary within the range of performance that can be attributed to measurement error are best interpreted as representing roughly the same level of performance.

Adequate and high scores on individual achievement tests.   Adequate and high scores on individually administered achievement tests are indicators of desirable outcomes and vouch for the adequacy of the educational placement. Administration of these tests is intended to yield a "best-effort" level of performance. Sometimes, students who earn failing grades in a classroom domain or skill directly related to a given subtest can actually attain strong scores in such an assessment. This result represents the difference between what an individual is able to do, and

what she is willing or able to do over a long period of time in classroom conditions. Classroom performance involves more than academic skills. Students who are unwilling or unable to complete homework assignments independently or participate in classroom activities such as discussions may have grades that are actually under-representations of their academic ability. Thus, individually administered achievement tests can help to discriminate between students needing additional academic support (low grades and low test scores) and students who are roughly on target in their skill development but in need of behavioral or organizational supports (low classroom grades but adequate test scores).

Low scores on individual achievement tests.   As was the case for state assessments, low scores can be the result of a variety of conditions unrelated to the student's actual competence. Therefore, the results of these tests, like the results of any other test, should not be taken at face value. In this case, it is easier for a student to underperform (attain a lower score than would be accurate) than it is to overperform (guess right often enough to substantially and meaningfully raise the test score).

All of the caveats for interpreting low scores on state tests apply to individual tests. Low scores suggest that educational programming may be inappropriate and that additional supports might be needed, which may necessitate a change in placement. However, a certain proportion of the population will always attain low normative scores for a variety of reasons (Kauffman & Konold, 2007). The emphasis of the educational goals in the IEP can help to determine the extent to which low scores alone call for additional effort. Like state assessments, individual standardized tests represent only one piece of the puzzle for making placement decisions. Other indicators must be used in conjunction with these kinds of scores.

Examples of Other Standardized Measures

Although IDEA and NCLB align to support academic outcomes and, thus, focus on tests of achievement, other measures of performance affect FAPE and LRE decisions. Among these are (a) behavior rating scales and (b) self-report measures of attitudes toward self and school-related constructs. Other classes of assessment measures exist, but we restrict our discussion here to these two examples.

Behavior rating scales.   A number of behavior rating scales are available to identify, categorize, and evaluate problem behaviors. Two examples that have substantial scientific validation are the Systematic Screening for Behavior Disorders (SSBD; Walker & Severson, 1992) and the Behavioral and Emotional Rating Scale (BERS; M. H. Epstein & Sharma, 1998). Teachers and parents complete such instruments by rating the frequency of a variety of behaviors during a given period of time (e.g., 6 months). The SSBD is an example of a "multiple-gating system" where each level of the assessment becomes progressively more precise and demanding. It moves from a general screening of behavior to actual comparison of the target student's behavior to norms constructed from more than 4,500 cases. The BERS is an example of a "strength-based assessment" that examines the presence of social abilities as well as deficits.

High levels of behavioral disorders or low levels of strength relative to the general population may signal the need for additional behavioral supports or instruction. As with academic instruction, some behavioral treatments require more specialized (restrictive) environments than the general education setting.

Self-report measures.   Students are sometimes asked to complete self-rating scales. The Student Self-Concept Scale (SSCS; Gresham, Elliott, & Evans-Fernandez, 1992) is one such instrument that possesses adequate psychometric properties. The SSCS collects information across three content domains (i.e., Self-Image, Academic, and Social) and creates ratings of (a) the individual's self-confidence in performing the behaviors, (b) the importance placed on the various behaviors, and (c) self-confidence that positive outcomes will result from carrying out the behaviors (Gresham, 1995). Although such self-report instruments are highly subjective and open to social expectancy effects (people may report in ways they think are beneficial to them rather than honestly), they may provide insights into the individual's emotional state, which would otherwise be unavailable or at least very difficult to obtain (S. N. Elliott & Busse, 2004).

Student perceptions of various placements are often overlooked in the process of assessment but potentially are useful. Students may express self-efficacy beliefs that suggest the need for more or different supports than are in their IEPs or general education programs. Student preference alone may not be the primary determinant in placement decisions. Nevertheless, when self-report measures suggest that students are developing feelings of inadequacy and hopelessness relative to their studies, the implication becomes clearer that additional support is desirable. Increases in intensity of program or frequency of evaluative interaction with teachers may require IEP changes in programming and placement.

Informal Measures

Informal measures differ from formal, standardized measures by a number of characteristics. In general, informal measures are less reliant on normative comparisons derived from large samples of the population, are more adaptable to immediate needs of educators, have less rigid and well-defined scoring criteria, and have less well-defined administration procedures (Bennett, 1982). The boundaries between formal, standardized assessments and informal assessments are not well-defined, and some procedures share characteristics of both classes of assessment (Vansickle, 2004). Curriculum-based measurement (CBM), for example, is a highly flexible approach to measurement that can be adjusted informally to adjust to classroom needs. CBM can also be standardized so that each student receives the same measure the same way, each time it is repeated. We have chosen to include CBM as an informal measure. Other forms of informal measures include but are not limited to (a) direct observation, (b) teacher opinion, (c) classroom grades, and (d) interviews with students and parents.

Direct Observation

Direct observation of behavior is by far the most frequently used tool for evaluating classroom behavior (Sasso, Conroy, Stichter, & Fox, 2001). Observations completed according to a predetermined structure including operational definitions of target behaviors and time parameters are usually more useful than general narrative observations. Frequently, in addition to observing the target student(s), observers will select one or two individuals who are also present in the environment and take data on their behaviors for comparison purposes. In that way, the behavior exhibited by the target student can be compared to others in the same environment. By examining the behavior of students within the context of the classroom, and relative to the teacher's actions, direct observation efforts can prompt suggestions for change in areas of need, which might be related to changes in placement (Slate & Saudargas, 1986).

Direct observation can range from relatively unstructured narrative approaches, in which the observer writes everything that is seen, heard, and perceived, to highly structured protocols, in which the variables to be observed and the schedule for observing them are specified (T. Thompson, Symons, & Felce, 2000). All observation procedures have their limitations and potential benefits, but the more structured methods appear to have the greatest utility for making decisions relative to placement.

When observational data suggest that other students in a given setting are engaged and responding appropriately to teacher directives, but the target student is unengaged or responding inappropriately, a number of possible implications regarding the adequacy of the educational program emerge. It is possible that the individual is unable to perform the behaviors expected of students in the class; it is possible that the individual does not value the reinforcers in the environment; it is also possible that the individual may believe he is incapable of attaining access to the reinforcers maintaining the behavior of other students. All of these possibilities suggest the need for alterations of instructional and behavioral programs available to the student. Increasing the intensity of instruction, for example, may require consideration of a more specialized and structured environment so that the student is working on missing skills. Conversely, a student may appear disengaged because the placement is overly restrictive and providing supports that the individual does not need. In such cases, a more typical or less-restrictive environment is indicated.

Teacher Opinions as Informal Assessments

The U.S. District Court of South Dakota considered teacher judgment that a student was performing at levels sufficient for reintegration as an adequate form of assessment data (*Geffre et al. v. Leola School District 44-2*, 2009). In this case, teacher opinion was a recognized form of assessment data that was considered when making placement decisions.

Teachers are often the first to notice the performance problems of students with frequently occurring disabilities such as mild intellectual disabilities and learning disabilities, and their judgment regarding the difficulties facing students relative to other classmates is often correct (M. M. Gerber, 2005; M. M. Gerber & Semmel, 1984). Elements such as the resources available to support learning (including materials for instruction and instructional expertise), and competing demands facing the teacher (clerical and other noninstructional duties, as well as the heterogeneity of students' learning needs) combine to form the boundaries of "teachability" in a classroom. Gerber and Semmel proposed that when students fall outside of the bounds of teachability, they are unlikely to receive appropriate instruction. In sum, characteristics of the individual student under consideration, as well as the context in which the student is taught, affect teacher judgment.

Factors affecting teacher judgment.   Contextual pressures on general education teachers (e.g., increased class size, or the behavioral challenges in the school population) are reflected in the number and severity of students referred for evaluation of a suspected disability (Hess & Brigham, 2007). Context can also affect the nature of students identified for special education and placed for instruction within different schools (Wiley, Siperstein, Bountress, Forness, & Brigham, 2009; Wiley, Siperstein, Forness, & Brigham, 2010).

Teachers are intimately familiar with how students interact with the learning environment in a way no assessment can adequately measure. Their informal observations comprise a data set much richer and more comprehensive than any other assessment measure, by taking into account many complex interactions between the student, the teacher, the curriculum, and the environment. Working with students on a daily basis puts teachers in a uniquely well-informed position to determine if a student can or cannot succeed in a given environment. Thus, teacher suggestions that the current educational environment is unsatisfactory should be considered relative to other decision-making data. The triangulation of teacher opinion with achievement and behavioral data can make a powerful case for determining the appropriateness of a placement option.

Classroom Grades as Informal Assessments

Classroom grades can influence educational placement decisions. The classroom teacher has a crucial role in determining the adequacy of educational programs and placements through awarding grades and evaluating student progress in other ways such as behavior reports and statements of a student's ability to manage learning and social behaviors independently.

Teacher grades are important indicators of placement and programmatic adequacy, but they are often constrained by various factors. For example, some schools use modified grading standards for students with IEPs, basing their grades not simply on performance but on a combination of performance and effort (Gersten, Vaughn, & Brengelman, 1996). Thus, it is not always clear what the grades awarded by a specific teacher to a given student mean. Nevertheless, grades should be considered relative to placement decisions. IEP teams should consider whether passing grades suggest that (a) a student has more support than is currently needed and might succeed in a less-restrictive placement, or (b) the current supports and placement are necessary to maintain passing grades. Failing grades may indicate that greater supports and a change of placement are appropriate, but need to be evaluated in terms of the possible reasons for the unsuccessful performance they indicate to make these decisions.

Interviews

Students and parents can provide useful information in support of FAPE and LRE placement decisions. Interviews of students and teachers as well as parents can yield insights that would not otherwise be available (De Groot, 2002). Students with learning disabilities frequently report a preference for more specialized (more-restrictive) settings for their special education programs over receiving supports in general education classes (Klingner, Vaughn, Schumm, Cohen, & Forgan, 1998; Vaughn & Klingner, 1998). Students with learning disabilities in inclusive settings also reported higher levels of alienation than did students with emotional/behavioral disorders in self-contained special education programs (Fulk, Brigham, & Lohman, 1998). More recently, groups of high school students with learning disabilities reported that they generally preferred to receive their services in "pull-out" settings (often considered more restrictive than general education settings) for two reasons: (a) special education teachers deliver distinctly different services than do general educators, and (b) it is often difficult to gain access to special education teachers in large co-taught classrooms (Leafstedt, Richards, LaMonte, & Cassidy, 2007).

Interview data provide another window on the adequacy of placements for individual students. In some cases, students and parents may be seeking more supportive or restrictive placements; in other cases, they may be seeking less-restrictive placements. When students are making adequate progress and they or their parents request a less-restrictive placement, educators are well-advised to consider the request. If school officials are uncertain that a less-restrictive placement will yield satisfactory results, they might initiate a trial placement and monitor the results for a set period of time. Continued success would indicate appropriate placement; declining performance would suggest an inappropriate program of instruction and accompanying placement.

Curriculum-Based Assessment and Measurement

Curriculum-based assessment (CBA) and CBM are kinds of formative evaluation that have been demonstrated to substantially raise the achievement of nearly all students with whom it is employed (L. S. Fuchs & D. Fuchs, 1986). These procedures also form a substantial component of Response to Intervention (RtI) programs, described in the following section (F. J. Brigham & Brigham, 2010; Wallace, Espin, McMaster, Deno, & Foegen, 2007).

CBA involves the observation and recording of student performance in a local curriculum in order to gather information to make instructional decisions. The test materials used in CBA are developed by the teacher on the basis of a task analysis of the curriculum and presented to students after pretesting identifies target skills for instruction. During instruction, students are repeatedly measured on the selected skills using alternative test forms. Mastery of a skill prompts a move to the next skill in the task analysis. With CBM, student performance is measured repeatedly (e.g., once or twice per week) with test materials that represent an entire curricular domain rather than specific subcomponents of the domain (Espin, Shin, & Busch, 2000).

CBA and CBM are particularly useful for demonstrating adequacy of intervention programs and the placements they require. Other chapters in this volume address CBA and CBM in greater detail (Chapters 8 and 3, respectively), but when student performance is consistently below the rate necessary to meet established goals by the end of a specified time period, some aspect of the instructional program (e.g., focus, method, duration, frequency of instruction) should be addressed. In some cases, increased instruction can necessitate a move to a different placement to facilitate the program.

Response to Intervention

Recent efforts to implement RtI approaches using multiple tiers of instructional support provide another opportunity for assessing students' needs and monitoring progress. RtI was developed through research efforts to (a) increase the accuracy of eligibility decisions for special education, (b) prevent students without disabilities from falling so far behind that they seem to require special education, (c) focus instructional attention on standards-based curricula, and (d) improve the professionalism of educational decision making (F. J. Brigham & Brigham, 2010; see also Chapter 2, this volume). The fundamental premise of RtI is that screening every child regularly on simple performance indicators related to important curricular outcomes allows teachers to recognize students who are showing signs of difficulty and respond to them with increasingly intense levels of support before their instructional problems become insurmountable (F. J. Brigham & Brigham, 2010).

Most RtI models operate in a three-tier model, with each tier involving more substantial supports and frequent progress monitoring (Mellard & Johnson, 2008). A student's responsiveness to intervention is judged according to both the actual performance level and the trajectory, or rate of improvement, compared to peers

(D. Fuchs, Mock, Morgan, & Young, 2003). That is, students who are nonresponsive to intervention not only perform at a lower level than their peers, but also improve at a slower rate. Tier 1 involves universal screening of performance in the general education program. Tiers 2 and 3 are devoted to increasingly intensive interventions for those who make inadequate progress at lower levels.

When students are found to be nonresponsive to Tier 3 interventions, implications arise for changing programming and placement. Nonresponsiveness to targeted treatments that resemble special education at this level suggests substantial amounts of time, and focused instruction needs to be allocated for progress to occur. Timely referral of struggling students for special education evaluations cannot be denied in the RtI process, and decision making that fosters appropriate programming in the LRE must not be delayed (U.S. Department of Education, 2010).

Using Assessments in Making Placement Decisions

The demonstration that school personnel have systematically considered the student's unique educational needs and the capacity of the program to confer educational benefit is fundamental to defensible decisions for placing students with disabilities in any instructional setting. The determination of a student's educational needs can be based on a variety of information sources, but should be based on careful consideration of meaningful assessment data.

Addressing Fundamental Questions with Assessment Data

Fundamental questions drive decisions about instructional placement for students with disabilities (Yell, 2006). In this section, we revisit these questions and examine assessment procedures that can be used to address them.

What Has Been Done to Maintain the Child in a General Education Class?

Given the legal preference for placements in general education settings, and the sentiments of many educators and parents, it is logical to ask what has been done to ensure that the student is responding to instruction with adequate levels of performance. What supplementary aides and services were used, what interventions were attempted, and how many interventions were tried?

Responding to this set of questions requires development of a historical record, and the assessment/intervention model used in multi-tiered levels of support such as RtI can provide useful tools for documenting (a) areas in need of interventions, (b) the instructional methods used, (c) the intensity (time) of the strategies, and (d) duration (weeks or months) of the interventions. Most RtI models compare student progress with intervention support against the progress expected of students' age- or grade-mates. When research-based interventions have been attempted with documented integrity (i.e., implemented as designed) over a sufficient amount of time, then continued low performance with a trajectory of improvement that is flatter than expected suggests the need to review the appropriateness of the student's programming and instructional placement.

RtI is carried out in the context of general education and can indicate the need to move to more intensive programming and possibly a more-restrictive placement option when students demonstrate poor response to even the best basic instruction. Reliable data on (a) what interventions and supports have been implemented and (b) the effects of those interventions and supports on student outcomes will be useful for IEP teams making justifiable and appropriate placement decisions. It is tempting to claim that data will trump opinion in every case, but that is unlikely. It is certain, however, that educators attempting to defend contentious decisions in the absence of data will find themselves on shaky legal and professional ground.

What Are the Relative Benefits of General Versus Special Education?

Addressing this question involves comparing the advantages of different program options; placement decisions must consider the potential costs and benefits of each environment. Recent policies (e.g., NCLB and IDEA) suggest that it is worth the social costs to address the academic benefits and nonacademic benefits of instruction delivered in either special or general education settings as long as the student's needs are met. In responding to these questions, educators must document the efforts made on the student's behalf, as well as her level of performance on academic measures in response to those efforts. Descriptions of expectations for behavior in a particular setting, as well as engagement in nonacademic activities during the day, could add to the evidence in favor of one setting (e.g., special education) over another (e.g., general education).

Using test data.   Scores from state tests and individual achievement tests can be used to compare the academic benefits of one setting over another. For example, students with low scores in basic skills may have more difficulty keeping pace with their peers in content area classes, even with supplementary aides and services. The student might have a significant need for reading instruction at a level of intensity and duration unlikely to be provided in a general education class, particularly in the upper grades. Difficult decisions might need to be made about the relative value of acquiring fundamental reading skills versus participating in social opportunities. In other cases, adequate scores for students in restrictive settings could suggest they might be able to prosper in a more typical placement with supports. Carr-George et al. (2009) reported that students with high-incidence disabilities taught in general education classrooms with in-class support were twice as likely to fail state tests as their general education classmates. Consequently, it should not be assumed that supplementary supports necessarily enable included students with disabilities to pass state proficiency tests.

Using classroom grades.   Before the rise of state testing programs, classroom grades determined a special education student's successful passage from grade to grade (*Board of Education v. Rowley, 1982*). Mead and Paige (2008) noted that the *Rowley* decision was inconclusive regarding the provision of FAPE and a student's progress in the curriculum. Foremost, it is unclear how much progress is sufficient. In a subsequent decision *(Alvin Independent School Dist. v. A.D. ex rel. Patricia F, 2007),* the court held that earning passing grades in the classroom and demonstrating proficiency on state assessments suggest that a general education student's program was *adequate* enough to not require special education. In cases where a special education student is unable to pass the state's achievement test, but is attaining passing grades, legislative language suggests that the IEP, which includes the student's instructional placement, is questionable (P. T. K. Daniel, 2008).

When grades and test scores align in a positive direction, it is difficult to contest the adequacy of the support. Situations in which grades are positive and test scores are low, or vice versa, could indicate the need for more intensive programming and placement. When both the test scores and classroom grades are low, there is little doubt that the educational program is in need of revision, and a more intensive and specialized placement should be considered.

Using student and teacher interviews.   Students may have clear preferences for one setting over

another. In cases where students strongly advocate for a general education setting, classroom descriptions and test information can be useful in prompting students to develop their own IEP supports (McGahee-Kovac, 1995; E. P. Snyder & Shapiro, 1997). In some cases, students may become more invested in their education, reducing the need for intensive services; in other cases, they may become more aware of the services they actually need.

There is also precedent for using teacher opinion and interview data in support of placement decisions. In *Geffre ex rel. S.G. v. Leola Sch. Dist.* (2009), the court found the school's unwillingness to consider the judgments of the direct service staff that the student could function well in a more typical environment to be a violation of the LRE provision of IDEA. This case supports the use of teacher judgment as one form of acceptable assessment data.

Combining data from state assessments, individual achievement tests, ongoing classroom performance (including progress-monitoring measures), and teacher judgment with the preferences of the student and the family can make a strong case for one placement over another. When indications point in the same direction, the decision is clear. When data from different sources suggest different options, the team must weigh the relative importance of each source against FAPE as developed in the student's IEP. Regardless of the placement decision, continued monitoring of conditions in the learning environment are essential to ensure adequate responses to instruction, and to make adjustments in the program. CBA and CBM are appropriate tools to use for this purpose because they are more sensitive to small changes over time. Teacher grades can also be an indicator, as can state and individual achievement tests, although grades may be influenced by other (subjective) factors, and achievement tests are not designed to measure small changes in student performance.

How Does This Student Affect the Environment?

Addressing this question acknowledges that the curricular and behavioral needs of a student might demand unusual attention from the classroom teacher. Consequently, the law permits IEP teams to consider the adverse impact on classmates (a) if the student is disruptive, or (b) if the student requires an inordinate amount of attention from the teacher. Responding to this set of questions is likely to be a sensitive issue. In essence, school officials are in the position of convincing a parent, hearing officer, or judge that the needs of the many outweigh the needs of the few. Using data can potentially reduce the adversarial nature of such discussions.

Using behavioral rating scales.   Having some indication that the student's behavior differs from that of age- or grade-mates is a logical place to start. Used for this purpose, behavioral rating scales can help to identify which behavioral domains are the most problematic, and also whether behaviors are consistent across teachers.

Using direct observation.   Data showing the amount of time the student remains on task with an age-appropriate level of independence, as well as the actual number of behaviors (e.g., out of seat, verbal outbursts) and the amount of time the teacher spends responding to the student, can be compelling. It is likely that several observations completed by personnel other than the classroom teacher, on different days and at different times, will be necessary to make the case that the student's presence has a detrimental effect on other students. Further, an observer can count the number of responses and total amount of time the teacher spends with the student. Using structured observation methods and protocols is likely to yield stronger evidence than will simple narrative observations.

Using teacher judgment.   Teacher judgment is part of any placement decision, as are the perspectives of the parents and the individual student. Teachers could be asked to estimate the amount of time and effort they spend with one individual as compared to other students in the class. Teachers might also be asked to compare the instructional needs of the target student with expectations for the curricular content or grade level they teach. Finally, teachers are in the position to observe the levels of social interaction and acceptance of individual students in relation to their classmates. Teacher judgment can be informative when the student's behavior differs considerably from normative expectations on valid rating scales, and direct classroom observations document that the behaviors are prominent, disruptive, and demanding of attention. A teacher's judgment that the student is inappropriately placed and might be better served in another setting is strengthened when supported by other assessment data.

Conclusion

Federal and state special education regulations favor but do not require that all educational programs be carried out in general education settings. These policies,

however, do require that all students with disabilities receiving special education services be provided with FAPE in the LRE for each student. With the reauthorizations of IDEA in 1997 and 2004, FAPE changed from being whatever the schools and parents wanted it to be, to a program of instruction as close as possible to what is provided to every other student in the school. Regardless of what is taught, however, students vary in their need for structure, explicitness, and a variety of other factors that affect educational progress. For special education students, such needs must be determined and addressed through the IEP process before instructional placement can be logically addressed. Addressing placement in an *a priori* manner independent of data and thought (i.e., determining placement on the basis of disability category) is arbitrary and unjustified. We have discussed several forms of data that can be considered when evaluating placement decisions. We suggest that each assessment tool works in concert with the others to support decisions that are logical, respectful of the student's needs, and likely to lead to enhanced educational outcomes.

No single source of data, test, or procedure can be used in making educational decisions (IDEA, 2004). Consequently, no single source of data (e.g., state assessment, individual achievement test, teacher opinion, classroom grades) is sufficient to guide instructional placement decisions for students with disabilities. When various forms of data align to suggest similar conclusions, IEP teams can feel more assured of making appropriate placement decisions. The following case serves as an example.

Consider an individual student who is unable to pass the state proficiency test, attains low scores on an individual achievement test, is earning failing grades, and whose teachers express doubts about the adequacy of the current educational program. With these features in alignment, it is difficult to argue that the student was receiving FAPE. Something in the program (e.g., goal, kinds of services, amount of services) needs to be changed. Changing the program sometimes necessitates a change in placement, because not all actions can be carried out in the same place.

Conversely, data from various sources can align, but when few interventions have been tried and documentation of the efforts to support the student in the current environment is sparse or lacking, changes in placement are difficult to support even if the teachers and family agree on a more-restrictive alternative. To justify placement in a more-restrictive yet supportive environment, it is necessary to demonstrate in each case that FAPE cannot be or was not provided in the learning environment despite the use of supports, not simply that an individual with a disability is doing poorly in school.

When the sources of data conflict, legislation and case law suggest that state tests are likely to trump other assessments, with classroom grades (if they are in agreement with state test results) following close behind (Gordon, 2006). Regardless of the data source, however, an appropriate education that meets the unique needs of a student with disabilities requires more than minimal progress, and adequate assessment requires more than token efforts to recognize and respond to students' learning needs. By delivering a FAPE with as few changes as necessary to the experiences provided to other students, instruction is provided in the LRE. In contrast, delivering a general education that fails to provide the personalized benefits of FAPE for a student with disabilities does not constitute that student's LRE.

CHAPTER 8

Curriculum-Based Assessment

John Venn | *University of North Florida*

Assessment is the use of tests and other measures to make educational decisions. Decision making is the key element in the process (Venn, 2007). One level of decision making involves identifying students with disabilities and developing initial individual education programs (IEPs). Traditional assessment instruments, especially formal, standardized tests, are widely used at this level. Other purposes of assessment include instructional intervention and progress monitoring. Norm-referenced, formal assessments measure broad curriculum areas (e.g., reading, math, writing), and they are not necessarily linked to school curriculum. Without a link to curriculum, their usefulness for assessing classroom instruction and monitoring student progress is limited. To address these limitations, a variety of classroom-based procedures have been developed to evaluate the impact of instructional interventions on students and to monitor the progress of students in their curricula. Curriculum-based assessment (CBA) is one of the most widely used of these alternative procedures. CBA relies on measurement strategies and techniques that enable teachers to link their evaluations of student performance with the curriculum they use with their students.

This chapter provides an overview of CBA including a definition and description of the characteristics of CBA, an overview of several CBA strategies and procedures, and a discussion of some current issues regarding implementation of CBA. The chapter concludes with recommendations for teachers, decision makers, and researchers.

Defining Curriculum-Based Assessment

The term *curriculum-based assessment* refers to evaluation processes and procedures that use content taken directly from the material taught (Hall & Mengel, 2002). It is one form of criterion-referenced assessment that directly links evaluation with instructional programs in ways that inform teachers about the learning progress and the learning difficulties of their students. CBA relies on observation and recording of student performance in the classroom as the basis for making instructional decisions. The CBA process is a form of direct measurement, because when teachers use it, they assess what they teach (Witt, Elliott, Daly, Gresham, & Kramer, 1998). This differs significantly from indirect assessment with norm-referenced tests, which may not reflect the material taught in a particular school or classroom.

Although teachers may know in a general sense when their students are making adequate progress, teachers are imperfect judges of the performance levels of the students in their classrooms (see Hoge & Coladarci, 1989, for a review). CBA provides a structured way to measure precisely how well students perform in relation to specific class materials and lessons. For example, when teachers need to know the progress of their students in literacy, they can directly assess their students' performance in reading, spelling, and writing based on what they have taught. Frequent, ongoing use of brief CBA measures enables teachers to quickly determine when students are making adequate progress or failing to master particular skills or concepts (Witt et al., 1998). As a result, CBA helps teachers make a variety of instructional decisions, including determining present levels of educational performance in the curriculum, identifying strengths and weaknesses in specific skill areas, establishing priorities for intervention and remediation, monitoring progress in the curriculum, and assisting in IEP planning (L. S. Fuchs & Fuchs, 1986).

E. D. Jones, Southern, and Brigham (1998) refer to CBA as testing what is taught and teaching what is tested. This description highlights the strong connection between assessment and instruction, and this is a defining characteristic of CBA. Although CBA is often referred to as a type of informal assessment, E. D. Jones et al. point out that many CBA procedures are quite systematic, structured, and formal in their approach. When practitioners standardize their use of CBA, effectiveness is enhanced, and more consistent results are obtained. Regardless of the specific type of CBA used, several stages are common to most procedures, including analyzing the curriculum and identifying specific learning outcomes and criteria for success, selecting or designing appropriate assessment procedures, determining present levels of performance in the curriculum, collecting and displaying the assessment results, and making decisions based on the results (Payne, Marks, & Bogan, 2007).

This process is essentially a diagnostic and prescriptive procedure that involves assessing student performance and then teaching students the skills they have not acquired but need to learn next in the curriculum or in a particular subject or learning area. Once students have received targeted instruction in the identified knowledge or skill area, then CBA is useful in quickly and accurately re-assessing the students to determine their progress. If the student has mastered the skills, then the teacher may move to the next skills in the curriculum. If the student has not made progress, then the intervention approach may need to be modified. Thus, CBA is a continuous test–teach–test–teach cycle that combines informal assessment with instructional intervention programs. For these reasons, CBA is useful in the IEP process, especially in establishing IEP goals by providing efficient and effective measures of present levels of performance in specific skill areas. The same CBA strategies and procedures used to establish goals can be used repeatedly to evaluate student progress in reaching those goals.

Characteristics of Curriculum-Based Assessment

A variety of CBA approaches have been developed, and they share several common characteristics. First, CBA involves brief, direct, and ongoing measurement in that teachers use probes, or small and discrete assessments, that may take only a few minutes to administer and score. Second, CBA measures the specific skills being taught by the teacher. This makes it context and content specific. Third, CBAs are grounded in good teaching practice by enabling teachers to assess student progress as an integral part of the teaching and learning process. Finally, CBAs are learner centered in that they help teachers focus on the particular skills with which individual children need help rather than more general skills.

Direct measurement of the skills being taught in the curriculum is the key characteristic of CBA. This is accomplished by assessing a sample of items using content and materials from the instructional lessons and learning activities in the curriculum. In other words, the skills assessed are the skills taught. For example, performance in oral reading and spelling are directly measured by assessing words read and spelled correctly using the words taught in the curriculum. Conducting assessment in this manner makes CBA more precise than traditional assessment and connects CBA with the goals for individual students and for groups of students. Most CBA techniques and procedures are brief, taking from 1 to 5 minutes to complete. This means they are usually quick and easy to accurately administer and score. As a result, they can be given frequently to obtain an ongoing measure of student performance over time. Frequent measurement gives CBA a distinct advantage over traditional testing.

In contrast to the traditional testing, which is episodic at best and usually given only once, CBA evaluates ongoing performance over time. This produces a more accurate picture of how much and what students are learning, and it is sensitive to small changes in student performance. CBA also produces more than test score results. Data may be charted for visual analysis or used in various item and error pattern analysis procedures for identifying current performance, pinpointing emerging skills, and targeting skills in need of remediation. These characteristics mean that CBA is grounded in good instructional practice as an integral part of the teaching and learning process.

Reliability, Validity, and Fairness

Reliability, validity, and fairness are important characteristics of all assessments, including curriculum-based evaluations. The goal is to conduct assessment in ways that produce reliable and valid results that are fair for all students and free from possible sources of bias. According to experts (National Council of Accreditation for Teacher Education, n.d.; Stiggins, 2001), reliability, validity, and fairness have specific meanings as applied to CBA. Assessments are reliable when they produce consistent score results. In other words, the scores are dependable and similar over more than one administration of the same test or assessment. For example, if a teacher assesses math performance using a procedure such as error analysis on several occasions within a few days of each other, the results should be similar on each assessment.

Assessments are said to be valid to the extent that they measure what they are supposed to measure. Validity is really a question of accuracy and fairness. Teachers can enhance accuracy by reviewing their assessments to ensure they reflect the standards, knowledge, and skills their students are expected to demonstrate. Similarly, assessments are fair when they assess what was taught in the curriculum. Content mapping is an example of a strategy teachers can use to help to ensure fairness. Content maps, or curriculum maps, involve identifying what one plans to teach (e.g., in a project map), as well as what one actually teaches (e.g., in a diary map) (J. A. Hale, 2008). By systematically and accurately recording what has actually been taught in class, teachers can design assessments that match their curriculum, thereby ensuring that students have had opportunities to learn and practice what is being assessed.

The notion of fairness is perhaps the key measurement characteristic that teachers should consider in CBA. Another aspect of fairness and validity is freedom from bias. Teachers may reduce the possible sources of bias in CBAs by minimizing distractions during assessment such as noise, discomfort, and inappropriate seating or lighting. Teachers should also ensure that all assessments have adequate instructions, well-written test questions, and materials that are neatly arranged and clearly copied. Ways to reduce bias also include providing assessments with appropriate language (e.g., using vocabulary and language that is at the students' comprehension levels) and consistent scoring procedures. Assessments that are fair avoid discriminating against students, including students from culturally and linguistically diverse backgrounds and students with disabilities. Fairness also refers to how the assessment results are used. Therefore, CBAs should also produce consistent scores and results that teachers can use effectively as part of instruction (Cole & Zieky, 2001; Joint Committee on Testing Practices, 2005; Whittington, 1999).

Representative CBA Strategies and Procedures

CBA strategies are available for general and special education classroom use and for assessing student performance in a number of specific areas, especially literacy (Gansle, Gilbertson, & VanDerHeyden, 2006; Garcia, 2007; Marcotte & Hintze, 2009; Otaiba & Lake, 2007). In this chapter we highlight CBA strategies and procedures for assessing reading performance. The particular CBA procedures described in the following sections are miscue and error analysis, cloze, informal reading inventories, checklists and rating scales, and portfolios. We chose these because they are CBA strategies teachers are most likely to use in their classrooms on a daily basis. Furthermore, although this chapter focuses on the application of CBA to reading, these procedures represent the kinds of assessments available for other subjects as well. For each procedure, we provide a definition of the process, a description of the characteristics of the procedures, and a discussion of how it may be implemented.

Miscue and Error Analysis

Miscue and error analysis are among the most commonly used curriculum-based strategies for assessing reading. The error analysis process described by McLoughlin and Lewis (2008) includes several steps, beginning with selection of appropriate material for the student to read. The materials may be from a word list or passages from graded books used in the curriculum. Several levels of graded passages should be used, including passages at the independent, instructional, and frustration levels. Two copies of each passage are needed. The student reads one copy, and the teacher records errors on the other. Teachers may also create an audio recording of the student reading the passage so that they can go back and make sure that they have recorded and coded all reading errors accurately. Common reading errors include additions, substitutions, omissions, and reversals. A variety of approaches are available for identifying and coding errors in miscue analysis (Jarmulowicz & Hay, 2009; Larsen & Nippold, 2007; Layton & Koenig, 1998; McGuinness, 1997; Watson & Willows, 1995).

Miscue analysis is similar to error analysis but focuses more on the qualitative aspects of the reading process. In subjects such as math, error analysis involves examining students' responses to a curriculum-based work sample, such as a computation worksheet, to identify patterns in errors and underlying skill deficits. The teacher identifies the errors and underlying skill deficit(s) and then addresses them in subsequent instruction. For example, if a student makes multiple errors by adding numbers on subtraction problems, subsequent instruction might involve teaching the student to highlight the operation sign in order to remediate this error pattern. K. S. Goodman (1965, 1967) initially developed miscue analysis from linguistic studies of cues and miscues in reading, describing it as providing teachers with "windows on the reading process" (K. S. Goodman, 1965, p. 123). Goodman used the term *miscue* instead of *mistake* or *error* to describe student reading responses that do not match expected responses. A reading miscue occurs when students read a word that is not the word in print. Miscues are not considered errors; rather, they represent a student's best attempt to read the given passage and can provide important information on the strategies that the student does and does not use to read difficult material.

In addition to recording the type of miscues made, teachers analyze miscues to determine whether they change the meaning of the text. According to K. S. Goodman and Burke (1973), miscues that change the meaning may include graphic similarity (e.g., reading *house* instead of *horse*), sound similarity (e.g., reading *wrist* instead of *waist*), and grammatical function (e.g., reading *besides* instead of *both sides*). Kucer (2008) reported that reading accurately might not be as important as the type of miscue and the pattern of errors. For example, although it involves errors, when a student reads, "We both got into the car," it does not change the essential meaning of the phrase in text, "We both hopped in the car." However, reading, "We both hoped to get a car" does change the meaning of the phrase, signals a comprehension problem, and is therefore considered a more important miscue. Furthermore, errors that change the meaning of an entire passage may be more significant than other types of errors. For example, errors in clauses are less likely to disrupt comprehension than errors in passages that contain a significant story event.

Teachers may develop their own analysis from reading materials in their classroom, but a formal, standardized Reading Miscue Inventory (Y. Goodman, Watson, & Burke, 2005) is available. Extensive research (Brown, Goodman, & Marek, 1996; Ehri & McCormick, 2004; McKenna & Picard, 2006) has been conducted using miscue analysis to assess student reading performance, to inform reading instruction, and to investigate how students learn to read. The overall results of these studies support the reliability and validity of the process. Ehri and McCormick indicated that teachers should use error totals in their analysis of students' reading. According to McKenna and Picard (2006), error totals are particularly helpful in identifying instructional and independent reading levels of students. These totals help teachers select appropriate reading materials for their students. Further, miscue analysis can help measure how well students use decoding skills.

Unlike formal, standardized tests, which are clinical and episodic in nature, miscue and error analyses assess reading in an authentic, genuine manner using reading materials that are part of the student's curriculum. This produces both quantitative data and qualitative information for evaluating reading performance as it occurs during instruction. Most miscue and error analysis procedures focus on assessing how students use cues in oral reading rather than on directly assessing reading comprehension. Cues are what students rely on to read words they don't know. For example, multiple miscues that exhibit high sound similarity but that change the meaning of the text indicate that the student may be using phonetic cues (e.g., trying to sound out the word) but not attending to whether the word choice makes sense. Evaluating the pattern of errors provides useful diagnostic information about areas in need of remediation. Although some aspects of comprehension may be evaluated using miscue analysis, many teachers rely on cloze procedures for assessing the comprehension skills of their students.

Cloze

Cloze is a diagnostic tool for assessing reading comprehension. The procedure involves deleting every *n*th word, usually every fifth word, in an appropriate grade-level passage and having the student read the material while filling in the missing words (Venn, 2007). Depending on the particular cloze procedure, word choices may or may not be provided. To complete the task, students must rely on background knowledge, context clues, word meanings, language structures, grammar skills, and general understanding of the material. Cloze provides teachers with data and information to determine whether specific reading material is on their students' instructional level. The cloze scoring process involves determining the percentage of words the students successfully supply.

According to Chatel (2001), students who correctly provide between 44% and 57% of the missing words are reading material at their instructional level. The instructional level refers to reading material that is challenging for a student to understand but is manageable with instructional support. If students fail to correctly supply at least 44% of the words in a passage, the material is too difficult for them, and they are likely to become frustrated. At the frustration level, students have difficulty understanding the meaning of what they are reading because the material is too difficult for them. Students who supply greater than 57% of the words correctly are at the independent level and can easily read and comprehend the reading passage without instructional support.

Like many curriculum-based tools, cloze is useful for identifying reading comprehension difficulties and planning instruction. Chatel (2001) indicated all teachers have the knowledge and skills necessary to develop and use cloze procedures and that the same reading material that teachers use for diagnostic purposes may be used instructionally to help students develop their skills in using background knowledge and language skills. Shin, Deno, and Espin (2000) reported that a derivation of the cloze procedure (maze, as described in the following paragraph) provided a reliable and valid method of assessing the reading growth of 43 second graders who were evaluated monthly for the entire school year.

Many variations of cloze procedures are used in literacy, including using the process as a visual way to assess spelling of the words the student supplies (Mercer & Pullen, 2005), and maze, which is a form of cloze with choices provided to the student for each of the missing words in the passage. The maze procedure (Shin et al., 2000) involves deleting every seventh word and providing the student with three, multiple-choice alternatives. One alternative is the correct word and the other two are incorrect. A critical feature of the maze procedure is that the rate at which the student reads the passage is timed. Busch and Lembke (2005) provide an excellent guide for preparing, administering, and scoring maze measures. Research evidence supports the use of maze procedures for assessing the reading progress of students, including students with severe reading deficits (Faykus & McCurdy, 1998; Parker, Hasbrouck, & Tindal 1992). As summarized by Busch and Lembke, research has shown that maze assessments demonstrate high alternate-forms reliability (i.e., student scores were consistent across different maze measures) and strong concurrent validity (i.e., students' scores on maze assessments correlated highly and positively with scores on other formal, standardized reading comprehension measures).

Informal Reading Inventories

Informal reading inventories (IRIs) are diagnostic tools for measuring reading performance. They consist of graded word lists for assessing word-decoding ability and graded reading passages for measuring oral reading, silent reading, and reading comprehension skills (Paris & Carpenter, 2003). The diagnostic procedure involves having students read passages that are below, at, and above their reading level to identify appropriate reading materials for students, to place students in reading groups, to determine strengths and areas in need of remediation, to evaluate progress over time, and to pinpoint gaps in the skills of struggling readers (Nilsson, 2008). In a review of informal reading inventories, Applegate, Quinn, and Applegate (2002) indicated that most IRIs are best at measuring reading recognition skills rather than reading comprehension abilities. Therefore, IRIs should be used together with other measures of reading to obtain a comprehensive picture of a student's reading strengths and weaknesses.

A variety of informal reading inventories are commercially available (e.g., Johns, 2005; Nilsson, 2008; Woods & Moe, 2006), but teachers may also construct their own IRIs from reading material in their curriculum (Venn, 2007). The process of constructing and using an IRI begins with the teacher's selecting appropriate passages from reading material in the curriculum. The passages should be about 50 to 100 words for elementary students and about 150 to 200 words for secondary students. Second, the teacher selects three to five passages; for example, two passages below the student's grade level, one passage on grade level, and two above the student's grade level. Next, the teacher makes two copies of each passage, and the student reads one copy aloud while the teacher records errors on the other copy. As an optional step, after the student finishes reading a passage, the teacher asks three to four comprehension questions a student should be able to answer. The questions include both factual (simple) and inferential (complex) questions. Finally, the teacher calculates the percentage of words read correctly.

Passages in which the student reads 95% or more of the words correctly can be considered to be at the student's independent level. *Independent* means the student can read the material easily. Teachers should make sure, for example, that students select material for pleasure reading that is at their independent reading level. Passages in which the student reads 90% to 95% of the words correctly can be considered to be at the student's instructional level, at which the student needs some support to read with fluency and for meaning. This means that reading material at this level is appropriate for use in instructional situations. Passages the student reads with an accuracy of below 90% are at the frustration level for the student. This means they are too difficult for the student to read independently and are generally not appropriate for instruction. In addition to calculating a percentage correct score, IRIs usually involve conducting a miscue analysis as part of the process of interpreting and analyzing the results for purposes of instruction and remediation. A summary of the steps in the process of conducting and scoring an IRI appears in Figure 8.1.

Figure 8.1   Steps in giving and scoring a teacher-made informal reading inventory.

1. Select two passages below, one passage at, and two above the student's grade level.
2. Make two copies of each passage.
3. Have the student read each passage, and record errors on a separate copy.
4. After the student is finished reading, ask three to four comprehension questions (optional).
5. Analyze the results.

Checklists and Rating Scales for Assessing Literacy

Teachers who want to systematically assess literacy behaviors in an efficient and effective manner often use diagnostic checklists and rating scales. A checklist is a list of skills or behaviors designed for recording student performance in a structured manner. Rating scales are like checklists except they include a scale or range of rating options for each item assessed (Oosterhof, 2009). Checklists and rating scales pinpoint behaviors quickly in an easily understood format. This makes them ideal tools for recording observations, documenting performance, and keeping progress data and notes. Diagnostic checklists are useful for assessing many literacy behaviors, including student reading strengths, areas for growth, and emerging skills. Checklists produce a permanent record and may be designed to measure improvement over time.

Checklists and rating scales are developed by taking broad skills and breaking them down into specific steps or subskills (McLoughlin & Lewis, 2008). For example, teachers often use informal diagnostic checklists to assess literacy skills such as oral reading. The diagnostic oral reading checklist appearing in Figure 8.1 (Hudson, Lane, & Pullen, 2005; Venn, 2007) provides a tool for assessing specific oral reading behaviors in a systematic, organized manner, and it provides a written record of student performance. Because checklists are quick and easy to create, administer, and score, teachers may use them to obtain data and information efficiently about student progress in ways that are connected with instruction. Teachers may use tools like this in a flexible manner, but they are perhaps most helpful when used systematically over time to measure progress (e.g., monthly or every other month).

The process of constructing a checklist begins with identifying the items that will make up the content. The content can be derived from the most important skills in a lesson or unit or the most important behaviors in a skill set, such as the oral reading behaviors in the sample in

Figure 8.2. The items may also be obtained from the objectives, outcomes, or standards in the curriculum. The items should be written in a way that is measureable and reliable. Reliability is a key to developing checklists that produce consistent, dependable results. Reliability is improved by providing operational definitions, examples, and nonexamples for each target behavior. A suitable format for displaying and scoring the behaviors or skills in checklist form should also be developed. In addition, the best checklists produce a score or result that can be used to monitor progress. One way to score checklists is to simply count the number of skills mastered out of the total number of skills. For example, a student may have mastered 8 of the 10 skills, objectives, or standards (or 80%).

Although a paucity of research supports the efficacy of checklists, this informal tool has high content validity (i.e., the degree to which the intended content is assessed) when teachers construct checklists and rubrics that reflect key competencies, outcomes, and standards that students are expected to acquire in their particular curriculum. Checklists provide a valuable tool for identifying the skills and knowledge that students have mastered and those areas in need of remediation.

Portfolio Assessment

A portfolio is a systematic collection of student work that provides evidence of student learning. Portfolios emphasize student performance, and most focus on literacy skills although they are useful in all subjects in the curriculum. Portfolio assessment is a type of curriculum-based evaluation that relies on genuine samples of authentic student work to assess academic performance (Venn, 2007). Tone and Farr (1998) suggested that portfolios facilitate reflective teaching, learning, and assessment by emphasizing student participation in the instructional process. Student self-assessment is a key feature of portfolio evaluation.

The two major types of portfolios are process and product portfolios. Process portfolios are the major and more dynamic type that teachers most commonly use in their classrooms. Process portfolios include evidence of the process students work through as they develop mastery of skills, standards, and outcomes. For example, students may include their "sloppy copy," rough draft, and final paper to show their progress in developing a writing sample. Product portfolios, in contrast, focus on the final products of student work such as the best or final writing samples.

Electronic and digital portfolios are becoming more widely used as an alternative approach to assessing student progress. Whereas paper portfolios are static documents, electronic portfolios are more dynamic because they may include links to a variety of sources. Students

Figure 8.2   Checklist of oral reading behaviors.

Student: _____   Teacher: _____

Date: _____   School: _____

Description of passage, including grade level and length:

Reading Behavior	*Yes*	*No*	*Notes*
1. Reads with expression and intonation.			
2. Reads clearly with good articulation.			
3. Reads fluently at an appropriate rate.			
4. Not easily distracted.			
5. Not easily discouraged.			
6. Reads in a flowing manner.			
7. Quick word identification.			
8. Attempts new words.			
9. Uses decoding to read unfamiliar words.			
10. Follows punctuation.			
11. Makes use of context clues.			
12. Demonstrates good comprehension.			
13. Other noticeable behaviors (list).			

Observations: _____

_____

also have the opportunity to develop their technology skills when they use electronic portfolios. Fitzsimmons (2008) identified several advantages of electronic portfolios, including efficient display of benchmark learning examples and effective links to state and local learning outcomes. For example, in the state of Rhode Island, digital portfolios have replaced high-stakes standardized tests as the accountability measure for student demonstration of their proficiency (Archer, 2007). The future clearly points to even more widespread use of electronic portfolios in classrooms, schools districts, and entire states.

The portfolio assessment process includes several steps (Venn, 2007) and begins with selecting the portfolio contents. Other steps include constructing a management system, developing appropriate scoring protocols, and holding student conferences. The management system should include teacher responsibilities for managing the portfolios and student duties related to organizing and managing the materials that are part of the portfolio. Portfolio scoring is usually conducted by the teacher, but most student portfolios include student self-assessment

materials such as writing and reading logs that include student reflections. Portfolios may be scored using holistic or analytic rubrics. Holistic scoring rubrics are usually brief forms that produce an overall score for the entire portfolio. In contrast, analytic rubrics are more detailed forms that score each portfolio entry individually, typically evaluating specific, prescribed aspects of each entry (e.g., grammar, spelling, cohesiveness, personal voice, completeness). Analytic scoring provides more specific data and information and is therefore more useful in instructional situations that require diagnosis and remediation of specific weaknesses.

Although portfolios are widely used in education, they tend to have low reliability, especially the informal portfolios developed by teachers (Miller, Linn, & Gronlund, 2009). For this reason, portfolios should be developed carefully, with attention to the scoring criteria and to using the most appropriate scoring rubric. The reliability of rubrics, especially holistic rubrics, has been examined (Jonsson & Svingby, 2007; Rezaei & Lovorn, 2010). In their review of research on scoring rubrics,

Jonsson and Svingby reported that although the reliability of rubrics was not always adequate, using rubrics generally improved the consistency of performance tests (e.g., portfolios). Moreover, their review indicated that factors such as using benchmarks (i.e., specific descriptions of what is required to earn each scoring point on a rubric), training in scoring rubrics, and using analytic and topic-specific rubrics are associated with more reliable scoring, More research is needed regarding how to make rubrics more useful as reliable and valid evaluation tools (N. Elliot, 2005; Hafner & Hafner, 2003).

Student self-assessment is a key element in all of these steps. For example, students should participate in the process of selecting the portfolio contents. Student conferences are a key part of portfolio teaching, learning, and assessment. In most portfolio systems, students have specific responsibilities to prepare for their conferences with the teacher, including identifying their learning goals and gauging their progress in meeting their goals. Students often write their goals on a portfolio conference record that can then become part of their portfolio contents after the conference is complete (Venn, 2007).

Issues in Curriculum-Based Assessment

Practitioners face a number of barriers in conducting CBA with high fidelity, or as designed. In addition to these barriers are concerns about how best to provide accommodations and modifications when using CBA. Each is considered in the following sections.

Barriers to High-Quality Curriculum-Based Assessment

The stumbling blocks that confront teachers in their efforts to conduct high-quality CBA are many, and these barriers are particularly evident with students who have special needs. In a review of these barriers, Stiggins (2001, 2007) identified negative feelings about assessment by teachers as a key obstacle. Problems may arise from the negative personal experiences many teachers have had with traditional assessment, which may have an impact on their view of the use of various assessment procedures in their classrooms. The teacher's negative experience may be coupled with similar negative assessment experiences of students with disabilities. Stiggins (2001, 2007) suggested that the general result is poor attitudes about assessment. More specifically, students with special needs often expect to fail tests based on their previous poor performance on many different assessments, including formal tests and informal curriculum-based evaluations.

Lack of institutional support for teachers who wish to conduct consistent and effective assessments is a second barrier cited by Stiggins (2007). Because students with special needs often present some of the most difficult assessment challenges, the need for support is especially evident in special education. Stiggins suggested that lack of support coupled with the many demands placed on teachers (e.g., pressure to focus on high-stakes testing) often result in incomplete classroom assessments simply because teachers do not have enough time to prepare, conduct, and analyze the results of CBAs of student performance. Best practices call for teachers to identify present levels of performance using appropriate assessments, develop individual learning goals and objectives for each student based on the assessment results, measure student progress in meeting the objectives, and revise the objectives based on student progress. It would appear that practitioners must receive meaningful support to successfully complete all of the complex and demanding assessment and intervention tasks expected of them.

Questions about Accommodations and Modifications

Accommodations provide students with disabilities the opportunity to demonstrate their skills and knowledge by removing the barriers preventing accurate measurement of a student's present levels of performance (Sireci, 2006). Similar to accommodations provided for high-stakes proficiency tests (see Chapter 9, this volume), accommodations in CBA may include changes in the setting, timing, scheduling, administration, or response method used (B. J. Case, 2005). Issues include how to identify appropriate accommodations, concerns about effectiveness, and how to create more flexible assessments that reduce the need for accommodations.

One ongoing issue is that teachers are often unsure about which accommodations to provide. Selecting the most appropriate accommodations is difficult because accommodations should be individualized to meet unique student needs, and there are many different accommodations (McKevitt & Elliott, 2003). Extended time and reduced distractions (e.g., using a separate room for the assessment) are two of the most common accommodations (Pitoniak & Royer, 2001). Sign language interpreters for deaf students, computers for word processing on essay tests, scribes who write for a student, and readers are other frequently used accommodations for classroom assessments. Further complicating the selection of accommodations is the absence of a sound research evidence base for many of the current policies guiding provision of accommodations (Sireci, Scarpati, & Li, 2005).

One possible solution to the problem of providing accommodations is the development of new, more flexible CBAs using Universal Design for Learning (UDL) techniques (Sireci, Li, & Scarpati, 2003). The term *UDL* refers to instruction that is accessible to all students including students with disabilities by presenting information in multiple and flexible formats and by providing multiple and flexible methods of expression and engagement for students (National Universal Design for Learning Task Force, 2007). It has been suggested that more widespread use of UDL would minimize the concerns about which accommodations should be available in different testing situations, though more research is clearly needed regarding the application of UDL principles and the use of CBA. UDL provides a way to develop CBAs and other assessments that are more flexible and can be adjusted to meet the unique and individual learning needs of many (although not all) students with disabilities without the need for accommodations. For example, the National Universal Design for Learning Task Force (2007) indicated that digital versions of student textbooks are becoming more readily available for students. Many digital textbooks are universally designed, and they provide text-to-speech decoding, research-based strategy supports, easily accessible glossary definitions for different levels of reading comprehension, and assessments that can be printed or taken on a computer.

Students with more severe disabilities may require modifications, which are more extensive changes in the assessment procedures than the changes typically afforded by accommodations. Modifications fundamentally change assessment procedures by altering the content, the level, or the administration procedure. Modifications, also referred to as *alternative assessments,* are provided to students with severe disabilities when it is determined typical assessments would not be appropriate, even with accommodations. Typical alternative assessments include portfolios, checklists, rating scales, or directly measuring skills using modified achievement standards (L. Cohen & Spenciner, 2007; Towles-Reeves, Kleinert, & Muhomba, 2009). Because guidelines, policies, and procedures for providing modifications are relatively new, clear and research-based guidelines for modifying CBAs for students with special needs do not yet exist.

Fortunately, teachers have considerable flexibility in how they provide accommodations and modifications in the classroom when using CBAs that are part of intervention programs. Teachers have much less flexibility when using formal, standardized, norm-referenced tests. Evidence (S. N. Elliott, McKevitt, & Kettler, 2002) supports the contention that most students with disabilities perform better on assessments when they receive accommodations. Therefore, teachers should implement appropriate accommodations when they use informal CBAs as well as when they give more formal, standardized tests.

Recommendations for Teachers, Decision Makers, and Researchers

Teachers, decision makers, and researchers face many challenges in further developing CBAs in ways that help students. The foremost challenge faced by teachers is building their knowledge and skills so that they can consistently and accurately use CBAs along with other assessments such as curriculum-based measurement (see Chapter 3, this volume) to plan and inform instruction, to develop remedial intervention programs, and to measure the progress of students with special needs. Given the current focus on inclusion of students with disabilities, teachers also need to become experts in providing accommodations and modifications for conducting CBAs in general education settings. For this to occur, decision makers must find new ways to support teachers as they build their competencies in using assessment as an integral part of the teaching and learning process.

The challenges faced by decision makers are many, including finding ways to provide additional support to practitioners as they strive to overcome the barriers to high-quality assessment in their classrooms. Some experts (Neil, 2008; Rothstein, Jacobsen, & Wilder, 2008) believe a major challenge is to develop policies that reduce the current overdependence on high-stakes test scores as the sole measure of school success. Rothstein et al. (2008) believe that state test-based, high-stakes accountability systems have failed to close the achievement gap, and they call for expansion of accountability measures to include local, curriculum-based evidence of student progress. According to Neil (2008), other nations with excellent educational systems rely either primarily on classroom assessments or on a combination of classroom evidence and results from high-stakes tests to account for student learning. For this to occur in the United States, decision makers, like teachers, need to develop their knowledge of CBA and measurement.

The challenges faced by researchers include conducting practical, applied investigations designed to assist teachers in strengthening the reliability and validity of CBA. This extends to the need for additional research on accommodations and modifications in the classroom. Although relatively new concepts to many educators, accommodations and modifications have much potential to assist students with special needs in the assessment process and during instruction. Researchers should also consider conducting more applied studies examining the efficacy of CBAs (e.g., does using CBAs result in improved student outcomes?). Findings from investigations such as these will clarify which CBAs are most effective in assessing student performance and improving student outcomes, which will in turn assist practitioners and decision makers in looking beyond high-stakes tests as the only useful measure of student progress.

Summary

This chapter has investigated a variety of topics associated with CBA for students with special needs. The chapter included discussions of representative procedures for assessing reading (i.e., miscue and error analysis, cloze, informal reading inventories, checklists and rating scales, and portfolios). Issues in CBA, including barriers to high-quality assessment and use of accommodations and modifications, were also addressed. The challenges that teachers, leaders, and researchers face in implementing CBA with fidelity were considered, with particular emphasis on the need to support teachers. Farr (1996), in a description of how to make assessment more

student centered, expressed the hope that teachers, along with support from policy makers and researchers, will develop new ways to use CBA and related assessments as valuable tools in planning and delivering instruction, remediating weaknesses, and measuring student progress. Farr indicated the need to place confidence in the validity of teachers' decision-making abilities as part of the assessment process. The goal is to use CBA to support student learning with the emphasis on student accomplishments (Farr, 1991). It will be necessary for teachers, decision makers, and researchers to work together to create, refine, administer, and apply the results of CBAs that focus on this goal in order to ensure that all students achieve, grow, and progress to the maximum extent possible. Researchers need to provide more practical, applied CBA information that directly informs instruction. Decision makers must provide additional support for teachers to implement CBA. Teachers need to build their skills and knowledge in using CBA as an assessment tool that can help them measure student performance accurately, efficiently, and effectively.

CHAPTER 9

Accommodations for Assessment

Martha L. Thurlow, Sheryl S. Lazarus, and **Laurene L. Christensen** |
National Center on Educational Outcomes, University of Minnesota

Accommodations have become an integral part of thinking about the participation of students with disabilities in assessment programs. Few books written today about state or district assessments fail to address in some way the need to provide accommodations to students with disabilities. In fact, several books have been written specifically about testing accommodations (Bolt & Roach, 2009; S. N. Elliott, Braden, & White, 2001; Laitusis & Cook, 2007).

Despite the increasing attention given to accommodations, confusion about terminology remains, complicated by the changing meaning of terms over time (Thurlow, 2007). As used today by most states and districts, *assessment accommodations* are defined as changes in test materials or procedures that *do not* alter the content being measured (Lazarus, Thurlow, Lail, & Christensen, 2009). *Assessment modifications,* in contrast, are defined as changes in test materials or procedures that *do* alter the content being measured. Federal law and regulations do not use the same terminology, instead referring almost exclusively to "accommodations," with clarification added as to whether the accommodation does or does not change the validity of assessment results. For consistency in this chapter, we use the term *accommodations* unless specifically citing a policy in which the term *modification* is used.

Accommodations generally are grouped into categories such as presentation, response, timing, scheduling, and setting. Sometimes categories are combined (e.g., timing and scheduling), and sometimes categories are added (e.g., technology). Regardless of the specific categories used, accommodations include changes such as large-print editions of a test, allowing the student to mark in the test booklet rather than on a bubble sheet, giving the student extended time, and having the student take the test in an area away from other students, perhaps in a separate room.

In this chapter we provide a historical picture of accommodations, along with the theoretical, legal, and policy contexts in which accommodations have existed and changed in meaning over time. Then we describe the research base for three accommodations—extended time, reading aloud/oral presentation, and computer-based testing—including the extent to which the evidence addresses classroom, district, or state assessments. We conclude with an analysis of the strengths and weaknesses of the literature on accommodations for students with disabilities, along with recommendations for practice and future research.

Historical, Theoretical, Legal, and Policy Contexts for Accommodations

Historical Context

Accommodations have been a part of special education practice for a long time. Starting before the first federal special education law for public schools (Public

Law 94-142, Education for All Handicapped Children Act of 1975), policy makers recognized the importance of making adjustments in the workplace and higher educational institutions to provide for the challenges that a disability might create for doing an activity in exactly the same way as all other individuals. Specifically, Section 504 of the 1973 Rehabilitation Act extended civil rights to individuals with disabilities. It required that programs receiving federal funds provide reasonable accommodations to individuals with disabilities so that they can participate in employment, education, and other activities (Cortiella & Kaloi, 2009; T. E. C. Smith & Patton, 1998).

Although debate continues about what *reasonable accommodations* means in various settings, the Individuals with Disabilities Education Act (IDEA; 1990) used the terms *accommodations* and *modifications* to refer to changes made to instructional materials and procedures in schools. It was not until the 1997 reauthorization of IDEA that state and district assessments were referenced in the law. Requirements for the participation of students with disabilities in state- and district-wide assessments included a short statement that students must be provided accommodations as appropriate, if necessary. And, in the section addressing individualized education programs (IEPs), additional statements were provided to indicate that modifications to be used in state and district assessments must be identified in the IEP. The use of the term *modifications* in the 1997 reauthorization of IDEA was inconsistent with the use of this term by most states and districts, and in fact, was changed in the 2004 reauthorization of IDEA to refer simply to *accommodations.*

In 2001, the Elementary and Secondary Act (ESEA) was reauthorized as the No Child Left Behind Act (NCLB). This reauthorization raised the importance of attending to the participation and performance of students with disabilities on state assessments. Although the previous reauthorization of ESEA in 1994 (the Improving America's Schools Act) required that students with disabilities must participate in state assessments and their results must be reported and disaggregated from those of other students, it took the accountability provisions of NCLB for districts and schools to attend to these requirements. NCLB reflected the requirements of IDEA, although it never used the term *modifications,* instead referring generally to accommodations that produced valid results and accommodations that produced invalid results. Subsequent guidance and regulations indicated that students who participated in assessments using accommodations that produced invalid results would no longer be counted as participants in the assessment. Counting assessment participants was an important piece of NCLB accountability, because any school, district, or state that had fewer than 95% participation of students with disabilities (as well as other groups) would automatically be designated as not meeting the adequate yearly progress (AYP) accountability measure.

As the NCLB requirements for accommodations were emerging, states were carefully setting policies to distinguish between changes in materials or procedures that would produce valid results (accommodations) and those that would produce invalid results (modifications). Nearly all states used this terminology (or the somewhat parallel terms, *standard accommodation* versus *nonstandard accommodation*) to clarify the distinction between accommodations and modifications. This distinction in the area of assessment created considerable angst among many educators, who believed that whatever students received during instruction (whether an accommodation or a modification) should be allowed during assessment. This misperception arose, in part, from best practices recommendations that an accommodation should not be used for the first time during an assessment, but rather should be part of typical classroom practice (J. L. Elliott & Thurlow, 2006; Thurlow, Elliott, & Ysseldyke, 2003).

Theoretical Context

The provision of "reasonable" accommodations has been a topic of civil rights advocates for years. Attention to accommodations in testing has raised questions about the function of accommodations and the procedures needed to determine whether a change in materials or procedures actually results in a test that produces valid or invalid results. Linn suggested that the purpose of accommodations for students with disabilities on assessments is to remove "disadvantages due to disabilities that are irrelevant to the construct the test is intended to measure without giving unfair advantage to those being accommodated" (2002, p. 36). Defining and identifying what constitutes an "unfair advantage" has led to considerable debate about the best way to determine whether test results are more accurate (valid) when accommodations are used than when not used. It is generally easy to understand how eyeglasses (which could be considered an accommodation) result in more accurate test results than would requiring a student to take an assessment without them—as long as the test is not measuring how well the student sees, and as long as the student has a vision problem that is addressed by glasses. Although this example seems simple, decisions about whether other accommodations produce valid assessment results have not been so simple to understand. Policy makers have looked to research to determine whether an assessment accommodation produces valid results.

The theoretical basis for research designed to determine whether an accommodation alters the content measured by the test (and thus produces invalid results) has changed over time. S. E. Phillips (1994) was the first to argue that to be considered an accommodation, a change in testing procedures or materials would have to increase the performance of students with disabilities and not change the performance of students without disabilities. Often, this is referred to as the *interaction hypothesis*. Since then, other researchers have suggested the need to identify a differential boost—in other words, the performance of students without disabilities increases some as the result of an accommodation, but the performance of students with disabilities increases more, indicating that students with disabilities gain a larger increase in their scores than do students without disabilities (L. S. Fuchs & Fuchs, 1999; Sireci, Scarpati, & Li, 2005). According to Laitusis (2007), the differential boost approach to research is the best for determining whether an accommodation produces valid results and whether it removes variance irrelevant to the construct being assessed.

Access to instruction and to assessments is critical for students with disabilities. Making decisions about accommodations for these students is the responsibility of the IEP team, but IEP teams often are challenged by the need to differentiate between instructional accommodations that provide access and assessment accommodations that provide both access and valid results (Thurlow, Lazarus, & Christensen, 2008). Information from research about the effects of accommodations, along with decision-making training and tools for IEP teams (J. L. Elliott & Thurlow, 2006; Minnesota Department of Education, 2009), all contribute to sound policies and decision making about accommodations.

Legal and Policy Context

Legal concerns about the provision of instructional accommodations arise most often in relation to Section 504 of the 1973 Rehabilitation Act and the Americans with Disabilities Act. Concerns about accommodations for state and district assessment generally arise in relation to those assessments that are considered high stakes for students (Heubert & Hauser, 1999). Cases on testing

accommodations within the K–12 education system in Oregon (Disability Rights Advocates, 2001) and Alaska (*Noon v. Alaska State Board of Education & Early Development*, 2004; Volz, 2004) were settled out of court by the states addressing (usually expanding) the accommodations allowed during testing, as well as providing alternative routes for students to show their knowledge and skills. In California, the ruling in *Juleus Chapman et al. v. California Department of Education*, 2001 (Disability Rights Advocates, 2008) indicated that accommodations were not being allowed for use on the California High School Exit Exam even though students had used them during instruction. In resolving the issues related to accommodations, the court decided that students with disabilities could use accommodations that state policy did not allow for other students. If the student passed the test using these accommodations, however, the student would need to go through a waiver process to earn a regular diploma.

Accommodations allowed by states for use during state assessments are described in state policies and guidelines. Policies and guidelines have changed considerably over time, reflecting changes in the policy framework that surrounds accommodations (Lazarus et al., 2009). The National Center on Educational Outcomes (NCEO) has studied state assessment policies on accommodations since the early 1990s (see Thurlow, Ysseldyke, & Silverstein, 1993, 1995). Since 1999, NCEO has examined accommodations policies every 2 years. In 1992, 21 states had written policies. Since 2001, all states have written accommodations policies that summarize the various accommodations that are allowed or not allowed, or have specified other restrictions that may apply to assessment situations.

Table 9.1 shows some of the most frequently mentioned accommodations and modifications in state assessment policies. Even though the accommodations and modifications listed are the most frequently mentioned within each category, they reflect different numbers of states mentioning them. For example, large print and braille are mentioned in the policies of 49 states.

Table 9.1   Frequently Mentioned Accommodations in State Assessment Policies for 2006 to 2007

Presentation	Response	Timing/Scheduling	Setting
Braille edition	Proctor/scribe	With breaks	Individual
Large print	Computer/machine	Extended time	Small group
Read-aloud questions	Write in booklet	Beneficial time	Carrel
Sign interpret directions	Communication device	Multiple sessions	Separate room
Sign interpret questions	Brailler	Multiple days	Seat location

Source: Information from Christensen, L. L., Lazarus, S. S., Crone, M., & Thurlow, M. L. (2008). *2007 state policies on assessment participation and accommodations for students with disabilities* (Synthesis Report 69). Minneapolis, MN: University of Minnesota, National Center on Educational Outcomes.

In contrast, "with breaks" is mentioned by 45 states and extended time is mentioned by 40 states.

In addition to states' accommodations policies for state tests, testing companies write policies for local and district assessments. For example in 2009, Northwest Educational Assessments' (NWEA) Measures of Academic Progress (MAP) allowed the extended-time accommodation (Northwest Evaluation Association, 2009), while the Metropolitan 8 (MAT-8) allowed an accommodation of up to twice the usual time (B. J. Case, 2003) when assessing students with disabilities. In contrast, the Dynamic Indicators of Basic Early Literacy Skills (DIBELS) measures instructed schools not to enter assessments conducted under untimed or with extended time into the DIBELS data system—and further instructed that any scores obtained under extended or untimed situations should be used with caution (Good & Kaminski, 2002/2003).

A frequently mentioned accommodation is not necessarily an accommodation that is frequently used (Bolt & Thurlow, 2004; Thurlow, 2007). Accommodations designed for sensory disabilities (e.g., braille, large print, sign language interpretation) are nearly always mentioned and allowed for use during state assessments but are among the most infrequently used—presumably because of the low incidence of sensory disabilities (see Albus, Thurlow, & Bremer, 2009, for state data on accommodations used in states).

Research Base for Assessment Accommodations

The research base for accommodation policies has changed over time and continues to change. It relies on various kinds of evidence, including surveys, extant data analyses, quasi-experimental studies, and experimental studies. Studies that examined early data (e.g., 2001) found a positive relationship between the number of accommodations allowed in state policies and the participation rates for students with disabilities (Cox, Herner, Demczyk, & Nieberding, 2006) and found that differences in National Assessment of Educational Progress (NEAP) participation rates could be tied to differences in state accommodations policies (N. E. Anderson, Jenkins, & Miller, 1996). These studies found general effects but did not necessarily show effects of specific accommodations.

Although attention to the effects of accommodations has increased since 2000, literally hundreds of accommodations still could be studied. Researchers have focused on relatively few accommodations—sometimes because they are frequently allowed, sometimes because they are frequently used, sometimes because they are easy to apply and study, and sometimes because they are controversial and need evidence to support or refute their use. Further complicating the study of accommodations, students who use accommodations rarely use just one accommodation, but instead frequently use a combination of accommodations. This reflects the fact that the disability characteristics of students almost always require more than one accommodation. In fact, some accommodations in themselves create a need for a second accommodation (e.g., receiving a read aloud from a human reader precludes the student from being in the traditional testing setting and instead requires an individualized or perhaps small-group administration). All of these factors, as well as others (e.g., grade level, disability category), make it difficult to identify specific accommodations with strong overall evidence to support their use. Nevertheless, evidence does exist when research findings are considered in detail.

We have selected three accommodations to highlight in this chapter. They reflect a frequently used accommodation (extended time), a controversial accommodation (read aloud/oral presentation), and a new approach to accommodations (computer-based testing). Each of these accommodations is explored in the next section, with clarification of exactly what the accommodation entails and the ways in which it is treated in state policies, as well as the nature of the research base for each accommodation. In recent years, researchers have increasingly focused on validating accommodations; however, research seldom provides conclusive evidence about the effects of accommodations on validity. In fact, comprehensive reviews of the literature have concluded that, of all the assessment accommodations that have been studied, only extended time has convincing evidence of a differential boost for students with disabilities (Sireci et al., 2005). As noted earlier, these research results may be attributable to many factors, including differences in the students who were included in studies, differences in the need for the accommodation among the tested students, and differences in the assessment tasks that students completed (Thurlow, 2007).

To summarize the literature for the three accommodations included in this chapter, we initially used the following criteria to select studies:

1. The study was conducted or published during or after 2000.

2. The study reported the results of empirical research.

3. The study was published in a peer-reviewed journal that could be obtained through a secure university library system.

4. The study focused on the effects of accommodations for students with disabilities in kindergarten through 12th grade.

5. The study examined the effects of accommodations on achievement tests or college entrance exams.

We used the NCEO online Accommodations Bibliography (http://apps.cehd.umn.edu/nceo/accommodations/) to identify empirical research studies, and we included those involving extant data only if the number of studies for an accommodation was limited without them (this occurred only for the extended-time accommodation). We also searched the ERIC online catalog to look for any studies that may have been missed in the Accommodations Bibliography. We coded each study by type of methodology used (i.e., randomized experimental, quasi-experimental, or correlational). We also compiled data on the grade levels of the study participants, the particular disability categories (e.g., learning disabilities [LD]) represented, the content area studied, and the study's reported results.

Extended Time

Extended time as an accommodation allows a student to take longer than the time typically allowed to complete an assessment. As indicated in Figure 9.1, in 2007 the policies of 34 states allowed the use of the extended-time accommodation with no restrictions, and 4 additional states allowed its use in certain circumstances (Christensen, Lazarus, Crone, & Thurlow, 2008). Similar to many other accommodations, states have frequently changed how extended time was included in policy over the years: 26 states allowed the use of extended time with no restrictions in 2001; the number gradually increased to 39 states in 2005, and then dropped to 34 states in 2007. In more recent years, some states probably dropped mention of extended time as they moved toward untimed tests (Lazarus et al., 2009).

Appendix 9.1 (appears at the end of this chapter) shows the eight extended-time studies we identified that included K–12 students with disabilities that were published in 2000 or later. The reported studies

do not include studies of accommodations packages (i.e., extended time provided with other accommodations). The eight studies (A. S. Cohen, Gregg, & Deng, 2005; Crawford, Helwig, & Tindal, 2004; S. N. Elliott & Marquart, 2004; L. S. Fuchs, Fuchs, Eaton, Hamlett, Binkley, & Crouch, 2000; L. S. Fuchs, Fuchs, Eaton, Hamlett, & Karns, 2000; Lewandowski, Lovett, Parolin, Gordon, & Codding, 2007; Lewandowski, Lovett, & Rogers, 2008; Lindstrom & Gregg, 2007) all examined whether students with disabilities received a differential boost in scores (when compared to students without disabilities) when provided with the extended-time accommodation. The studies also examined whether both groups of students received a boost.

None of the studies conclusively found a differential boost for students with disabilities; though L. S. Fuchs, Fuchs, Eaton, Hamlett, and Karns (2000) found a differential boost on problem-solving classroom-based measures (CBMs) but not on the conventional test. Four of the eight studies (S. N. Elliott & Marquart, 2004; L. S. Fuchs, Fuchs, Eaton, Hamlett, Binkley, & Crouch, 2000; Lewandowski et al., 2007, 2008) concluded that a general (rather than differential) increase in the scores of both students with disabilities and students without disabilities occurred when extended time was used.

As shown in Appendix 9.1 (at the end of this chapter), the studies examined the effect of extended time on different content areas. Five studies examined the effect on math assessments (A. S. Cohen et al., 2005; S. N. Elliott & Marquart, 2004; L. S. Fuchs, Fuchs, Eaton, Hamlett, & Karns, 2000; Lewandowski et al., 2007; Lindstrom & Gregg, 2007); three studies examined the effect on a reading assessment (L. S. Fuchs, Fuchs, Eaton, Hamlett, Binkley, & Crouch, 2000; Lewandowski et al., 2008; Lindstrom & Gregg, 2007), and two studies examined the effect on a writing assessment (Crawford et al., 2004; Lindstrom & Gregg, 2007). The Lindstrom and Gregg study examined all three of these content areas.

Six of the studies included students with LD (A. S. Cohen et al., 2005; Crawford et al., 2004; L. S. Fuchs, Fuchs, Eaton, Hamlett, Binkley, & Crouch, 2000; L. S. Fuchs, Fuchs, Eaton, Hamlett & Karns, 2000; Lewandowski et al., 2008; Lindstrom & Gregg, 2007). Lindstrom and Gregg and Lewandowski et al. also included students with attention deficit hyperactivity disorder (ADHD). The S. N. Elliott and Marquart (2004) study included students with mild LD, emotional disabilities, behavior disabilities, mild physical disabilities, speech and language disabilities, and mild cognitive disabilities.

Two studies (A. S. Cohen et al., 2005; Lindstrom & Gregg, 2007) were correlational studies that used large extant data sets to compare the scores of accommodated students with the scores of nonaccommodated students. To explore whether students with extended time

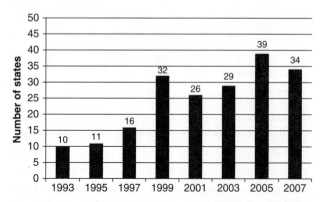

Figure 9.1 States that allow the use of extended time with no restrictions.

Source: Data from Christensen et al., 2008; Lazarus et al., 2009.

performed differently from other students, A. S. Cohen et al. analyzed data for ninth-grade students from the 2003 administration of the mathematics Florida Comprehensive Assessment Test (FCAT). Half were randomly selected from the group of students identified as having LD who used extended time (and no additional accommodations); the other half were randomly selected from the group of students without LD who used no accommodations. A. S. Cohen et al. found that "the results suggest that students' accommodation status is not a sufficiently useful explanatory variable for determining the cause of differential item functioning" (p. 231). Lindstrom and Gregg (2007) analyzed scores from the Scholastic Aptitude Reasoning Test for students with LD and/or ADHD who used extended time and for students without disabilities who did not use extended time. The analysis was conducted for the Critical Reading, Math, and Writing sections of the test. Although differences in mean scores were found across groups and there was greater variability in scores for students with disabilities, results of invariance analyses indicated that "the items measuring the constructs of critical thinking, reasoning, and writing appear to function in the same way for the two groups" (p. 92). Therefore, the authors suggested that extended time did not alter the constructs being assessed for students with LD and ADHD.

As is evident in Appendix 9.1 (at the end of this chapter), six studies had quasi-experimental designs (Crawford et al., 2004; S. N. Elliott & Marquart, 2004; L. S. Fuchs, Fuchs, Eaton, Hamlett, Binkley, & Crouch, 2000; L. S. Fuchs, Fuchs, Eaton, Hamlett, & Karns, 2000; Lewandowski et al., 2007, 2008). Lewandowski et al. (2007) compared how scores were affected for fifth- and seventh-grade students with ADHD and students without disabilities on a mathematics assessment when they had the extended-time accommodation. The extended-time accommodation was one and one half times the normal length of the test. The students with disabilities did not receive a differential boost, and the authors concluded that "although students with ADHD tended to work with less overall efficiency in terms of processing speed and task fluency, they do not benefit significantly more than nondisabled students when given extended time on a speed-based math task" (p. 17). Lewandowski et al. (2008) examined whether extended time affected the performance of high school students on a reading comprehension test. Half of the students had LD; half did not have an identified disability. Lewandowski et al. found that the scores of both groups of students were boosted, though the scores of students without disabilities were boosted more than the scores of the students with LD. The students with LD attempted the same number of questions as the other students when provided with the extended-time accommodation.

Two of the earliest studies examined the effect of extended time on fourth- and fifth-grade students' performance on CBMs. L. S. Fuchs, Fuchs, Eaton, Hamlett, Binkley, and Crouch (2000) analyzed how students with and without LD did on a reading assessment under standard and extended-time conditions. Both groups of students received a boost from the accommodation. L. S. Fuchs, Fuchs, Eaton, Hamlett, and Karns (2000) administered a short mathematics CBM to a group of fourth- and fifth-grade students, half without disabilities and half with LD. The measures covered three domains: computations, concepts and applications, and problem solving. The analysis found that students with LD tended to have a differential boost from extended time on problem-solving CBMs but not on the other CBMs.

S. N. Elliott and Marquart (2004) compared performance with and without extended time for three groups of eighth-grade students (students with disabilities, students without identified disabilities who were educationally at risk on the math test, and students without disabilities). The researchers found that the scores of all students were boosted when the extended-time accommodation was provided, though the scores were boosted the most for the struggling students who did not have identified disabilities. They also surveyed the participating students and found that most students preferred the extended-time administration; in general, however, students with disabilities less strongly supported the extended-time accommodation than the other two groups of students.

Crawford et al. (2004) was the only extended-time study of the eight that examined how a multiple-day administration affected performance. Crawford et al. compared how two groups of fifth- and eighth-grade students (students with LD, students without disabilities) performed on a 30-minute writing assessment with how they performed on an assessment completed over 3 days. The study included 213 fifth graders (including 42 students with LD) and 140 eighth graders (including 6 with LD). The findings were mixed. Crawford et al. reported a significant time by disability status interaction for fifth-grade participants, indicating that both groups of students performed better with extended time, but that students with LD received a greater benefit from the accommodation. The authors found no effect of extended time for eighth graders; however, few students with LD in this grade participated in the study.

Results vary across studies, and the results are inconclusive. The literature base does not provide conclusive evidence that the extended-time accommodation provides differential boost for students with disabilities. In fact, some evidence shows that extended time may often boost the scores of both students with and without disabilities. This suggests that it may be appropriate to allow extended time for all students.

Read-Aloud/Oral Presentation

Reading a test, or portion of a test, aloud to a student may occur in a variety of ways. One consideration is the portion of the test being read. It is often a good testing practice to read the directions aloud; still, in some states reading directions aloud is considered an accommodation. More controversial is the reading aloud of test questions and test passages. When these are read aloud, they may be read by a human reader, or they may be read by a computer. In some situations, these items may be provided orally via audio or video. In some cases, the read-aloud accommodation may be bundled with another accommodation, like extended time, small-group setting, or individual administration. Tindal and Fuchs (2000) also reported that having the test read aloud may be accompanied by cueing, rephrasing, and dictation (p. 55).

In their analysis of state accommodations policies, Christensen et al. (2008) noted that a majority of states (*n* = 31) allowed directions to be read aloud as an accommodation without any restrictions; of course, in some states reading the directions aloud is not considered an accommodation but rather is standard testing practice available for all students. Reading the questions aloud is allowed in nearly all states (*n* = 49); however, most states put some restriction on its use. For example, in 24 states, the accommodation is allowed only in certain circumstances, such as only in certain grades (e.g., high school) or in certain subject areas (e.g., science or mathematics). In 20 states, reading the questions aloud is allowed in limited circumstances; however, when students have questions read to them, their scores may be thrown out, or the students may be counted as nonparticipants. Only in three states is this accommodation allowed without any restrictions. Subtle changes have occurred over time in the number of states allowing the read-aloud accommodation without restrictions (see Figure 9.2).

The controversial nature of the read-aloud accommodation makes it an interesting subject of research.

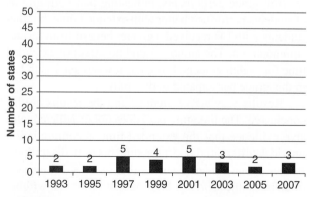

Figure 9.2 States that allow read-aloud/oral presentation with no restrictions.

Appendix 9.2 (at the end of this chapter) shows the eight studies of the read-aloud accommodation selected for review here. Studies that used a speech-to-text computer-based approach were excluded because they were confounded with the computer-based approach. In the studies reviewed here, the nature of the read-aloud accommodation itself varied. Two studies (Ketterlin-Geller, Yovanoff, & Tindal, 2007; McKevitt & Elliott, 2003) presented the read-aloud accommodation via audiotape. One study, conducted by Helwig, Rozek-Tedesco, and Tindal (2002), used a videotape to present the accommodation to students. Four studies (Elbaum, 2007; L. S. Fuchs, Fuchs, Eaton, Hamlett, & Karns, 2000; Johnson, 2000; Meloy, Deville, & Frisbie, 2002) described giving the accommodation to students by having someone read the questions aloud directly to the students. Of these four, only the Johnson and Meloy et al. studies mentioned using a process to train the readers to read a script verbatim. One additional study (Schulte, Elliott, & Kratochwill, 2001) did not describe the means by which the students received the read-aloud accommodation.

The study designs used to research the read-aloud accommodation were primarily experimental and quasi-experimental. Although the participants themselves were not chosen through a randomized control process, the determination of who received the accommodation was often made randomly. For example, Ketterlin-Geller, Yovanoff, et al. (2007) investigated two accommodations, the read-aloud questions accommodation and the simplified-language accommodation. The students in their study were assigned to one of the two accommodations randomly. Then, students took the assessment both with and without the accommodation. Ketterlin-Geller, Yovanoff, et al. found that students benefited from the read-aloud accommodation only when the level of language in the questions was challenging enough to interfere with the student's understanding of the content.

All eight studies considered here examined differential boost. Of these, five studies (L. S. Fuchs, Fuchs, Eaton, Hamlett, & Karns, 2000; Helwig et al., 2002; Johnson, 2000; Ketterlin-Geller, Yovanoff, et al., 2007; Schulte et al., 2001) found some support for using the accommodation in elementary school. For example, Schulte et al. (2001) found that elementary students with disabilities benefited more than their peers without disabilities when the math test was read aloud to them. In her meta-analysis of eight studies examining read-aloud accommodations for students with disabilities on math tests, Elbaum (2007) found that elementary students with LD received a differential boost from the read-aloud accommodation.

Studies examining the effect of the accommodation for middle school or high school (Elbaum, 2007;

Helwig et al., 2002; McKevitt & Elliott, 2003; Meloy et al., 2002) yielded more divided findings. Meloy et al. found that the read-aloud accommodation did provide a differential boost for students with LD in middle school. The other studies concluded that middle school students with disabilities received no differential boost with the use of this accommodation. For example, McKevitt and Elliott (2003) found no significant differential boost for students with disabilities who used the read-aloud accommodation, although all of the students (both those with and without disabilities) who used the accommodation did somewhat better than the students who used other teacher-recommended accommodations.

The content areas included in the read-aloud studies varied. Seven of the studies (Elbaum, 2007; L. S. Fuchs, Fuchs, Eaton, Hamlett, & Karns, 2000; Helwig et al., 2002; Johnson, 2000; Ketterlin-Geller, Yovanoff, et al., 2007; Meloy et al., 2002; Schulte et al., 2001) looked at the effect of the read-aloud accommodation for math. All of the studies found some benefit for students with disabilities when used in math, although the effects varied somewhat by grade, as noted earlier. Two of the studies also looked at effects for reading (McKevitt & Elliott, 2003; Meloy et al., 2002). Both of these studies found no differential boost for students with disabilities. Thus, the research suggests some benefit occurs for elementary students using the accommodation in math but not in reading.

Five of the studies included here (Elbaum, 2007; L. S. Fuchs, Fuchs, Eaton, Hamlett, & Karns, 2000; Helwig et al., 2002; Ketterlin-Geller, Yovanoff, et al., 2007; Meloy et al., 2002) identified students with LD as the target population. Helwig et al. found that elementary students with LD benefited from the accommodation. L. S. Fuchs et al. found that students with LD benefited on CBM when the CBM involved problem solving. Ketterlin-Geller, Yovanoff, et al., Meloy et al., and Elbaum found less conclusive results. Meloy et al. reported that both students with and without LD benefited from the accommodation. In the Ketterlin-Geller, Yovanoff, et al. study, students benefited from the accommodation only when the language level limited their interaction with the more challenging content. At the secondary level, Elbaum reported that students without disabilities benefited more from read-aloud accommodations than did students with LD. In conclusion, these five studies suggest that some benefit may exist in using the read-aloud accommodation with students who have LD. Still, many considerations, such as the conditions under which students will benefit, need further exploration before strong conclusions are drawn.

In both research and practice, the read-aloud accommodation has been, and remains, controversial. Since the beginning of the standards-based reform movement, states have frequently refined their policies on reading the test or parts of it to the student (see Lazarus et al., 2009). States look to research to show conclusive evidence that an accommodation is appropriate. Conclusive evidence has not yet emerged from research on read-aloud accommodations. Of those studies that have been conducted, a variety of approaches to implementing the accommodation have been used. Furthermore, most of the studies focused on mathematics as the content area, even though reading is the area of most interest to states setting policies. Just two of the studies reviewed here, McKevitt and Elliott (2003) and Meloy et al. (2002), looked at the read-aloud accommodation for reading.

Computer-Based Testing

Computer-based testing as an accommodation involves the provision of the assessment on a computer and may or may not include allowing the use of other accommodations (e.g., screen reader, highlighting key terms, spell-checker) via the computer. In an early summary of the empirical basis for defining accommodations, Tindal and Fuchs (2000) indicated that some of the changes that may be incorporated into computer-based testing might not typically be considered as accommodations but can nevertheless be "used to enhance access to tests for students with disabilities because changes are made in the manner in which items are displayed, sequenced, or presented (sequenced or paced)" (p. 30).

Figure 9.3 shows the number of states that allowed computer-based testing as an accommodation with no restrictions from 1993 to 2007. Figure 9.3 shows that the number of states that permitted this accommodation fluctuated. Just 11 states mentioned this accommodation in 1993, but by 1999, 28 states allowed the use of computer-based testing without restrictions. By 2003 the number was 37; after that the number dropped to 25 in 2005 and then increased again to 31 in 2007. These

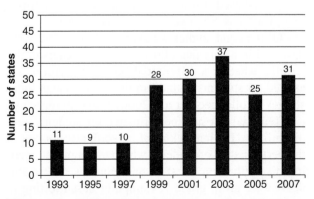

Figure 9.3   States that allow computer-based testing with no restrictions.

fluctuations are consistent with those observed for the extended-time and read-aloud accommodations.

Christensen et al. (2008) found that computer-based testing was identified as a response accommodation (i.e., used by students in documenting their response to test questions) for state-wide assessments by 43 states. Most states ($n = 31$) allowed this accommodation without restriction; the remaining states ($n = 12$) imposed some type of limitation on the accommodation (e.g., spell-checker must be disabled, cannot be used for writing assessment). States' accommodations policies generally did not identify computerized testing as a presentation accommodation but instead referred specifically to the use of screen readers or other approaches to reading the assessment to the student via computer.

Appendix 9.3 (at the end of this chapter) shows the computer-based accommodations studies that included students with disabilities of school age. The eight studies included in our analysis (Calhoon, Fuchs, & Hamlett, 2000; Dolan, Hall, Bannerjee, Chun, & Strangman, 2005; Hasselbring & Crossland, 1982; Hollenbeck, Rozek-Tedesco, Tindal, & Glasgow, 2000; Horton & Lovitt, 1994; Keen & Davey, 1987; Poggio, Glasnapp, Yang, & Poggio, 2005; Varnhagen & Gerber, 1984) examined whether a differential boost occurred for students with disabilities or a general increase in performance occurred for all students; the studies also examined the perceptions of the accommodation by students. All of these studies appeared in published journals, but at least half were published before 2000. We extended the dates we reviewed for this accommodation so that we could obtain a reasonable number of studies to examine. The limitation of including only those studies that were in journals available through the secure University of Minnesota library system eliminated several older studies that had been cited in summaries of accommodations research by Tindal and Fuchs (2000) and S. Thompson, Blount, and Thurlow (2002), including studies that specifically examined the effects of computer-based testing for students with disabilities (e.g., Barton & Sheinker, 2003; Burk, 1999).

Of the eight studies we examined, only four were designed in a way that allowed the researchers to determine whether a differential boost in performance existed for students with disabilities. Just one of these studies (Hollenbeck et al., 2000) found evidence of a differential boost in performance for students with disabilities. Hollenbeck et al. specifically looked at the performance of students who had diagnosed reading disabilities on a test of mathematics. These students were all in grade 7. Computer-based testing in which students determined their own pace in working through problems produced a differential boost

over a paper-and-pencil test for which a videotaped teacher presented information and paced test completion. Hollenbeck et al. actually found that not only was there a differential boost for students with reading disabilities, but that for those students without disabilities, there was a slight but nonsignificant negative effect on performance for the computer-based self-paced testing.

Five of the studies we examined (Calhoon et al., 2000; Dolan et al., 2005; Hasselbring & Crossland, 1982; Horton & Lovitt, 1994; Varnhagen & Gerber, 1984) showed a general (rather than differential) increase in performance. Three studies (Horton & Lovitt, 1994; Poggio et al., 2005; Varnhagen & Gerber, 1984) that could have detected a differential boost did not. Two studies (Dolan et al., 2005; Hasselbring & Crossland, 1982) included only students with disabilities.

As is evident in Appendix 9.3 (at the end of this chapter), the five studies that showed a general increase in performance varied widely in terms of content area (mathematics, one study; social studies, two studies, with one also looking at science; spelling, two studies), and student grade level (study grades: 9–12, 11 and 12, 3–8, 6–12, and 3). All students with disabilities in these studies had either LD or learning "handicaps." Two of the five studies provided additional information about the nature of the general increase in performance that they found. For example, Dolan et al. (2005) found that the difference between computer-based and paper-and-pencil tests emerged only when the item passages (in a social studies test) were "long" (meaning greater than 100 words in this study). In their study, students with LD were administered equivalent forms of the test in counterbalanced order for paper-and-pencil and computer-based tests. Students without disabilities were not included in this study. Also, the computer-based form had optional text-to-speech capability, meaning that students could use that feature or not, depending on their preferences. Students in this study reported that they would recommend the use of computer-based testing (with text to speech) for other students, and that they thought they performed better on the computer-based test.

Horton and Lovitt (1994) also found an increase in performance with computer-based testing, but results were mixed in their examination of social studies and science tests. Horton and Lovitt studied three groups of middle and high school students (students with LD, students in remedial programs, and normally achieving students). All students participated in each condition through an equivalent time-samples design in which students were "randomly assigned four times each to all experimental and control groups" (paragraph 30). The researchers found no differences between computer-based and paper-and-pencil tests when the items were interpretive questions; when the items were factual questions, computer-based testing produced increased performance over the paper-and-pencil format.

The finding of a general boost in performance for computer-based testing—higher performance for test takers regardless of whether they had a disability—is consistent with the concept of universally designed assessments (see S. J. Thompson, Thurlow, & Malouf, 2004). Universally designed assessments are designed to be accessible to the widest range of students, including those with and without disabilities, as long as what the test is intended to measure does not change.

Only two of the eight studies we examined (Keen & Davey, 1987; Poggio et al., 2005) indicated no statistical difference between computer-based and paper-and-pencil tests. The Keen and Davey study was published in the late 1980s, and the computer-based system may have not been as easy to use as more recent computer-based tests. Yet the study by Hasselbring and Crossland (1982) also was published in the 1980s and found an increase in performance with the computer-based test. Another unique aspect of the Keen and Davey study was that it focused on a test of reading—the only one of the eight studies that addressed this content area. It may be that something about a test of reading precludes a boost in performance from the computer-based platform.

The Poggio et al. (2005) study is a relatively recent study that was clearly designed to detect a differential boost if one existed. The researchers found, however, no statistical difference between the computer-based and the paper-and-pencil version on a math test. This study involved students taking equivalent forms of the test, with each student taking both the computer-based and the paper-and-pencil, with order counterbalanced across students. Poggio et al. also examined possible effects by type of question (i.e., knowledge, application) and found that performance was virtually identical for the two question types.

The variability in studies is typical of accommodations research; this variability was evident not only in the computer-based testing studies, but also in those focused on extended time and read aloud. In fact, similar variability exists in the research on many other accommodations that have been studied (see Johnstone, Altman, Thurlow, & Thompson, 2006; S. Thompson et al., 2002; Tindal & Fuchs, 2000; Zenisky & Sireci, 2007). Nevertheless, one can take away from this research that computer-based testing is a viable accommodation for students with disabilities. Beyond that, research suggests that computer-based testing may be an approach that provides greater accessibility for all students and something that should be pursued in the name of universally designed assessments.

This conclusion does not, on the other hand, detract from the suggestion that caution must be observed in implementing a computer-based test. Many accommodations and design features must first be explored (Dolan et al., 2009; S. J. Thompson, Quenemoen, & Thurlow, 2006).

Conclusion

Accommodations are an essential part of the instruction and assessment of students with disabilities. Yet, they are surrounded by controversy and confusion, especially when applied to assessments. Historically, assessment accommodations have taken a wandering pathway. First they were considered necessary just to provide access to assessments for students whose disabilities interfered with their ability to take the test (regardless of what happened to the construct being measured). They now are considered to be an essential part of the validity argument for assessments; to obtain valid results for students with disabilities, it is necessary to provide accommodations that help them show what they know and can do without interference from the barriers that their disabilities pose, as long as the accommodations do not change what the assessment is intended to measure.

The crux of the challenge for policy makers and educators is to determine which changes in testing materials or procedures actually alter what the test is intended to measure. The theory behind how this is shown has changed over time, from an interaction hypothesis to a differential-boost hypothesis. Nevertheless, research-based evidence has not produced clear results. In part, the lack of clarity about accommodations and their effects is due to all the confounding factors that surround the identification of students as having disabilities, the nature of specific disability categories, and the challenges of determining whether an individual student needs an accommodation. The research evidence presented in this chapter for three accommodations—extended time (which is frequently used), read aloud (which is controversial), and computer-based testing (which is relatively new)—dramatically reflects the variability in research findings. The variability spans not only the number and types of students included (although most participants with disabilities have LD), the content of the assessment, and the grade levels in which the studies were conducted, but also the nature of the research itself and whether packages of accommodations were included or just a single accommodation. All of these factors, and others, have an impact on the results obtained.

The accommodations research literature has shown many strengths in recent years. For example, there has been a general progression in methods toward more re-fined randomized experimental and quasi-experimental designs. Increasingly, studies include greater numbers of students and often attempt to reflect actual testing situations.

The weaknesses in the literature on the effects of accommodations are related in many ways to the challenges of conducting this research. For example, researchers study accommodations in numerous content areas, resulting in studies of an accommodation being conducted in content other than where the greatest practical questions actually exist (e.g., the read aloud, where many studies are in content areas other than reading). An additional weakness is that many studies involve relatively small numbers of students. This limitation reflects the difficulty of identifying students who may need an accommodation, and then securing their participation in a study.

Implications for Practice

Practitioners can take away from this review of accommodations both the conclusion that accommodations are important research-based practices for supporting the participation and performance of students with disabilities (Crawford, 2007) and the conclusion that the three accommodations that we included in this chapter are supported by some of the research. This is true despite the fact that research on most accommodations is still relatively limited, though the number of studies has increased over time, and that the research varies in terms of the students who are included, the nature of the test, and the methodology used to study the accommodation. It is the conditions of the research to which practitioners must attend as they consider how to use specific accommodations in their own environments. These conditions also suggest the importance of practitioners engaging in a process of checking the effects of specific accommodations for individual students during classroom instruction and assessments (see J. L. Elliott & Thurlow, 2006; Thurlow et al., 2003).

It is important for practitioners also to realize that additional research, not reviewed here, suggests educators have difficulties making decisions about accommodations and implementing accommodations during instruction and assessment (Shriner & DeStefano, 2003). This research indicates that even with the improvements that have occurred in accommodations research, many contextual issues remain that contribute to the challenge of conducting research, as well as to the challenge of actually implementing accommodations effectively. Implementation research suggests a need for greater emphasis on training on appropriate accommodations and decision making about accommodations for instruction and assessment. Further, some research suggests the need for monitoring of the provision and effects of accommodations in actual testing situations (Christensen, Thurlow, & Wang, 2009; Thurlow et al., 2008).

Across the time that research on accommodations has been conducted, dating back to some of the early work at Educational Testing Services (Willingham et al., 1988), policy increasingly has pushed accommodation practices for testing. Some accommodations (e.g., extended time) have over time become considered good testing practice rather than accommodations (e.g., providing untimed tests). As good testing practices, they are available to all students. This trend supports the emphasis now being placed on universally designed assessments (S. J. Thompson et al., 2004), in which all students are considered from the beginning of test development, and tests are designed to meet the needs of the widest range of students, as long as the intent of the assessment is not compromised.

Appendix 9.1

Extended Time: Study Descriptions

Study	Type	Grades	Disabilities	Package	Content	Results
A. S. Cohen, Gregg, & Deng (2005)	C[1]	9	LD (n = 2,500; 1,250 per group)	No	M	Accommodated/ nonaccommodated status did little to explain differences in performance between students with LD and students without disabilities.
Crawford, Helwig, & Tindal (2004)	QE[2]	5, 8	LD (Grade 5: n = 213; 42 with LD; Grade 8: n = 140; 6 with LD)	No	W	Mixed results; grade-5 students (both students with LD and students without disabilities) benefited from extended time (over multiple days) on a writing performance assessment, and students with disabilities benefited the most; at grade 8, there was little effect of extended time.
S. N. Elliott & Marquart (2004)	QE[3]	8	Multiple[4] (n = 97; 23 with disabilities, 23 at risk in math, 51 without disabilities)	No	M	Scores of all three groups were boosted when the extended-time accommodation was provided—though the scores were boosted the most for the struggling students who did not have identified disabilities.
L. S. Fuchs, Fuchs, Eaton, Hamlett, Binkley, & Crouch (2000)[5]	QE[3]	4–5	LD (n = 365; approximately half with LD; 59 received extended time[5])	No	R	Scores of both groups (both students with LD and students without disabilities) boosted when extended time was provided.
L. S. Fuchs, Fuchs, Eaton, Hamlett, & Karns (2000)	QE[3]	4–5	LD (n = 400; approximately 200 per with LD; 145 received extended time[5])	No	M	Mixed results: Students with LD tended to have a differential boost on problem-solving CBMs, but not on conventional CBMs.
Lewandowski, Lovett, Parolin, Gordon, & Codding (2007)	QE[3]	5–7	ADHD (n = 65[6]; 27 in each group)	No	M	Scores of both groups (both students with ADHD and students without disabilities) boosted when extended time was provided.

Study	Type	Grades	Disabilities	Package	Content	Results
Lewandowski, Lovett, & Rogers (2008)	QE[3]	10–12	LD (*n* = 64; 32 per group)	No	R	Scores of both groups (both students with LD and students without disabilities) boosted when extended time was provided—but the scores of students without disabilities were boosted more. Students with LD were able to attempt as many items as students without disabilities.
Lindstrom & Gregg (2007)	C	HS[7]	LD, ADHD (1,517 with LD, 588 with ADHD, 371 with both)	No	R, M, W	Invariance analyses indicated that extended time did not alter the constructs of critical thinking, reasoning, and writing for students with LD and ADHD.

Note: Study Type: C = correlational; QE = quasi-experimental.
Grades: HS = high school.
Disabilities: ADHD = attention deficit/hyperactivity disorder; LD = learning disability.
Package: Yes = effect of more than one accommodation; No = effect of a single accommodation.
Content: M = math; R = reading; W = writing.
Results: CBM = curriculum-based measurement.
[1]Used extant data from the mathematics Florida Comprehensive Assessment Test (FCAT). Half of the cases were randomly selected from the group of students identified as having LD who used extended time (and no additional accommodations); the other half were randomly drawn from the group of students without LD who used no accommodations.
[2]All students participated in both conditions. Students completed the Oregon Statewide Assessment Test-Writing (OSAT-W) over a 3-day period; the 30-minute writing task was approximately 2 weeks before or after the OSAT-W.
[3]Study did not use random assignment to conditions, but instead had all students in all conditions, with counterbalancing of order.
[4]Included students with mild learning disabilities; emotional disabilities, behavior disabilities, mild physical disabilities, speech and language disabilities, and mild cognitive disabilities.
[5]Several accommodations were included in the study. Data-based rules and teacher judgment were used to determine which students would receive extended time.
[6]Several students were later excluded from study due to high scores on ADHD rating scales or high processing speed scores.
[7]Used extant data from the SAT Reasoning Test. Half of the cases were the group of students with LD, ADHD, or both who used extended time; the other half were randomly drawn from the group of students who used no accommodations.

Appendix 9.2

Read-Aloud/Oral Administration Study Descriptions

Study	Type	Grades	Disabilities[1]	Package	Content	Results
Elbaum (2007)	QE[2]	6–10	LD (*n* = 388)	No	M	Test administrator read each item aloud twice. Students without disabilities benefited more from accommodations than did students with LD, which was consistent with results of accompanying meta-analysis. Meta-analysis showed that elementary students with LD made greater gains with the accommodation than peers.
L. S. Fuchs, Fuchs, Eaton, Hamlett, & Karns (2000)[3]	QE	4–5	LD (*n* = 200)	Extended time, calculators	M	Teacher read the questions aloud. Students with LD benefited from accommodations on problem-solving CBMs but not on conventional CBMs.
Helwig, Rozek-Tedesco, & Tindal (2002)	QE[4]	4–8	LD (*n* = 200)	No	M	Read aloud was given through a video. Elementary students benefited from the accommodation; middle school students experienced no significant interaction.
Johnson (2000)	QE[4]	4	Students with IEPs (*n* = 38)	No	M	Trained proctors read the items verbatim. Study supports the use of the accommodation for math when students have a reading disability.
Ketterlin-Geller, Yovanoff, & Tindal (2007)	RE[5]	3	EBD (*n* = 1), CD (*n* = 10), LD (*n* = 11), UNS (*n* = 6)	Extended time	M	Students received the accommodation via audiotape. Students benefited from the accommodation only when the level of language limited interaction with challenging content.
McKevitt & Elliott (2003)	RE[6]	8	Students with IEPs (*n* = 40)	Small group	R	Students received the accommodation via audiotape. No differential benefit for students with disabilities using the accommodation was observed.

Study	Type	Grades	Disabilities[1]	Package	Content	Results
Meloy, Deville, & Frisbie (2002)	RE[7]	6–8	LD (*n* = 62)	No	R, M, S, U&E	Students were given the read-aloud accommodation as read via a script. Test scores were higher for both the LD group and the non-LD group in this study.
Schulte, Elliott, & Kratochwill (2001)	QE[4]	4	UNS (*n* = 43)	Yes	M	Test was read aloud to student. Students with disabilities benefited more from the accommodations than students without disabilities.

Note: Study Type: QE = quasi-experimental; RE = randomized experimental.
Disabilities: CD = communication disorder; EBD = emotional and behavioral disorder; IEP = individualized education program; LD = learning disability; UNS = unspecified.
Content: M = math; R = reading; S = science; U&E = usage and expression.
Results: CBM = curriculum-based measurement.
[1]Number is the number of students with disabilities; other groups (e.g., general education students, gifted students) are not reflected in this number.
[2]Classrooms were randomly assigned to one of four testing conditions.
[3]This study examined differential boost.
[4]Study did not use random assignment to conditions, but instead had all students in all conditions with counterbalancing of order.
[5]Study used a convenience sample of students, with random assignment to one of two accommodations under investigation. All students in each accommodation group took the assessment with and without accommodations.
[6]Students were selected to receive one of two treatment conditions using random assignment. In addition, two versions of the assessment were used, and selection of the assessment version was determined by a flip of a coin.
[7]Students who were LD and students who were not LD were randomly assigned to one of two treatment groups (with the read-aloud accommodation and without the accommodation).

Appendix 9.3

Computerized Testing Study Descriptions

Study	Type	Grades	Disabilities[1]	Package	Content	Results
Calhoon, Fuchs, & Hamlett (2000)	QE[2]	9–12	LD ($n = 81$)	Yes	M	Computer-based with computer reading or computer reading with video showed same increases in performance as teacher-read without computer; all produced higher scores than standard administration. No students without disabilities were included.
Dolan, Hall, Bannerjee, Chun, & Strangman (2005)	QE[2]	11, 12	LD ($n = 10$)	Yes	SS	No statistical difference overall for computer based versus paper-and-pencil, but a significant difference favoring the computer-based test when item passages were long (>100 words). No students without disabilities were included.
Hasselbring & Crossland (1982)	RE	3–8[3]	LD ($n = 28$; 14 per group)	No	SP	Computerized test boosted scores more than paper-and-pencil for students with LD. No students without disabilities were included.
Hollenbeck, Rozek-Tedesco, Tindal, & Glasgow (2000)	QE[2]	7	RD ($n = 25$)	No	M	Computer-based test with student pacing produced a differential boost over teacher-paced video presentation for students with disabilities compared to students without disabilities for whom a slight negative effect was found.
Horton & Lovitt (1994)	QE[4]	6–12[5]	LD ($n = 13$)	No	Sc, SS	Mixed results: computer-based favored for factual questions; no difference for interpretive questions for all students overall. No significant effects were observed for students with disabilities versus other groups.
Keen & Davey (1987)	RE	9–12	LD ($n = 51$; 25 computer, 26 paper/pencil)	No	R	No differences in performance between computer-based and paper-and-pencil. No students without disabilities were included.

Study	Type	Grades	Disabilities[1]	Package	Content	Results
Poggio, Glasnapp, Yang, & Poggio (2005)	QE[2]	7	LD (*n* = 31–32)	No	M	No statistical difference for computer-based versus paper-and-pencil for either students with disabilities or students without disabilities.
Varnhagen & Gerber (1984)	QE[1]	3	LH (*n* = 9)	No	SP	Paper-and-pencil boosted scores more than computerized test for both students with learning handicaps and students without disabilities.

Note: Study Type: QE = quasi-experimental; RE = randomized experimental.
Disabilities: LD = learning disability; LH = learning handicap; RD = reading disability.
Content: M = math; R = reading; Sc = science, SP = spelling, SS = social studies.
[1]Number is the number of students with disabilities; other groups (e.g., general education students, gifted students) are not reflected in this number.
[2]Study did not use random assignment to conditions, but instead had all students in all conditions, with counterbalancing of order.
[3]Study included ages 9 yr 9 mo to 14 yr 6 mo. Table shows estimated grades covered by those ages.
[4]Study design was an equivalent time samples design, with the computer-based and paper-and-pencil tests randomly assigned to all experimental and control groups.
[5]Student included middle school and high school students. Table shows estimated grades covered by those school levels.

References

Achenbach, T. (1991). *Manual for the Child Behavior Checklist/4–18 and 1991 Profile.* Burlington, VT: University of Vermont Department of Psychiatry.

Ahearn, E. M. (2009). State eligibility requirements for specific learning disabilities. *Communication Disorders Quarterly, 30*(2), 120–128.

Albus, D., Thurlow, M., & Bremer, C. (2009). *Achieving transparency in the public reporting of 2006–2007 assessment results* (Technical Report 53). Minneapolis, MN: University of Minnesota, National Center on Educational Outcomes.

Allen, S. K., Smith, A. C., Test, D. W., Flowers, C., & Wood, W. M. (2001). The effects of self-directed IEP on student participation in IEP meetings. *Career Development for Exceptional Individuals, 24*(2), 107–120.

Allen-Meares, P. (2008). Assessing the adaptive behavior of youths: Multicultural responsivity. *Social Work, 53*(4), 307–316.

Alvin Independent School Dist. v. A.D. ex rel. Patricia F, 30. 503 M33d7 8 (5th Cir. 2007).

Amanda J. v. Clark County School District, 260 F.3d 1106 (9th Cir. 2001).

Analysis of Comments and Changes to 2006 IDEA Part B Regulations, 71 *Federal Register,* 46565 and 46664, August 14, 2006.

Anderson, N. E., Jenkins, F. F., & Miller, K. E. (1996). *NAEP inclusion criteria and testing accommodations: Findings from the NAEP 1995 field test in mathematics.* Washington, DC: National Center for Education Statistics.

Applegate, M. D., Quinn, K. B., & Applegate, A. J. (2002). Levels of thinking required by comprehension questions in informal reading inventories. *The Reading Teacher, 56,* 174–180.

Archer, J. (2007). Digital portfolios: An alternative approach to assessing progress. *Education Week, 26*(30), 38.

Artiles, A. J. (2003). Special education's changing identity: Paradoxes and dilemmas in views of culture and space. *Harvard Educational Review, 73*(2), 164–202.

Arunachalam, V. (2001). The science behind tradition. *Current Science, 80,* 1272–1275.

Baker, S., & Smith, S. (1999). Starting off on the right foot: The influence of four principles of professional development in improving literacy instruction in two kindergarten programs. *Learning Disabilities Research and Practice, 14,* 239–253.

Baker, S., & Smith, S. (2001). Linking school assessments to research-based practices in Beginning Reading: Improving programs and outcomes for students with and without disabilities. *Teacher Education and Special Education, 24,* 315–322.

Barnard-Brak, L., & Lechtenberger, D. (2009). Student IEP participation and academic achievement across time. *Remedial and Special Education, 30,* 1–7.

Barnett, D., Elliot, N., Graden, J., Ihlo, T., Macmann, G., Natntais, M., & Prasse, D. (2006). Technical adequacy for response to intervention practices. *Assessment for Effective Intervention, 32,* 20–31.

Barton, K. E., & Sheinker, A. (2003). *Comparability and accessibility: On line versus on paper writing prompt administration and scoring across students with various abilities.* Monterey, CA: CTB-McGraw-Hill.

Bateman, B. D. (2007a). *From gobbledygook to clearly written IEP goals.* Verona, WI: IEP Resources/Attainment.

Bateman, B. D. (2007b). Law and the conceptual foundations of special education practice. In J. B. Crockett, M. M., Gerber, & T. J., & Landrum (Eds.), *Achieving the radical reform of special education: Essays in honor of James M. Kauffman* (pp. 95–114). Mahwah, NJ: Erlbaum.

Bateman, B. D. (2011). Individual education programs for students with disabilities. In J. M. Kauffman & D. P. Hallahan (Eds.), *Handbook of special education* (pp. 91–106). New York: Routledge.

Bateman, B. D., & Linden, M. A. (2006). *Better IEPs: How to develop legally correct and educationally useful programs* (4th ed.). Verona, WI: IEP Resources/Attainment.

Behar, L., & Stringfield, S. (1974). *Preschool Behavior Questionnaire, Scale and Manual.* Durham, NC: Learning Institute of North Carolina.

Bennett, R. E. (1982). Cautions for the use of informal measures in the educational assessment of exceptional children. *Journal of Learning Disabilities, 15,* 337–339.

Bergeron, R., Floyd, R. G., & Shands, E. I. (2008). States' eligibility guidelines for mental retardation: An update and consideration of part scores and unreliability of IQs. *Education and Training in Developmental Disabilities, 43*(1), 123–131.

Bird, H. R., Canino, G. J., Davies, M., Ramirez, R., Chavez, L., Duarte, C., & Shen, S. (2005). The Brief Impairment Scale (BIS): A multidimensional scale of functional impairment for children and adolescents. *Journal of the American Academy of Child and Adolescent Psychiatry, 44*, 699–707.

Blachman, B. A., Tangel, D. M., Bail, E. W., Black, R., & McGraw, C. K. (1999). Developing phonological awareness and word recognition skills: A two-year intervention with low-income, inner-city children. *Reading and Writing: An Interdisciplinary Journal, 11*, 239–273.

Blue-Banning, M., Summers, J. A., Frankland, H. C., Nelson, L. L., & Beegle, G. (2004). Dimensions of family and professional partnerships: Constructive guidelines for collaboration. *Exceptional Children, 70*, 167–184.

Board of Education of the Hendrick Hudson School District v. Rowley, 458 U.S. 176 (1982).

Boardman, A. G., Arguelles, M. E., Vaughn, S., Hughes, M. T., & Klingner, J. (2005). Special education teachers' views of research-based practices. *Journal of Special Education, 39*, 168–180.

Bolt, S., & Roach, A. T. (2009). *Inclusive assessment and accountability: A guide to accommodations for students with diverse needs.* New York: Guilford Press.

Bolt, S. E., & Thurlow, M. L. (2004). Five of the most frequently allowed testing accommodations in state policy: Synthesis of research. *Remedial and Special Education, 25*, 141–152.

Bolt, S. E., & Ysseldyke, J. E. (2006). Comparing DIF across math and reading/language arts tests for students receiving a read-aloud accommodation. *Applied Measurement in Education, 19*, 329–355.

Boone, R. (1992). Involving culturally diverse parents in transition planning. *Career Development for Exceptional Individuals, 15*, 205–221.

Botvin, G. (2004). Advancing prevention science and practice: Challenges, critical issues, and future directions. *Prevention Science, 5*, 69–72.

Brigham, F. J., & Brigham, M. S. P. (2010). Preventive instruction: Response to intervention can catch students before their problems become insurmountable. *The American School Board Journal, 197*(6), 32–33.

Brigham, M. M., Brigham, F. J., & Lloyd, J. W. (2002). *Balancing interventions and accommodations: Educating, equalizing, or equivocating?* Paper presented at the annual conference of Teacher Educators of Children with Behavior Disorders, Tempe, AZ.

Brophy, J., & Good, T. L. (1986). Teacher behavior and student achievement. In M. C. Wittrock (Ed.), *Handbook of research on teaching* (3rd ed., pp. 328–375). New York: Macmillan.

Brown, J., Goodman, K. S., & Marek, A. M. (Eds.). (1996). *Studies in miscue analysis: An annotated bibliography.* Newark, DE: International Reading Association.

Brown-Chidsey, R., & Steege, M. W. (2005). *Response to intervention: Principles and strategies for effective practice.* New York: Guilford Press.

Bruder, M. B. (2000). Family-centered early intervention: Clarifying our values for the new millennium. *Topics in Early Childhood Special Education, 20*, 105–115.

Bruininks, R. H., Woodcock, R.W., Weatherman, R. F., & Hill, B. K. (1996). *Scales of Independent Behavior—Revised.* Itasca, IL: Riverside Publishing.

Burk, M. (1999). *Computerized test accommodations.* Washington, DC: A.U. Software, Incorporated.

Burke, M. D., & Hagen-Burke, S. (2007). Concurrent criterion-related validity of early literacy for middle of first grade. *Assessment for Effective Intervention, 32*, 66–77.

Burns, M. K., Appleton, J. A., & Stehouwer, J. D. (2005). Meta-analytic review of responsiveness-to-intervention research: Examining field-based and research-implemented models. *Journal of Psychoeducational Assessment, 23*, 381–394.

Burns, M. K., & Coolong-Chaffin, M. (2006). Response-to-intervention: Role for and effect on school psychology. *School Psychology Forum, 1*(1), 3–15.

Burns, M. K., Dean, V. J., & Klar, S. (2004). Using curriculum-based assessment in the responsiveness to intervention diagnostic model for learning disabilities. *Assessment for Effective Intervention, 29*(3), 47–56.

Burns, M. K., Deno, S. L., & Jimerson, S. R. (2007). Toward a unified response-to-intervention model. In S. R. Jimerson, M. K., Burns, & A. M. VanDerHeyden (Eds.), *Handbook of response to intervention* (pp. 428–440). New York: Springer.

Burns, M. K., & Gibbons, K. (2008). *Response to intervention implementation in elementary and secondary schools: Procedures to assure scientific-based practices.* New York: Routledge.

Burns, M. K., Jacob, S., & Wagner, A. R. (2008). Ethical and legal issues associated with using response-to-intervention to assess learning disabilities. *Journal of School Psychology, 46*(3), 263–279.

Burns, M. K., Peters, R., & Noell, G. H. (2008). Using performance feedback to enhance the implementation integrity of the problem-solving team process. *Journal of School Psychology, 46*, 537–550.

Burns, M. K., Scholin, S. E., Kosciolek, S., & Livingston, S. (2010). Reliability of decision-making frameworks for response to intervention for reading. *Journal of Psychoeducational Assessment, 28*, 102–114.

Burns, M. K., & Senesac, B. K. (2005). Comparison of dual discrepancy criteria for diagnosis of unresponsiveness to intervention. *Journal of School Psychology, 43*, 393–406.

Burns, M. K., & Symington, T. (2002). A meta-analysis of prereferral intervention teams: Systemic and student outcomes. *Journal of School Psychology, 40*, 437–447.

Burns, M. K., Tucker, J. A., Frame, J., Foley, S., & Hauser, A. (2000). Interscorer, alternate-form, internal consistency, and test–retest reliability of Gickling's model of curriculum-based assessment for reading. *Journal of Psychoeducational Assessment, 18*, 353–360.

Burns, M. K., & VanDerHeyden, A. M. (2006). Using response to intervention to assess learning disabilities: Introduction to the special series.

Assessment for Effective Intervention, 32, 3–5.

Burns, M. K., VanDerHeyden, A. M., & Boice, C. H. (2008). Best practices in delivery intensive academic interventions. In A. Thomas & J. Grimes (Eds.), *Best practices in school psychology* (5th ed.). Bethesda, MD: National Association of School Psychologists.

Burns, M. K., VanDerHeyden, A. M., & Jiban, C. (2006). Assessing the instructional level for mathematics: A comparison of methods. *School Psychology Review, 35,* 401–418.

Burns, M. K., & Wagner, D. (2008). Determining an effective intervention within a brief experimental analysis for reading: A meta-analytic review. *School Psychology Review, 37,* 126–136.

Burns, M. K., Wiley, H. I., & Viglietta, E. (2008). Best practices in facilitating problem-solving teams. In A. Thomas & J. Grimes (Eds.), *Best practices in school psychology* (5th ed.). Bethesda, MD: National Association of School Psychologists.

Burns, M. K., & Ysseldyke, J. E. (2009). Reported prevalence of evidence-based instructional practices in special education. *Journal of Special Education, 43,* 3–11.

Busch, T. W., & Lembke, E. S. (2005). *Teaching tutorial 5: Progress monitoring in reading using the CBM maze procedure.* Web-based tutorial published on the Council for Exceptional Children, Division for Learning Disabilities, Web site. Available from http://www.dldcec.org

Caldarella, P., Young, E. L., Richardson, M. J., Young, B. J., & Young, K. R. (2008). Validation of the Systematic Screening for Behavior Disorders in middle and junior high school. *Journal of Emotional and Behavioral Disorders, 16*(2), 105–117.

Calhoon, M. B., Fuchs, L. S., & Hamlett, C. L. (2000). Effects of computer-based test accommodations on mathematics performance assessments for secondary students with learning disabilities. *Learning Disability Quarterly, 23,* 271–282.

Callicott, K. J. (2003). Culturally sensitive collaboration within person-centered planning. *Focus on Autism and Other Developmental Disabilities, 18*(1), 60–68.

Carnine, D. (1997). Bridging the research-to-practice gap. *Exceptional Children, 63,* 513–521.

Carr-George, C., Vannest, K. J., Willson, V., & Davis, J. L. (2009). The participation and performance of students with emotional and behavioral disorders in a state accountability assessment in reading. *Behavioral Disorders, 35,* 66–78.

Carson, P. M., & Eckert, T. L. (2003). An experimental analysis of mathematics instructional components: Examining the effects of student-selected versus empirically-selected interventions. *Journal of Behavioral Education, 12,* 35–54.

Case, B. J. (2003). *Accommodations for the Metropolitan8: Meeting the needs of all students.* Upper Saddle River, NJ: Pearson Education. Retrieved from http://pearsonassess.com/NR/rdonlyres/1E23DAFB-0131046C2-938F-E077F4900777/0/AccommodationfortheMAT8_Rev1_Final.pdf

Case, B. J. (2005). *Accommodations to improve instruction and assessment of students who are deaf or hard of hearing.* Retrieved from http://pearsonassess.com/NR/rdonlyres/318B76DB-853A-449F-A02E-CC53C8CFD1DB/0/Deaf.pdf

Catone, W. V., & Brady, S. A. (2005). The inadequacy of individual educational program (IEP) goals for high school students with word-level reading difficulties. *Annals of Dyslexia, 55*(1), 53–78.

Chabris, C., & Simons, D. (2010). *The invisible gorilla: And other ways our intuitions deceive us.* New York: Crown.

Chambers, C. R., & Childre, A. L. (2005). Fostering family-professional collaboration through person-centered IEP meetings: The "true directions" model. *Young Exceptional Children, 8*(3), 20–28.

Chandler, M. A. (2009, November 19, 2009). Alternative test may inflate score gains. *The Washington Post.* Retrieved from http://www.washingtonpost.com/wp-dyn/content/article/2009/11/18/AR2009111801796.html

Chard, D. J., & Kame'enui, E. J. (2000). Struggling first-grade readers: The frequency and progress of their reading. *The Journal of Special Education, 34,* 28–38.

Charlebois, P., & Leblanc, M. (1994). Methodological issues in multiple-gating screening procedures for antisocial behaviors in elementary students. *Remedial and Special Education, 15*(1), 44–54.

Chatel, R. G. (2001). Diagnostic and instructional uses of the Cloze procedure. *New England Reading Association Journal, 37,* 3–7.

Chiang, B., Rylance, B. J., Bongers, J., & Russ, S. (1998). *School psychologist ratio and caseload: A statewide survey.* (Wisconsin Educators' Caseload Efficacy Project Research Report No. 3) Oshkosh, WI: University of Wisconsin Oshkosh.

Childre, A., & Chambers, C. R. (2005). Family perceptions of student centered planning and IEP meetings. *Education and Training in Developmental Disabilities, 40,* 217–233.

Christ, T. J. (2006). Short term estimates of growth using curriculum-based measurement of oral reading fluency: Estimates of standard error of the slope to construct confidence intervals. *School Psychology Review, 35,* 128–133.

Christensen, L. L., Lazarus, S. S., Crone, M., & Thurlow, M. L. (2008). *2007 state policies on assessment participation and accommodations for students with disabilities* (Synthesis Report 69). Minneapolis, MN: University of Minnesota, National Center on Educational Outcomes.

Christensen, L. L., Thurlow, M. L., & Wang, T. (2009). *Improving accommodations outcomes: Monitoring assessment accommodations for students with disabilities.* Minneapolis, MN: National Center on Educational Outcomes with Council of Chief State School Officers.

Christle, C. A., & Yell, M. L. (2010). Individualized educational programs: Legal requirements and research findings. *Exceptionality, 18*(3), 109–123.

Claes, C., Van Hove, G., Vandevelde, S., van Loon, J., & Schalock, R. L. (2010) Person-centered planning: Analysis of research and effectiveness. *Intellectual and Developmental Disabilities, 48,* 432–453.

Clark, E. (1995). Review of the Developing Skills Checklist. In J. C. Conoley & J. C. Impara (Eds.), *The twelfth mental measurements yearbook* (pp. 278–281). Lincoln, NE: Buros Institute of Mental Measurements.

Cohen, A. S., Gregg, N., & Deng, M. (2005). The role of extended time and item content on a high-stakes mathematics test. *Learning Disabilities Research and Practice, 20,* 225–233.

Cohen, L., & Spenciner, L. (2007). *Assessment of children and youth with special needs* (3rd ed.). Upper Saddle River, NJ: Merrill/Pearson Education.

Coie, J. D., Watt, M. F., West, S. G., Hawkins, J. D., Asarnow, J. R., Markman, H. J., . . . Long, B. (1993). The science of prevention: A conceptual framework and some directions for a national research program. *American Psychologist, 48,* 1013–1022.

Cole, N. S., & Zieky, M. J. (2001). The new faces of fairness. *Journal of Educational Measurement, 38,* 369–382.

Compton, D. L., Fuchs, D., Fuchs, L. S., & Bryant, J. D. (2006). Selecting at-risk readers in first grade for early intervention: A two-year longitudinal study of decision rules and procedures. *Journal of Educational Psychology, 98,* 394–409.

Cone, J. D., Delawyer, D. D., & Wolfe, V. V. (1985). Assessing parent participation: The parent/family involvement index. *Exceptional Children, 51,* 417–424.

Conway, T. (2001). Intensive remedial instruction for children with severe reading disabilities: Immediate and long-term outcomes for two instructional approaches. *Journal of Learning Disabilities, 34,* 33–58.

Cook, B. G., Landrum, T. J., Tankersley, M., & Kauffman, J. M. (2003). Bringing research to bear on practice: Effecting evidence-based instruction for students with emotional or behavioral disorders. *Education and Treatment of Children, 26,* 325–361.

Cook, B. G., & Schirmer, B. R. (2006). An overview and analysis of the role of evidence-based practices in special education. In B. G. Cook & B. R. Schirmer (Eds.), *What is special about special education: The role of evidence-based practices* (pp. 175–185). Austin, TX: Pro-Ed.

Cook, B. G., & Smith, G. J. (2012).Leadership and instruction: Evidence-based practices in special education. In J. B. Crockett, B. S. Billingsley, & M. L. Boscardin (Eds.), *Handbook of leadership and administration for special education.* London: Routledge.

Cook, B. G., Tankersley, M., Cook, L., & Landrum, T. J. (2008). Evidence-based practices in special education: Some practical considerations. *Intervention in School & Clinic, 44*(2), 69–75.

Cook, B. G., Tankersley, M., & Harjusola-Webb, S. (2008). Evidence-based special education and professional wisdom: Putting it all together. *Intervention in School and Clinic, 44,* 105–111.

Cook, B. G., Tankersley, M., & Landrum, T. J. (2009). Determining evidence-based practices in special education. *Exceptional Children, 75,* 365–383.

Cook, L., Cook, B. G., Landrum, T. J., & Tankersley, M. (2008). Examining the role of group experimental research in establishing evidenced-based practices. *Intervention in School & Clinic, 44*(2), 76–82.

Cortiella, C. (2006). *NCLB and IDEA: What parents of students with disabilities need to know and do.* Minneapolis, MN: University of Minnesota: National Center on Educational Outcomes.

Cortiella, C., & Kaloi, L. (2009). *Understanding the Americans with Disabilities Act Amendments Act and Section 504 of the Rehabilitation Act* (Panel Advocacy Brief). New York: National Center for Learning Disabilities.

Council for Exceptional Children. (2009). *What every special educator must know: Ethics, standards, and guidelines* (6th ed.). Arlington, VA: Council for Exceptional Children.

Cox, M. L., Herner, J. G., Demczyk, M. J., & Nieberding, J. L. (2006). Provision of testing accommodations for students with disabilities on statewide tests: Statistical links with participation and discipline rates. *Remedial and Special Education, 27*(6), 346–354.

Crawford, L. (2007). *State testing accommodations: A look at their value and validity.* New York: National Center for Learning Disabilities.

Crawford, L., Helwig, R., & Tindal, G. (2004). Writing performance assessments: How important is extended time? *Journal of Learning Disabilities, 37,* 132–142.

Crockett, J. B. (2008). IEPs, the least restrictive environment, and placement. In K. E. Lane, M. A. Gooden, J. F. Mead, P. Pauken, & S. Eckes (Eds.), *The principal's legal handbook* (4th ed., pp. 243–268). Dayton, OH: Education Law Association.

Cutler, W. W. (2000). *Parents and schools: The 150-year struggle for control in American education.* Chicago: University of Chicago Press.

Dabkowski, D. M. (2004). Encouraging active parent participation in IEP team meetings. *TEACHING Exceptional Children, 36*(3), 34–39.

Dacy, B. J. S., Nihalani, P. K., Cestone, C. M., & Robinson, D. H. (2011). (Lack of) support for prescriptive statements in teacher education textbooks. *The Journal of Educational Research, 104,* 1–6.

Daly, E. J., III, Witt, J. C., Martens, B. K., & Dool, E. J. (1997). A model for conducting a functional analysis of academic performance problems. *School Psychology Review, 26,* 554–574.

Dammann, J. E., & Vaughn, S. (2001). Science and sanity in special education. *Behavioral Disorders, 27,* 21–29.

Daniel, P. T. K. (2008). "Some benefit" or "Maximum benefit": Does the No Child Left Behind Act render greater educational entitlement to students with disabilities. *Journal of Law & Education, 37,* 347–365.

De Groot, E. V. (2002). Learning through interviewing: Students and teachers talk about learning and schooling. *Educational Psychologist, 37*I 41–52.

Della Toffalo, D. A., & Milke, R. M. (2008). Test reviews: Dynamic assessment of test accommodations. *Journal of Psychoeducational Assessment, 26,* 83–91.

Dennis, R., & Giangreco, M. F. (1996). Creating conversation: Reflections on cultural sensitivity in family interviewing. *Exceptional Children, 63,* 103–116.

Dennis, R. E., Williams, W., Giangreco, M. F., & Cloninger, C. J. (1993). Quality of life as a context for planning and evaluation of services for people with disabilities. *Exceptional Children, 59,* 499–512.

Deno, S. L. (1985). Curriculum-based measurement: The emerging alternative. *Exceptional Children, 52,* 219–232.

Deno, S. L. (2003). Developments in curriculum-based measurement. *Journal of Special Education, 37,* 184–192.

Deno, S. L. (2006). Developments in curriculum-based measurement. In B. G. Cook & B. R. Schirmer (Eds.), *What is special about special education: The role of evidence-based practices* (pp. 100–112). Austin, TX: Pro-Ed.

Deno, S. L., Fuchs, L. S., Marston, D., & Shin, J. (2001). Using curriculum-based measurement to establish growth standards for students with learning disabilities. *School Psychology Review, 30,* 507–526.

Deno, S. L., Marston, D., & Mirkin, P. K. (1982). Valid measurement procedures for continuous evaluation of written expression. *Exceptional Children, 48,* 368–371.

Deno, S. L., & Mirkin, P. K. (1977). *Data-based program modification: A manual.* Minneapolis, MN: National School Psychology Inservice Network.

Deno, S. L., Mirkin, P. K., & Chiang, B. (1982). Identifying valid measures of reading. *Exceptional Children, 49,* 36–45.

Deno, S. L., Mirkin, P. K., Lowry, L., & Kuehnle, K. (1980). *Relationships among simple measures of spelling and performance on standardized achievement tests* (Research Report No. 21). Minneapolis: Institute for Research on Learning Disabilities, University of Minnesota.

Dickson, D. (2003). Let's not get too romantic about traditional knowledge. *Science Development Network.* Retrieved from http://www.scidev.net/en/editorials/lets-not-get-too-romantic-about-traditional-knowl.html

Disability Rights Advocates. (2001). *Do no harm—High stakes testing and students with learning disabilities.* Oakland, CA: Author.

Disability Rights Advocates. (2008). *Chapman v. California Department of Education.* Retrieved from http://www.dralegal.org/cases/education_testing/chapman_v_ca.php

Dolan, R. P., Burling, K. S., Harms, M., Beck, R., Hanna, E., Jude, J., Murray, E. A., Rose, D. H., & Way, W. (2009). *Universal design for computer-based testing guidelines.* Iowa City, IA: Pearson.

Dolan, R. P., Hall, T. E., Bannerjee, M., Chun, E., & Strangman, N. (2005). Applying principles of universal design to test design: The effect of computer-based read-aloud on test performance of high school students with learning disabilities. *The Journal of Technology, Learning, and Assessment, 3*(7). Retrieved from http://www.jtla.org

Donovan, M. S., & Cross, C. T. (2002). *Minority students in special and gifted education.* Washington, DC: National Academy Press.

Doyle, W. (1986). Classroom organization and management. In M. C. Wittrock (Ed.), *Handbook of research on teaching* (3rd ed., pp. 392–431). New York: Macmillan.

Drasgow, E., Yell, M. L., & Robinson, T. R. (2001). Developing legally and educationally appropriate IEPs: Federal law and lessons learned from the Lovaas hearings and cases. *Remedial and Special Education, 22,* 359–373.

Dunst, C. J. (2000). Revisiting "Rethinking early intervention." *Topics in Early Childhood Special Education, 20,* 95–104.

Dyson, A. H. (1986). What are we teaching? Applying error analysis to school activities. *Reading Research and Instruction, 25,* 71–79.

Edelman, S., Knutson, J., Osborn, D., & Giangreco, M. F. (1995). Heidi's inclusion in junior high: Transition and educational planning for a student with deaf-blindness. *Deaf-Blind Perspectives, 2*(3), 1–6.

Education for All Handicapped Children Act of 1975 § 1401 *et seq.*

Ehri, L. C., & McCormick, S. (2004). Phases of word learning: Implications for instruction with delayed and disabled readers. In R. B. Ruddell, M. R. Ruddell, & H. Singer (Eds.), *Theoretical models and processes of reading* (5th ed., pp. 365–389). Newark, DE: International Reading Association.

Elbaum, B. (2007). Effects of an oral testing accommodation on the mathematics performance of secondary students with and without learning disabilities. *The Journal of Special Education, 40,* 218–229.

Elbaum, B., Vaughn, S., Hughes, M. T., Moody, S. W., & Schumm, J. S. (2000). How reading outcomes of students with disabilities are related to instructional grouping formats: A meta-analytic review. In R. M. Gersten, E. P. Schiller, & S. Vaughn (Eds.), *Contemporary special education research: Syntheses of the knowledge base on critical instructional issues* (pp. 105–135). Mahwah, NJ: Erlbaum.

Elliot, N. (2005). *On a scale: A social history of writing assessment in America.* New York: Peter Lang.

Elliot, S. N., Braden, J. P., & White, J. (2001). *Assessing one and all: Educational accountability and students with disabilities.* Alexandria, VA: Council for Exceptional Children.

Elliott, J., Lee, S. W., & Tollefson, N. (2001). A reliability and validity study of the Dynamic Indicators of Basic Early Literacy Skills—Modified. *School Psychology Review, 30,* 33–49.

Elliott, J., & Morrison, D. (2008). *Response to intervention blueprints for implementation: District level.* Alexandria, VA: National Association of State Directors of Special Education.

Elliott, J. L., & Thurlow, M. L. (2006). *Improving test performance of students with disabilities on district and state assessments* (2nd ed.). Thousand Oaks, CA: Corwin.

Elliot, S. N., Braden, J. P., & White, J. (2001). *Assessing one and all: Educational accountability and students with disabilities.* Alexandria, VA: Council for Exceptional Children.

Elliott, S. N., & Busse, R. T. (2004). Assessment and evaluation of students' behavior and intervention outcomes: The utility of rating scale methods. In R. B. Rutherford, M. M. Quinn, & S. R. Mathur (Eds.), *Handbook of research in emotional and behavioral disorders* (pp. 123–142). New York: Guilford Press.

Elliott, S. N., & Marquart, A. M. (2004). Extended time as a testing accommodation: Its effects and perceived consequences. *Exceptional Children, 70,* 349–367.

Elliott, S. N., McKevitt, B. C., & Kettler, R. J. (2002). Testing accommodations research and decision-making: The case of "good" scores being highly valued but difficult to achieve for all students. *Measurement and Evaluation in Counseling and Development, 35,* 153–166.

Ellis, A. K. (2005). *Research on educational innovations* (4th ed.). Larchmont, NY: Eye on Education.

Engelmann, S. (1997). Theory of mastery and acceleration. In J. W. Lloyd, E. J. Kameenui, & D. J. Chard (Eds.), *Issues in educating students with disabilities* (pp. 177–195). Mahwah, NJ: Erlbaum.

Epstein, J. S. (2009). *School, family and community partnerships.* Thousand Oaks, CA: Corwin Press.

Epstein, M., Patton, J. R., Polloway, E. A., & Foley, R. (1992). Educational services for students with behavior disorders: A review of Individualized Education Programs. *Teacher Education and Special Education, 15*(1), 41–48.

Epstein, M. H., & Sharma, H. M. (1998). *Behavioral and Emotional Rating Scale (BERS).* Austin, TX: Pro-Ed.

Ervin, R., Schaughency, E., Goodman, S., McGlinchey, M., & Matthews, A. (2006). Merging research and practice agendas to address reading and behavior school-wide. *School Psychology Review, 35,* 198–223.

Espin, C. A., Busch, T. W., Shin, J., & Kruschwitz, R. (2001). Curriculum-based measurement in the content areas: Validity of vocabulary-matching as an indicator of performance in social studies. *Learning Disabilities Research and Practice, 16(3),* 142–151.

Espin, C. A., De La Paz, S., Scierka, B. J., & Roelofs, L. (2005). Relation between curriculum-based measures in written expression and quality and completeness of expository writing for middle-school students. *Journal of Special Education, 38,* 208–217.

Espin, C., Shin, J., & Busch, T. W. (2000). *Formative evaluation* (Current Practice Alerts No. 2). Reston, VA: Division for Learning Disabilities & Division for Research of the Council for Exceptional Children.

Espin, C. A., Shin, J., & Busch, T. W. (2005). Curriculum-based measurement in the content areas: Vocabulary-matching as an indicator of social studies learning. *Journal of Learning Disabilities, 38,* 353–363.

Espin, C. L., & Wallace, T. (2004). *Descriptive analysis of curriculum-based measurement literature.* Working Document. University of Minnesota Institute for Research on Progress Monitoring.

Espin, C., Wallace, T., Campbell, H., Lembke, E. S., Long, J. D., & Ticha, R. (2008). Curriculum-based measurement in writing: Predicting the success of high-school students on state standards tests. *Exceptional Children, 74,* 174–193.

Espin, C., Wallace, T., Lembke, R., Campbell, H., & Long, J. D. (2010). Creating a progress-monitoring system in reading for middle-school students: Tracking progress toward meeting high-stakes standards. *Learning Disabilities Research & Practice, 25,* 60–75.

Etscheidt, S., & Curran, C. M. (2010). Peer-reviewed research and individualized education programs: An examination of intent and impact. *Exceptionality, 18,* 138–150.

Farr, R. (1991). The assessment puzzle. *Educational Leadership, 49,* 95.

Farr, R. (1996). I have a dream about assessment. *The Reading Teacher, 49,* 424.

Faykus, S. P., & McCurdy B. L. (1998). Evaluating the sensitivity of the maze as an index of reading proficiency for students who are severely deficient in reading. *Education and Treatment of Children, 21,* 1–21.

Feil, E. G., & Severson, H. H. (1995). Identification of critical factors in the assessment of preschool behavior problems. *Education and Treatment of Children, 18*(3), 261–272.

Feil, E. G., Walker, H., Severson, H., & Ball, A. (2000). Proactive screening for emotional/behavioral concerns in Head Start preschools: Promising practices and challenges in applied research. *Behavioral Disorders 26*(1), 13–25.

Ferguson, C. (2008). *The school–family connection: Looking at the larger picture.* Austin, TX: Southwest Educational Development Laboratories.

Finn, J. E., & Kohler, P. D. (2009). A compliance evaluation of the Transition Outcomes Project. *Career Development for Exceptional Individuals, 32*(1), 17–29.

Fitzsimmons, D. (2008). Digital portfolios in visual arts classrooms. *Art Education, 61*(5), 47–55.

Flannery, K. B., Newton, S., Horner, R. H., Slovic, R., Blumberg, R., & Ard, W. R. (2000). The impact of person centered planning on the content and organization of individual supports. *Career Development of Exceptional Individuals, 23,* 123–137.

Fletcher, J. M., Coulter, W. A., Reschly, D. J., & Vaughn, S. (2004). Alternative approach to the definition and identification of learning disabilities: Some questions and answers. *Annals of Dyslexia, 54,* 304–331.

Foegen, A. (2008). Algebra progress monitoring and interventions for students with learning disabilities. *Learning Disability Quarterly, 31,* 65–78.

Foegen, A., & Deno, S. L. (2001). Identifying growth indicators for low-achieving students in middle-school mathematics. *Journal of Special Education, 35,* 4–16.

Foegen, A., Jiban, C., & Deno, S. (2007). Progress monitoring in mathematics: A review of the literature. *Journal of Special Education, 41,* 121–139.

Foegen, A., Olson, J. R., & Impecoven-Lind, L. (2008). Developing progress monitoring measures for secondary mathematics: An illustration in algebra. *Assessment for Effective Intervention, 33,* 240–249.

Foorman, B. R., Francis, D. J., Fletcher, J. M., Schatschneider, C., & Mehta, P. (1998). The role of instruction in learning to read: Preventing reading failure in at-risk children. *Journal of Educational Psychology, 90,* 37–55.

Foster, M., Berger, M., & McLean, M. (1981). Re-thinking a good idea: A reassessment of parent involvement. *Topics in Early Childhood Special Education, 1,* 55–65.

Forest, M., & Lusthaus, E. (1987). The kaleidoscope: Challenge to the cascade. In M. Forest (Ed.), *More education/integration* (pp. 1–16). Downsview, Ontario: G. Allan Roeher Institute.

Francis, D. J., Shaywitz, S. E., Stuebing, K. K., Shaywitz, B. A., & Fletcher, J. M. (1996). Developmental lag versus deficit models of reading disability: A longitudinal, individual growth curve analysis. *Journal of Educational Psychology, 88,* 3–17.

Freedman, D. H. (2010). *Wrong: Why experts keep failing us—and how to know when not to trust them.* New York: Little, Brown.

Fuchs, D., & Deshler, D. D. (2007). What we need to know about responsiveness to intervention and shouldn't be afraid to ask. *Learning Disabilities Research & Practice, 22*(2), 129–136.

Fuchs, D., & Fuchs, L. S. (2005). Peer-assisted learning strategies: Promoting word recognition, fluency, and reading comprehension in young children. *Journal of Special Education, 39,* 34–44.

Fuchs, D., & Fuchs, L. S. (2006). New directions in research, introduction to response to intervention: What, why, and how valid is it? *Reading Research Quarterly, 41,* 93–99.

Fuchs, D., Fuchs, L. S., Mathes, P. G., & Simmons, D. C. (1997). Peer-assisted learning strategies: Making classrooms more responsive to diversity. *American Educational Research Journal, 34,* 174–206.

Fuchs, D., Mock, D., Morgan, P. L., & Young, C. L. (2003). Responsiveness-to-intervention: Definitions, evidence, and implications for the learning disabilities construct. *Learning Disablilities Research & Practice, 18,* 157–171.

Fuchs, L. S. (2003). Assessing intervention responsiveness: Conceptual and technical issues. *Learning Disabilities: Research & Practice, 18,* 172–186.

Fuchs, L. S. (2004). The past, present, and future of curriculum-based measurement research. *School Psychology Review, 33,* 188–192.

Fuchs, L. S. & Deno, S. L. (1991). Effects of curriculum within curriculum-based measurement. *Exceptional Children, 58,* 232–244.

Fuchs, L. S., & Deno, S. L. (1994). Must instructionally useful performance assessment be based in the curriculum? *Exceptional Children, 61,* 15–24.

Fuchs, L. S., Deno, S. L., & Mirkin, P. K. (1984). Effects of frequent curriculum-based measurement and evaluation on

pedagogy, student achievement, and student awareness of learning. *American Educational Research Journal, 21,* 449–460.

Fuchs, L. S., & Fuchs, D. (1986). Effects of systematic formative evaluation on student achievement: A meta-analysis. *Exceptional Children, 53,* 199–208.

Fuchs, L. S., & Fuchs, D. (1992). Identifying a measure for monitoring student progress. *School Psychology Review, 21,* 45–58.

Fuchs, L. S., & Fuchs, D. (1999). Fair and unfair testing accommodations. *School Administrator, 56,* 24–29.

Fuchs, L. S., & Fuchs, D. (2001). Helping teachers formulate sound test accommodation decisions for students with learning disabilities. *Learning Disabilities Research & Practice, 16,* 174–181.

Fuchs, L. S., & Fuchs, D. (2002). *What is scientifically-based research on progress monitoring?* (Technical report). Nashville, TN: Vanderbilt University.

Fuchs, L. S., Fuchs, D., Compton, D. L., Bryant, J. D., Hamlett, C. L., & Seethaler, P. M. (2007). Mathematics screening and progress monitoring at first grade: Implications for response to intervention. *Exceptional Children, 73,* 311–330.

Fuchs, L., Fuchs, D., Eaton, S., & Hamlett, C. (2003). *Dynamic Assessment of Test Accommodations.* San Antonio TX: PsychCorp.

Fuchs, L. S., Fuchs, D., Eaton, S. B., Hamlett, C., Binkley, E., & Crouch, R. (2000). Using objective data sources to enhance teacher judgments about test accommodations. *Exceptional Children, 67,* 67–81.

Fuchs, L. S., Fuchs, D., Eaton, S. B., Hamlett, C. L., & Karns, K. M. (2000). Supplementing teacher judgments of mathematics test accommodations with objective data sources. *School Psychology Review, 29*(1), 66–85.

Fuchs, L. S., Fuchs, D., & Hamlett, C. L. (1989). Effects of instrumental use of curriculum-based measurement to enhance instructional programs. *Remedial and Special Education, 10,* 42–52.

Fuchs, L. S., Fuchs, D., & Hamlett, C. L. (1993). Technological advances

linking the assessment of students' academic proficiency to instructional planning. *Journal of Special Education Technology, 12,* 49–62.

Fuchs, L. S., Fuchs, D., Hamlett, C. L., Phillips, N. B., & Bentz, J. (1994). Classwide curriculum-based measurement: Helping general educators meet the challenge of student diversity. *Exceptional Children, 60,* 518–537.

Fuchs, L. S., Fuchs, D., Hamlett, C. L., & Stecker, P. M. (1990). The role of skills analysis in curriculum-based measurement in math. *School Psychology Review, 19,* 6–22.

Fuchs, L. S., Fuchs, D., Hosp, M. K., & Hamlett, C. L. (2003). The potential for diagnostic analysis within curriculum-based measurement. *Assessment for Effective Intervention, 28*(3–4), 13–22.

Fuchs, L. S., Fuchs, D., & Maxwell, S. (1988). The validity of informal reading comprehension measures. *Remedial and Special Education, 9*(2), 20–28.

Fuchs, L. S., Tindal, G., & Deno, S. L. (1984). Methodological issues in curriculum-based reading assessment. *Diagnostique, 9,* 191–207.

Fulk, B. M., Brigham, F. J., & Lohman, D. (1998). Motivation and self-regulation: A comparison of students with learning and behavior problems. *Remedial & Special Education, 19,* 300–309.

Furney, K. S., & Salembier, G. (2000). Rhetoric and reality: A review of the literature on parent and student participation in the IEP and transition planning process. In D. R. Johnson & E. J. Emanuel (Eds.), *Issues influencing the future of transition programs and services in the United States* (pp. 111–126). Minneapolis: National Transition Network, Institute on Community Integration.

Galagan, J. E. (1985). Psychoeducational testing: Turn out the lights, the party's over. *Exceptional Children, 52,* 288–299.

Gallagher, J., & Desimone, L. (1995). Lessons learned from implementation of the IEP: Applications to the IFSP. *Topics in Early Childhood Education, 15*(3), 353–378.

Gallagher, W. (1993). *The power of place: How our surroundings shape our thoughts, emotions, and actions.* New York: Poseidon Press.

Gansle, K. A., Gilbertson, D. N., & VanDerHeyden, A. M. (2006). Elementary school teachers' perceptions of curriculum-based measures of written expression. *Practical Assessment, Research & Evaluation, 11*, 1–17.

Gansle, K. A., & Noell, G. H. (2007). The fundamental role of intervention implementation in assessing resistance to intervention. In S. Jimerson, M. K. Burns, & A. M. VanDerHeyden (Eds.), *Handbook of response to intervention: The science and practice of assessment and intervention* (pp. 244–254). New York: Springer.

Gansle, K. A., Noell, G. H., VanDer Heyden, A. M., Naquin, G. M., & Slider, N. J. (2002). Moving beyond total words written: The reliability, criterion validity, and time cost of alternative measure for curriculum-based measurement in writing. *School Psychology Review, 31*(4), 477–497.

Garcia, T. (2007). Facilitating the reading process. *Teaching Exceptional Children, 39,* 12–17.

Geenan, S., Powers, L. E., & Lopez-Vasquez, A. (2001). Multicultural aspects of parent involvement in transition planning. *Exceptional Children, 67,* 265–282.

Geffre et al., v. Leola School District 44-2 CIV 06-1047 (U.S. Dist. LEXIS 88278 2009).

Gerber, M. M. (2005). Teachers are still the test. Limitations of response to instruction strategies for identifying children with learning disabilities. *Journal of Learning Disabilities, 38,* 516–524.

Gerber, M. M., & Semmel, M. I. (1984). Teacher as imperfect test: Reconceptualizing the referral process. *Educational Psychologist, 19,* 137–148.

Gerber, P. L., Banbury, M. M., & Miller, J. H. (1986). Special educators' perceptions of parental participation in the Individual Education Plan process. *Psychology in the Schools, 23,* 158–163.

Gersten, R., Vaughn, S., & Brengelman, S. U. (1996). Grading and academic feedback for special education students and students with learning difficulties. In T. R. Guskey (Ed.), *Communicating student learning: ASCD yearbook, 1996* (pp. 47–57). Alexandria, VA: Association for Supervision and Curriculum Development.

Giangreco, M. F., Cloninger, C. J., Dennis, R. E., & Edelman, S. W. (1993). National expert validation of COACH: Congruence with exemplary practice and suggestions for improvement. *Journal of the Association for Persons with Severe Handicaps, 18*, 109–120.

Giangreco, M. F., Cloninger, C. J., & Iverson, V. S. (2011). *Choosing outcomes and accommodations for children (COACH): A guide to educational planning for students with disabilities* (3rd ed.). Baltimore: Brookes.

Giangreco, M. F., Cloninger, C., Mueller, P., Yuan, S., & Ashworth, S. (1991). Perspectives of parents whose children have dual sensory impairments. *Journal of the Association for Persons with Severe Handicaps, 16,* 14–24.

Giangreco, M. F., Dennis, R., Edelman, S., & Cloninger, C. (1994). Dressing your IEPs for the general education climate: Analysis of IEP goals and objectives for students with multiple disabilities. *Remedial and Special Education, 15,* 288–296.

Giangreco, M. F., Edelman, S., Dennis, R., & Cloninger, C. J. (1995). Use and impact of COACH with students who are deaf-blind. *Journal of the Association for Persons with Severe Handicaps, 20,* 121–135.

Giangreco, M. F., Edelman, S.W, Nelson, C., Young, M. R., & Kiefer-O'Donnell, R. (1999). Improving support service decision-making: Consumer feedback regarding updates to VISTA. *International Journal of Disability, Development and Education, 46,* 463–473.

Giangreco, M. F., Whiteford, T., Whiteford, L., & Doyle, M. B. (1998). Planning for Andrew: A case study of COACH and VISTA use in an inclusive early childhood program. *International Journal of Disability, Development and Education, 45,* 375–396.

Glover, T. A., & Albers, C. A. (2007). Considerations for evaluating universal screening assessments. *Journal of School Psychology, 45,* 117–135.

Goldman, R. W. (1994). A free appropriate education in the least restrictive environment: Promises made, promises broken by the Individuals with Disabilities Education Act. *Dayton Law Review, 20,* 243–291.

Goldstein, S., Strickland, B., Turnbull, A. P., & Curry, L. (1980). An observational analysis of the IEP conference. *Exceptional Children, 46,* 278–286.

Good, R. H., Gruba, J., & Kaminski. R. A. (2001). Best practices in using Dynamic Indicators of Basic Early Literacy Skills (DIBELS) in an outcomes-driven model. In A. Thomas & J. Grimes (Eds.), *Best practices in school psychology* (vol. 4, pp. 679–700). Washington, DC: National Association of School Psychologists.

Good, R. H., & Kaminski, R. A. (2002, rev.2003). *Dynamic Indicators of Basic Literacy Skills*TM *6th Edition DIBELS*TM. Eugene, OR: Institute for the Development of Educational Achievement. Retrieved from http://dibels.uoregon.edu/Dibels

Good, R. H., & Kaminski, R. A. (Eds.). (2007). *Dynamic Indicators of Basic Early Literacy Skills* (6th ed.). Eugene, OR: Institute for the Development of Educational Achievement.

Good, R. H., III, Simmons, D. C., & Kame'enui, E. J. (2001). The importance and decision- making utility of a continuum of fluency-based indicators of foundational reading skills for third-grade high-stakes outcomes. *Scientific Studies of Reading, 5,* 257–289.

Goodman, K. S. (1965). A linguistic study of cues and miscues in reading. *Elementary English, 42,* 639–643.

Goodman, K. S. (1967). Reading: A psycholinguistic guessing game. *Journal of the Reading Specialist, 6,* 126–135.

Goodman, K. S. (1969). Analysis of oral reading miscues: Applied psycholinguistics. *Reading Research Quarterly, 5,* 9–30.

Goodman, K. S., & Burke, C. L. (1973). *Theoretically based studies of patterns of miscues in oral reading performance.* Washington, DC: U.S. Department of Health, Education and Welfare. (ERIC Document Reproduction Service No. ED 079 708)

Goodman, Y., Watson, D., & Burke, C. (2005). *Reading miscue inventory.* Katonah, NY: Richard C. Owen.

Gordon, S. (2006). Making sense of the inclusion debate under IDEA. *Brigham Young University Education and Law Journal, 189*(1), 176–213.

Graden, J. L., Stollar, S. A., & Poth, R. L. (2007). The Ohio integrated systems model: Overview and lessons learned. In S. Jimerson, M. K. Burns, & A. M. VanDerHeyden (Eds.), *Handbook of response to intervention: The science and practice of assessment and intervention* (pp. 288–299). New York: Springer.

Gravois, T. A., & Gickling, E. (2008). Best practices in instructional assessment. In A. Thomas & J. Grimes (Eds.), *Best practices in school psychology* (vol. 4, pp. 503–518). Bethesda, MD: National Association of School Psychologists.

Gravois, T. A., & Rosenfield, S. A. (2006). Impact of instructional consultation teams on the disproportionate referral and placement of minority students in special education. *Remedial and Special Education, 27,* 45–52.

Greene, G. (1996). Empowering culturally and linguistically diverse families in the transition planning process. *Journal for Vocational Special Needs Education, 19*(l), 26–30.

Greenspan, S. (2006). Functional concepts in mental retardation: Finding the natural essence of an artificial category. *Exceptionality, 14*(4), 205–224.

Greenwood, C. R., & Abbott, M. (2001). The research-to-practice gap in special education. *Teacher Education and Special Education, 24,* 276–289.

Gresham, F. M. (1995). Student Self-Concept Scale: Description and relevance to students with emotional and behavioral. *Journal of Emotional & Behavioral Disorders, 3,* 19–26.

Gresham, F. M. (2002). Responsiveness to intervention: An alternative approach to the identification of learning disabilities. In R. Bradley & L. Danielson (Eds.), *Identification of learning disabilities: Research to practice. The LEA series on special education and disability* (pp. 467–519). Mahwah, NJ: Erlbaum.

Gresham, F. M. (2005). Response to intervention: An alternative means of identifying students as emotionally disturbed. *Education and Treatment of Children, 28*(4), 328–344.

Gresham, F. M. (2007). Evolution of the response-to-intervention concept: Empirical foundations and recent developments. In S. R. Jimerson, M. K., Burns, & A. M. VanDerHeyden (Eds.), *Handbook of response to intervention* (pp. 10–24). New York: Springer.

Gresham, F. M., Elliott, S. N., & Evans-Fernandez, S. (1992). *Student Self-Concept Scale.* Circle Pine, MN: American Guidance Service.

Grimes, J., Kurns, S., Tilly W. D., III. (2006). Sustainability: an enduring commitment to success. *School Psychology Review, 35,* 224–243.

Grisham-Brown, J., Pretti-Frontczak, K., Hemmeter, M. L., & Ridgley, R. (2002). Teaching IEP goals and objectives in the context of classroom routines and activities. *Young Exceptional Children, 6*(1), 18–27.

Hafner, J. C., & Hafner, P. M. (2003). Quantitative analysis of the rubric as an assessment tool: An empirical study of student peer-group rating. *International Journal of Science Education, 25*(12), 1509–1528.

Hage, S. M., Romano, J. L., Conye, R. K., Kenny, M., Matthews, C., Schwartz, J. P., & Waldo, M. (2007). Best practice guidelines on prevention, practice, research, training, and social advocacy for psychologists. *Journal of Counseling Psychologists, 35,* 493–566.

Hale, J. A. (2008). *Curriculum mapping: Planning, implementing, and sustaining the process.* Thousand Oaks, CA: Corwin Press.

Hale, J. B., Naglieri, J. A., Kaufman, A. S., & Kavale, K. A. (2004). Specific learning disability classification in the new Individuals with Disabilities Education Act: The danger of good ideas. *The School Psychologist, 58*(1), 6–13.

Hall, T., & Mengel, M. (2002). *Curriculum-based evaluations.* Wakefield, MA: National Center on Accessing the General Curriculum. Retrieved from http://www.cast.org/publications/ncac/ncac_curriculumbe.html

Hallenbeck, B. A., & Kauffman, J. M. (1995). How does observational learning affect the behavior of students with emotional or behavioral disorders? A review of research. *Journal of Special Education, 29,* 45–71.

Halpern, A. S., Herr, C. M., Wolf, N. K., Doren, B., Johnson, M. D., & Lawson, J. D. (1997). *Next S.T.E.P.: Student transition and educational planning.* Austin, TX: Pro-Ed.

Hammer, M. R. (2004). Using the self-advocacy strategy to increase student participation in IEP conferences. *Intervention in School and Clinic, 39,* 295–300.

Harris-Murri, N., King, K., & Rostenberg, D. (2006). Reducing disproportionate minority representation in special education programs for students with emotional disturbances: Toward a culturally responsive response to intervention model. *Education and Treatment of Children, 29*(4), 779–799.

Harrison, P., & Oakland, T. (2003). *Adaptive Behavior Assessment System, 2nd Edition.* San Antonio, TX: Psychological Corporation.

Harry, B. (1992a). An ethnographic study of cross-cultural communication with Puerto Rican-American families in the special education system. *American Educational Research Journal, 29,* 471–494.

Harry, B. (1992b). Making sense of disability: Low-income, Puerto Rican parents' theory of the problem. *Exceptional Children, 59,* 27–40.

Harry, B. (2008). Collaboration with culturally and linguistically divers families: Ideal vs. reality. *Exceptional Children 74,* 372–388.

Harry, B., Allen, N., & McLaughlin, M. (1995). Communication versus compliance: African-American parents' involvement in special education. *Exceptional Children, 61,* 364–377.

Harry, B., Klingner, J. K., Sturges, K. M., & Moore, R. F. (2002). Of rocks and soft places: Using qualitative methods to investigate disproportionality. In D. J. Losen & G. Orfield (Eds.), *Racial inequity in special education* (pp. 71–92). Cambridge, MA: Civil Rights Project at Harvard University, Harvard Education Press.

Hasazi, S., Furney, K. S., & DeStefano, L. (1999). Implementing the IDEA transition mandates. *Exceptional Children, 65,* 555–566.

Hasbrouck, J., & Tindal, G. (2005). *Oral reading fluency: 90 years of measurement* (Tech. Rep. No. 33). Eugene, OR: University of Oregon, College of Education, Behavioral Research and Teaching.

Hasselbring, T. S., & Crossland, C. L. (1982). Application of microcomputer technology to spelling assessment of learning disabled students. *Learning Disability Quarterly, 5,* 80–82.

Heflinger, C. R., Cook, V. J., & Thackrey, M. (1987). Identification of mental retardation by the System of Multicultural Pluralistic Assessment: Nondiscriminatory or nonexistent? *Journal of School Psychology, 25,* 177–183.

Heller, K. A., Holtzman, W. H., & Messick, S. (1982). *Placing children in special education: Theories and recommendations.* Washington, DC: National Academy Press.

Helwig, R., Rozek-Tedesco, M., & Tindal, G. (2002). An oral versus a standard administration of a large-scale mathematics test. *The Journal of Special Education, 36,* 39–47.

Henderson, A. T., & Mapp, K. L. (2002). *A new wave of evidence: The impact of school, family, and community connection on student achievement.* Austin, TX: Southwest Education Development Laboratory.

Henry, M. (1996). *Parent–school collaboration: Feminist organizational structures and school leadership.* Albany, NY: State University of New York Press.

Heshusius, L. (2004). Special education knowledges: The inevitable struggle with the "self." In D. J. Gallagher, L. Heshusius, R. P. Iano, & T. M. Skrtic (Eds.), *Challenging orthodoxy in special education: Dissenting voices.* (pp. 283–309). Denver, CO: Love.

Hess, F. M., & Brigham, F. J. (2007). How federal special education policy affects schooling in Virginia. In M. Burns (Ed.), *Taking sides: Clashing views in special education* (3rd ed., pp. 139–149). New York: McGraw-Hill.

Hess, F., & Petrilli, M. (2006). *No Child Left Behind primer.* New York: Peter Lang.

Heubert, J. P., & Hauser, R. M. (1999). *High stakes: Testing for tracking, promotion, and graduation.* Washington, DC: National Academy Press.

Hill, C. C. (2006). *The individualized education program: An analysis of IEP litigation from 2000 to present* (Doctoral dissertation). (UMI No. 3252012)

Hintze, J. M., Christ, T. J., & Keller, L. A. (2002). The generalizability of CBM survey-level mathematics assessments: Just how many samples do we need? *School Psychology Review, 31,* 514–528.

Hoge, R. D., & Coladarci, T. (1989). Teacher-based judgments of academic achievement: A review of literature. *Review of Educational Research, 59,* 297–313.

Hogue, A., Henderson, C. E., Dauber, S., Barajas, P. C., Fried, A., & Liddle, H. A. (2008). Treatment adherence, competence, and outcome in individual and family therapy for adolescent behavior problems. *Journal of Consulting and Clinical Psychology, 76,* 544–555.

Holdnack, J. A., & Weiss, L. G. (2006). IDEA 2004: Anticipating implications for clinical practice—Integrating assessment and intervention. *Psychology in the Schools, 43,* 871–882.

Hoover-Dempsey, K. V., Walker, J. M. T., Jones, K. P., & Reed, R. P. (2002). Teachers involving parents (TIP): Results of an in-service teacher education program for enhancing parental involvement. *Teaching and Teacher Education, 18,* 843–867.

Hollenbeck, K., Rozek-Tedesco, M. A., Tindal, G., & Glasgow, A. (2000). An exploratory study of student-paced versus teacher-paced accommodations for large-scale math tests. *Journal of Special Education Technology, 15,* 27–36.

Horn, E., Lieber, J., Li, S., Sandall, S., & Schwartz, I. (2000). Supporting young children's IEP goals in inclusive settings through embedded learning opportunities. *Topics in Early Childhood Education, 20,* 208–223.

Horton, S. V., & Lovitt, T. C. (1994). A comparison of two methods of administering group reading inventories to diverse learners. *Remedial and Special Education, 15,* 378–390.

Hosp, J. L. (2008). Best practice in aligning academic assessment with instruction. In A. Thomas & J. Grimes (Eds.), *Best practices in school psychology* (vol. 5, pp. 363–376). Bethesda, MD: National Association of School Psychologists.

Hosp, J. L., & Hosp, M. K. (2001). Behavior differences between African-American and Caucasian students: Issues for assessment and intervention. *Education & Treatment of Children, 24*(3), 336–350.

Hosp, M. K., & Fuchs, L. S. (2005). Using CBM as an indicator of decoding, word reading, and comprehension: Do the relations change with grade? *School Psychology Review, 34,* 9–26.

Howell, K. W., & Nolet, V. (2000). *Curriculum-based evaluation: Teaching and decision making.* Atlanta, GA: Wadsworth.

Hudson, R. F., Lane, H. B., & Pullen, P. C. (2005). Reading fluency assessment and instruction: What, why, and how? *The Reading Teacher, 58,* 702–715.

Huebner, E. S., & Gould, K. (1991) Multidisciplinary teams revisited: Current perceptions of school psychologists regarding team functioning. *School Psychology Review, 20*(3), 428–434.

Huefner, D. S. (2000). The risks and opportunities of the IEP requirements of IDEA '97. *Journal of Special Education, 33,* 195–204.

Huefner, D. S. (2008). Updating the FAPE standard under IDEA. *Journal of Law & Education, 37,* 367–379.

Hughes, C. A., & Ruhl, K. L. (1987). The nature and extent of special educator contacts with students' parents. *Teacher Education and Special Education, 10*(4), 180–184.

Hunt, P., Goetz, L., & Anderson, J. (1986). The quality of IEP objectives associated with placement on integrated versus segregated school sites. *The Journal of the Association for Persons with Severe Handicaps, 11,* 125–130.

Huynh, H., & Barton, K. (2006). Performance of students with disabilities under regular and oral administration of a high stakes reading examination. *Applied Measurement in Education, 19,* 21–39.

Huynh, H., Meyer, J. P., & Gallant, D. J. (2004). Comparability of student performance between regular and oral administrations for a high-stakes mathematics test. *Applied Measurement in Education, 17,* 39–57.

Ikeda, M. J., & Gustafson, J. K. (2002). *Heartland AEA 11's problem solving process: Impact on issues related to special education* (Research Report. No. 2002-01). Johnston, IA: Heartland Area Education Agency.

Ikeda, M. J., Rahn-Blakeslee, A., Niebling, B. C., Gustafson, J. K., Allison, R., & Stumme, J. (2007). The Heartland Area Educational Agency 11 problem-solving approach: An overview and lesson learned. In S. R. Jimerson, M. K., Burns, & A. M. VanDerHeyden (Eds.), *Handbook of response to intervention* (pp. 255–268). New York: Springer.

Inclusive Solutions. (n.d.). *Person centered planning*. Retrieved from http://www.inclusive-solutions.com/pcplanning.asp

Individuals with Disabilities Education Act of 1990, Pub. L. No. 101-476, 104 Stat. 1142.

Individuals with Disabilities Education Act of 1997, Pub. L. No. 105-17, 105 Stat. 37.

Individuals with Disabilities Education Improvement Act of 2004, Pub. L. No. 108-446, 118 Stat. 2647.

Interactive Collaborative Autism Network. (n.d.). *Person centered planning*. Retrieved from http://www.autismnetwork.org/modules/social/pcp/index.html

Jackson, L., Ryndak, D. L., & Billingsly, F. (2000). Useful practices in inclusive education: A preliminary view of what experts in moderate to severe disabilities are saying. *Journal of the Association for Persons with Severe Handicaps, 25,* 129–141.

Jacob, S., & Hartshorne, T. S. (2007). *Ethics and law for school psychologists* (5th ed.). Hoboken, NJ: John Wiley & Sons.

Jarmulowicz, L., & Hay, S. E. (2009). Derivational morphophonology: Exploring morphophonology: Exploring errors in third graders' production [part of a forum on morphology and literacy]. *Language, Speech, and Hearing Services in Schools, 40,* 299–311.

Jegatheesan, B., Miller, P., & Fowler, S. (2010). Autism from a religious perspective: A study of parental beliefs in South Asian Muslim immigrant families. *Focus on Autism and Other Developmental Disabilities, 25*(2), 98–109.

Jenkins, J. R., Graff, J. J., & Miglioretti, D. L. (2009). Estimating reading growth using intermittent CBM progress monitoring. *Exceptional Children, 75*(2), 151–163.

Jenkins, J. R., & Jewell, M. (1993). Examining the validity of two measures for formative teaching: Reading aloud and maze. *Exceptional Children, 59,* 421–432.

Jennings, J. L., & Beveridge, A. A. (2009). How does test exemption affect schools' and students' academic performance? *Educational Evaluation and Policy Analysis, 31,* 153–175.

Jeynes, W. H. (2005). A meta-analysis of the relation of parental involvement to urban elementary school student academic achievement. *Urban Education, 40,* 237–239.

Jitendra, A. K., Sczesniak, E., & Deatline-Buchman, A. (2005). An exploratory validation of curriculum-based mathematical word problem-solving tasks as indicators of mathematics proficiency for third graders. *School Psychology Review, 34,* 358–371.

Johns, J. L. (2005). *Basic reading inventory* (9th ed.). Dubuque, IA: Kendall/Hunt.

Johnson, E. (2000). The effects of accommodations on performance assessments. *Remedial and Special Education, 21,* 261–267.

Johnstone, C. J., Altman, J., Thurlow, M. L., & Thompson, S. J. (2006). *A summary of research on the effects of test accommodations: 2002 through 2004* (Technical Report 45). Minneapolis, MN: University of Minnesota, National Center on Educational Outcomes.

Joint Committee on Testing Practices. (2005). Code of fair testing practices in education (Revised). *Educational Measurement, 24,* 2–9.

Jones, E. D., Southern, W. S., & Brigham, F. J. (1998). Curriculum-based assessment: Testing what is taught and teaching what is tested. *Intervention in School and Clinic, 33,* 239–249.

Jones, M. L. (2009). A study of novice special educators' views of evidence-based practices. *Teacher Education and Special Education, 32*(2), 101–120.

Jonsson, A., & Svingby, G. (2007). The use of scoring rubrics: Reliability, validity and educational consequences. *Educational Research Review, 2,* 130–144.

Jordan, N. C., & Hanich, L. (2000). Mathematical thinking in second-grade children with different forms of LD.

Journal of Learning Disabilities, 33, 567–578.

Juel, C. (1988). Learning to read and write: A longitudinal study of 54 children from first through fourth grades. *Journal of Educational Psychology, 80,* 437–447.

Juleus Chapman et al. v. California Department of Education et al., 2001, No. C01-1780.

Kaestle, C. F. (2001). The common school. In S. Mondale & S. B. Patton (Eds.), *School: The story of American public education* (pp. 11–17). Boston: Beacon Press.

Kalyanpur, M., & Harry, B. (1999). *Culture in special education: Building reciprocal family–professional relationships.* Baltimore, MD: Brookes.

Kauffman, J. M. (1996). Research to practice issues. *Behavioral Disorders, 22,* 55–60.

Kauffman, J. M., & Konold, T. R. (2007). Making sense in education: Pretense (including No Child Left Behind) and realities in rhetoric and policy about schools and schooling. *Exceptionality, 15,* 75–96.

Kauffman, J. M., & Lloyd, J. W. (1995). A sense of place: The importance of placement issues in contemporary special education. In J. M. Kauffman, J. W. Lloyd, D. P. Hallahan & T. A. Astuto (Eds.), *Issues in educational placement: Students with emotional and behavioral disorders* (pp. 3–19). Hillsdale, NJ: Erlbaum.

Kaufman, A. S., & Kaufman, N. L. (2004). *Kaufman Test of Educational Achievement, Second Edition (KTEA-II).* Circle Pines, MN: American Guidance Service.

Kavale, K. A. (2002). Mainstreaming to full inclusion: From orthogenesis to pathogenesis of an idea. *International Journal of Disability, Development and Education, 49,* 201–214.

Kavale, K. A., & Forness, S. R. (1985). *The science of learning disabilities.* San Diego, CA: College-Hill Press.

Kavale, K. A., & Forness, S. R. (2000). Policy decision in special education: The role of meta-analysis. In R. M. Gersten, E. P. Schiller, & S. Vaughn (Eds.), *Contemporary special education research: Syntheses of the knowledge base on critical instructional issues* (pp. 281–326). Mahwah, NJ: Erlbaum.

Kavale, K. A., Kauffman, J. M., Bachmeier, R. J., & LeFever, G. B. (2008). Response-to-intervention: Separating the rhetoric of self-congratulation from the reality of specific learning disability identification. *Learning Disability Quarterly, 31*(3), 135–150.

Kazdin, A. E. (2010). *Single case research designs: Methods for clinical and applied settings* (2nd ed.). New York: Oxford University Press.

Keen, S., & Davey, B. (1987). Effects of computer-presented text on LD adolescents reading behaviors. *Learning Disabilities Quarterly, 19,* 283–290.

Ketterlin-Geller, L. R., Alonzo, J., Braun-Monegan, J., & Tindal, G. (2007). Recommendations for accommodations: Implications of (in)consistency. *Remedial and Special Education, 28,* 194–206.

Ketterlin-Geller, L., Yovanoff, P., & Tindal, G. (2007). Developing a new paradigm for conducting research on accommodations in mathematics testing. *Exceptional Children, 73*(3), 331–347.

Keyes, M. W., & Owens-Johnson, L. (2003). Developing person-centered IEPs. *Intervention in School & Clinic, 38,* 145–152.

Kilpatrick, J., Swafford, J., & Finell, B. (Eds.). (2001). *Adding it up: Helping children learn mathematics.* Washington, DC: National Academy Press.

Kirby v. Cabell Board of Education, 46 IDELR 156 (D. W.VA. 2006).

Kleinert, H. L., Haig, J., Kearns, J. F., & Kennedy, S. (2000). Alternate assessments: Lessons learned and roads to be taken. *Exceptional Children, 67,* 51–66.

Klingner, J. K., & Edwards, P. A. (2006). Cultural considerations with response to intervention models. *Reading Research Quarterly, 41*(1), 108–117.

Klingner, J. K., Vaughn, S., Schumm, J. S., Cohen, P., & Forgan, J. W. (1998). Inclusion or pull-out: Which do students prefer? *Journal of Learning Disabilities, 31,* 148–158.

Kortteinen, H., Närhi, V., & Ahonen, T. (2009). Does IQ matter in adolescents' reading disability? *Learning and Individual Differences, 19,* 257–261. doi: 10.1016/j.lindif.2009.01.003

Kratochwill, T. R., Clements, M. A., & Kalymon, K. M. (2007). Response to intervention: Conceptual and methodological issues in implementation. In S. R. Jimerson, M. K. Burns, & A. M. VanDerHeyden (Eds.), *Handbook of response to intervention* (pp. 25–52). New York: Springer.

Krom, D. M., & Prater, M. A. (1993). IEP goals for intermediate-aged students with mild mental retardation. *Career Development for Exceptional Individuals, 16,* 87–95.

Kucer, S. B. (2008). Speed, accuracy, and comprehension in the reading of elementary students. *Journal of Reading Education, 34,* 33–38.

Kurns, S., & Tilly, W. D. (2008). *Response to intervention blueprints for implementation: School building level.* Alexandria, VA: National Association of State Directors of Special Education.

Laitusis, C. C. (2007). Research designs and analysis for studying accommodations on assessments. In C. C. Laitusis & L. L. Cook (Eds.), *Large-scale assessment and accommodations: What works?* (pp. 67–79). Arlington, VA: Council for Exceptional Children.

Laitusis, C. C., & Cook, L. L. (2007). *Large-scale assessment and accommodations: What works?* Arlington, VA: Council for Exceptional Children.

Lake, S. E. (2010). *Slippery slope! The IEP missteps every team must know—and how to avoid them.* Horsham, PA: LRP Publications.

Lambert, N., Nihira, K., & Leland, H. (1993). *AAMR Adaptive Behavior Scale—School: 2nd Edition.* Austin, TX: American Association on Mental Retardation.

Lamory, S. (2002). The effects of culture on special education services: Evil eyes, prayer meetings, and IEPs. *TEACHING Exceptional Children, 34*(5), 67–71.

Lancaster, P., & Lancaster, S. (2003). *The self-advocacy strategy* [CD-ROM]. Lawrence, KS: Edge Enterprises.

Landrum, T. J. (2000). Assessment for eligibility: Issues in identifying students with emotional or behavioral disorders. *Assessment for Effective Intervention 26*(1), 41–49.

Landrum, T. J., Cook, B. G., Tankersley, M. T., & Fitzgerald, S. (2002). Teachers' perceptions of the trustworthiness, useability, and accessibility of information from different sources. *Remedial and Special Education, 23*(1), 42–48.

Landrum, T. J., Cook, B. G., Tankersley, M., & Fitzgerald, S. (2007). Teacher perceptions of the usability of intervention information from personal versus data-based sources. *Education and Treatment of Children, 30,* 27–42.

Landrum, T. J., & McDuffie, K. A. (2010). Learning styles in the age of differentiated instruction. *Exceptionality, 18,* 6–17.

Landrum, T. J., & Tankersley, M. (2004). Science at the schoolhouse: An uninvited guest. *Journal of Learning Disabilities, 37,* 207–212.

Larsen, J. A., & Nippold, M. A. (2007). Morphological analysis in school-age children: Dynamic assessment of a word learning strategy. *Language, Speech, and Hearing Services in Schools, 38,* 201–212.

Lau, M. Y., Sieler, J. D., Muyskens, P., Canter, A., Vankeuren, B., & Marston, D. (2006). Perspectives on the use of the problem-solving model from the viewpoint of a school psychologist, administrator, and teacher from a large Midwest urban school district. *Psychology in the Schools, 43,* 117–127.

Layton, C. A., & Koenig, A. J. (1998). Increasing reading fluency in elementary students with low vision through repeated readings. *Journal of Visual Impairment & Blindness, 92,* 276–292.

Lazarus, S. S., Thurlow, M. L., Lail, K. E., & Christensen, L. (2009). A longitudinal analysis of state accommodations policies: Twelve years of change 1993–2005. *Journal of Special Education, 43,* 67–80.

Leafstedt, J. M., Richards, C., LaMonte, M., & Cassidy, D. (2007). Perspectives on co-teaching: Views from high school students with learning disabilities. *Learning Disabilities: A Multidisciplinary Journal, 14*(3), 177–184.

Lembke, E. S., & Foegen, A. (2009). Identifying early numeracy indicators for kindergarten and first-grade students. *Learning Disabilities Research & Practice, 24,* 12–20.

Lembke, E. S., Foegen, A., Whittaker, T. A., & Hampton, D. (2008). Establishing technically adequate measures of progress in early numeracy. *Assessment for Effective Intervention, 33,* 206–214.

Lerner, J. W. (2002). *Learning disabilities: Theories, diagnosis, and teaching strategies* (8th ed.). Boston: Houghton-Mifflin.

Levine, D. U., & Lezotte, L. W. (1990). *Unusually effective schools: A review and analysis of research and practice.* Madison, WI: National Center for Effective Schools Research and Development.

Lewandowski, L. J., Lovett, B. J., Parolin, R., Gordon, M., & Codding, R. S. (2007). Extended time accommodations and the mathematics performance of students with and without ADHD. *Journal of Psychoeducational Assessment, 25,* 17–28.

Lewandowski, L. J., Lovett, B. J., & Rogers, C. L. (2008). Extended time as a testing accommodation for students with reading disabilities: Does a rising tide lift all ships? *Journal of Psychoeducational Assessment, 26,* 315–324.

Lindstrom, J. H., & Gregg, N. (2007). The role of extended time on the SAT for students with learning disabilities and/or attention-deficit/hyperactivity disorder. *Learning Disabilities Research and Practice, 22,* 85–95.

Linn, R. L. (2002). Validation of the uses and interpretations of results of state assessment and accountability systems. In G. Tindal & M. Haladyna (Eds.), *Large-scale assessment programs for all students.* Mahwah, NJ: Erlbaum.

Lloyd, J. W. (2002). There's more to identifying learning disability than discrepancy. In R. Bradley, L., Danielson, & D. P. Hallahan (Eds.), *Identification of learning disabilities: Research to practice* (pp. 427–435). Mahwah, NJ: Erlbaum.

Lloyd, J. W., Pullen, P. C., Tankersley, M., & Lloyd, P. A. (2006). Critical dimensions of experimental studies and research syntheses that help define effective practice. In B. G. Cook & B. R. Schirmer (Eds.), *What is special about special education? Examining the role of evidence-based practices* (pp. 136–153). Austin, TX: Pro-Ed.

Loeber, R., Dishion, T. J., & Patterson, G. R. (1984). Multiple gating: A multistage assessment procedure for identifying youths at risk for delinquency. *Journal of Research on Crime and Delinquency, 21,* 7–32.

Lusthaus, C. S., Lusthaus, E. W., & Gibbs, H. (1981). Parents' role in the decision process. *Exceptional Children, 48,* 256–257.

Lynch, E. C., & Beare, P. L. (1990). The quality of IEP objectives and their relevance to instruction for students with mental retardation and behavioral disorders. *Remedial and Special Education, 11*(2), 48–55.

Lynch, E. W., & Stein, R. (1983). Perspectives on parent participation in special education. *Exceptional Education Quarterly, 3,* 56–63.

Lyon, G. R., Fletcher, J. M., Shaywitz, S. E., Shaywitz, B. A., Torgesen, J. K., Wood, F. B., . . . Olson, R. K. (2001). Rethinking learning disabilities. In C. E. Finn, Jr., R. A. J. Rotherham, & C. R. Hokanson, Jr. (Eds.), *Rethinking special education for a new century* (pp. 259–287). Washington, DC: Thomas B. Fordham Foundation and Progressive Policy Institute.

Lytle, R. K., & Bordin, J. (2001). Enhancing the IEP team: Strategies for teachers and professionals. *TEACHING Exceptional Children, 33*(5), 40–44.

MacMillan, D. L., & Forness, S. R. (1998). The role of IQ in special education placement decisions: Primary and determinative or peripheral and inconsequential? *Remedial and Special Education, 19*(4), 239.

MacMillan, D. L., & Siperstein, G. N. (2002). Learning disabilities as operationally defined by schools. In R. Bradley, L. Danielson, & D. P. Hallahan (Eds.), *Identification of learning disabilities: Research to practice* (pp. 287–333). Mahwah, NJ: Erlbaum.

MacMillan, D., & Turnbull, A. P. (1983). Parent involvement in special education: Respecting individual preferences. *Education and Training of the Mentally Retarded, 18,* 4–9.

Madelaine, A., & Wheldall, K. (2005). Identifying low-progress readers: Comparing teacher judgment with a curriculum-based measurement procedure. *International Journal of Disability, Development and Education, 52,* 33–42.

Madison Wisconsin Metropolitan School District. (n.d.). Student intervention monitoring system. Retrieved from http://dpi.wi.gov/rti/sims2.html

Mager, R. (1962). *Preparing instructional objectives.* Palo Alto, CA: Fearon Press.

Malecki, C. K., & Demaray, M. K. (2007). Social behavior assessment and response to intervention. In S. R. Jimerson, M. K. Burns, & A. M. VanDerHeyden (Eds.), *Handbook of response to intervention* (pp. 161–171). New York: Springer.

Malouf, D. B., & Schiller, E. P. (1995). Practice and research in special education. *Exceptional Children, 61,* 414–424.

Marcotte, A. M., & Hintze, J. M. (2009). Incremental and predictive utility of formative assessment methods of reading comprehension. *Journal of School Psychology, 47,* 315–335.

Mardell, C., & Goldenberg, D. S. (1998). *DIAL-3: Developmental Indicators for the Assessment of Learning, 3rd Edition.* Bloomington, MN: Pearson Assessment.

Marston, D. (1982). *The technical adequacy of direct, repeated measurement of academic skills in low-achieving elementary students.* Unpublished doctoral dissertation, University of Minnesota, Minneapolis.

Marston, D. B. (1989). A curriculum-based measurement approach to assessing academic performance: What it is and why do it. In M. R. Shinn (Ed.), *Curriculum-based measurement: Assessing special children.* New York: Guilford Press.

Marston, D., Muyskens, P., Lau, M., & Canter, A. (2003). Problem-solving model for decision making with high-incidence disabilities: The Minneapolis experience. *Learning Disabilities: Research & Practice, 18*(3), 187–200.

Martin, J. E., Marshall, L. H., Maxson, L. M., & Jerman, R. L. (1997). *The Self-Directed IEP.* Longmont, CO: Sopris West.

Martin, J. E., Marshall, L. H., & Sale, P. (2004). A 3-year study of middle, junior high and high school IEP meetings. *Exceptional Children, 70,* 285–297.

Martin, J. E., Van Dycke, J. L., Christensen, W. R., Greene, B. A., Gardner, J. E., & Lovett, D. L. (2006). Increasing student participation in IEP meetings: Establishing the Self-Directed IEP as an evidenced-based practice. *Exceptional Children, 72,* 299–316.

Martin, J. E., Van Dycke, J. L., Greene, B. A., Gardner, J. E., Christensen, W. R., Woods, L. L., & Lovett, D. L. (2006). Direct observation of teacher-directed IEP meetings: Establishing the need for student IEP meeting instruction. *Exceptional Children, 72,* 187–200.

Martin, K. F., Lloyd, J. W., Kauffman, J. M., & Coyne, M. (1995). Teachers' perceptions of educational placement decisions for pupils with emotional or behavioral disorders. *Behavioral Disorders, 20,* 106–117.

Mather, N., & Kaufman, N. (2006). Introduction to the special issue, part one: It's about the *what,* the *how well,* and the *why. Psychology in the Schools, 43*(7), 747–752.

Mattingly, D. J., Prislin, R., McKenzie, T. L., Rodriguez, J. L., & Kayzar, B. (2002). Evaluating evaluations: The case of parent involvement programs. *Review of Educational Research, 72,* 549–576.

May, K. (2009). By reason thereof: Causation and eligibility under the Individuals with Disabilities Education Act, *BYU Education and Law Journal,* (1), 173–195.

McComas, J. J., Wacker, D. P., Cooper, L. J., Asmus, J. M., Richman, D., & Stoner, B. (1996). Brief experimental analysis of stimulus prompts for accurate responding on academic tasks in an outpatient clinic. *Journal of Applied Behavior Analysis, 29,* 397–401.

McConaughy, S. H., Kay, P. L., & Fitzgerald, M. (1999). The achieving, behaving, caring project for preventing ED: Two-year outcomes. *Journal of Emotional and Behavioral Disorders, 7,* 224–239.

McGahee-Kovac, M. (1995). *Student-led IEPs.* Washington DC: National Information Center for Children and Youth with Disabilities.

McGuinness, D. (1997). Decoding strategies as predictors of reading skill: a follow-on [study of first- and third-grade children]. *Annals of Dyslexia, 47,* 117–150.

McKenna, M. C., & Picard, M. (2006). Revisiting the role of miscue analysis in effective teaching. *The Reading Teacher, 60,* 378–380.

McKevitt, B. C., & Elliott, S. N. (2003). Effects and perceived consequences of using read-aloud and teacher-recommended test accommodations on a reading achievement test. *School Psychology Review, 32,* 583–600.

McLaughlin, M. J., & Warren, S. H. (1995). *Individual education programs: Issues and options for change* (Final Report for the Office of Special Education Programs). Alexandria, VA: National Association of State Directors of Special Education.

McLoughlin, J. A., & Lewis, R. B. (2008). *Assessing students with special needs* (7th ed.). Upper Saddle River, NJ: Merrill/Pearson.

McMaster, K. L., Fuchs, D., Fuchs, L. S., & Compton, D. L. (2005). Responding to nonresponders: An experimental field trial of identification and intervention methods. *Exceptional Children, 71,* 445–464.

McMaster, K. L., Fuchs, D., Saenz, L., Lemons, C., Kearns, D., Yen, L., . . . Fuchs, L. S. (2010). Scaling up PALS: The importance of implementing evidence-based practice with fidelity and flexibility. *New Times for DLD, 28*(1), 1–3. Retrieved from http://www.teachingld.org/pdf/NewTimes_ScalingUpPals2010.pdf

McMaster, K. L., & Wagner, D. (2007). Monitoring response to general education instruction. In S. R. Jimerson, M. K. Burns, & A. M. VanDerHeyden (Eds.), *Handbook of response to intervention: The science and practice of assessment and intervention* (pp. 223–233). New York: Springer.

McNair, J., & Rusch, F. R. (1991). Parent involvement in transition programs. *Mental Retardation, 29,* 93–101.

McNamara, K., & Hollinger, C. (2003). Intervention-based assessment: Evaluation rates and eligibility findings. *Exceptional Children, 69,* 181–194.

McWilliam, R. A., Tocci, L., & Harbin, G. L. (1998). Family-centered services: Service providers' discourse and behavior. *Topics in Early Childhood Special Education, 18,* 206–221.

Mead, J. F., & Paige, M. A. (2008). *Board of Education of Hendrick Hudson v. Rowley*: An examination of its precedential impact. *Journal of Law & Education, 37,* 329–345.

Mellard, D. F., & Johnson, E. (2008). *RTI: A practitioner's guide to implementing response to intervention.* Thousand Oaks, CA: Corwin Press.

Meloy, L., Deville, C., & Frisbie, D. (2002). The effect of a read aloud accommodation on test scores of students with and without a learning disability in reading. *Remedial and Special Education, 23,* 248–255.

Menlove, R. R., Hudson, P. J., & Suter, D. (2001). A field of IEP dreams: Increasing general education teacher participation in the IEP development process. *Teaching Exceptional Children, 33*(5), 28–33.

Mercer, C. D., & Pullen, P. C. (2005). *Students with learning disabilities* (7th ed.). Upper Saddle River, NJ: Merrill/Pearson Education.

Merulla, E., & McKinnon, A. (1982). 'Stuck' on Deno's cascade. *Journal of Learning Disabilities, 15,* 94–96.

Messick, S. (1988). The once and future issues of validity: Assessing the meaning and consequences of measurement. In H. Wainer & H. I. Braun (Eds.), *Test validity* (pp. 22–45). Hillsdale, NJ: Erlbaum.

Messick, S. (1995). Validity of psychological assessment: Validation of inferences from persons' responses and performances as scientific inquiry into score meaning. *American Psychologist, 50,* 741–749.

Michnowicz, L. L., McConnell, S. R., Peterson, C. A., & Odom, S. L. (1995). Social goals and objectives of preschool IEPs: A content analysis. *Journal of Early Intervention, 19,* 273–282.

Miller, D., Linn, R., & Gronlund, N. (2009). *Measurement and assessment in teaching,* (10th ed.). Upper Saddle River, NJ: Allyn & Bacon/Pearson.

Miner, C. A., & Bates, P. E. (1997). The effect of person centered planning on the IEP/Transition Planning process. *Education and Training in Mental Retardation and Developmental Disabilities, 32,* 105–112.

Minnesota Department of Education. (2009). *Minnesota manual of* accommodations: A guide to selecting, administering, and evaluating the use of test administration accommodations for students with disabilities. Roseville, MN: Author.

Mostert, M. P. (Ed.). (2010). Empirically unsupported interventions in special education [special issue]. *Exceptionality, 18*(1).

Mostert, M. P., & Crockett, J. B. (2000). Reclaiming the history of special education for more effective practice. *Exceptionality, 8,* 133–143.

Mount, B., & Zwernik, K. (1988). *It's never too early, it's never too late: A booklet about personal futures planning.* St. Paul, MN: Minnesota Governor's Planning Council on Developmental Disabilities.

Musson, J. E., Thomas, M. K., Towles-Reeves, E., & Kearns, J. F. (2010). An analysis of state alternate assessment participation guidelines. *The Journal of Special Education, 44,* 67–78.

Naglieri, J. A. (1997). *Naglieri Nonverbal Ability Test.* San Antonio, TX: Psychological Corporation.

National Council of Accreditation for Teacher Education. (n.d.). *Assessing the assessments: Fairness, accuracy, consistency, and the avoidance of bias in NCATE standard 2.* Washington, DC: Author.

National Reading Panel. (2000). *Teaching children to read: An evidence-based assessment of the scientific research literature on reading and its implications for reading instruction. reports of the subgroups.* Bethesda, MD: National Institute for Literacy.

National Secondary Transition Technical Assistance Center. (n.d.). Research to practice lesson plan starter: IEP meeting involvement using person-centered planning. Retrieved from http://www.nsttac.org/LessonPlanLibrary/2_27_35.pdf

National Universal Design for Learning Task Force. (2007). Universal design for learning classroom scenarios. Retrieved from http://www.advocacyinstitute.org/UDL/classroom_scenarios.shtml

Neil, M. (2008). *Improving accountability: A review of grading education.* Boston: National Center for Fair and Open Testing. Retrieved from http://www.fairtest.org/improving-accountability-review-grading-education

Newborg, J. (2005). *Battelle Developmental Inventory, 2nd Edition: Examiner's manual.* Itasca, IL: Riverside.

Nickles, J. L., Cronis, T. G., Justen, J. E. I., & Smith, G. J. (1992). Individualized education programs: A comparison of students with BD, LD, and MMR. *Intervention in School and Clinic, 28*(1), 41–44.

Nilsson, N. L. (2008). A critical analysis of eight Informal Reading Inventories. *The Reading Teacher, 61,* 526–536.

Nishioka, V. (2001). *Similarities and differences in the personal and ecological characteristics of middle school boys with emotional disturbance, learning disabilities, and social maladjustment.* Eugene: Institute on Violence and Destructive Behavior, University of Oregon.

No Child Left Behind Act of 2001, Pub. L. No. 107-110, 115 Stat. 1425 et seq. (2001). Noell, G. H., Duhon, G. J., Gatti, S. L., & Connell, J. E. (2002). Consultation, follow-up, and implementation of behavior management interventions in general education. *School Psychology Review, 31,* 217–234.

Noell, G. H., & Gansle, K. A. (2006). Assuring the form has substance: Treatment plan implementation as the foundation of assessing response to intervention. *Assessment for Effective Intervention, 32*(1), 32–39.

Noell, G. H., Gresham, F. M., & Gansle, K. A. (2002). Does treatment integrity matter? A preliminary investigation of instructional implementation and mathematics performance. *Journal of Behavioral Education, 11,* 51–67.

Noell, G. H., Witt, J. C., Slider, N. J., Connell, J. E., Gatti, S. L., Williams, K. L., & Duhon, G. J. (2005). Treatment implementation following behavioral consultation in schools: A comparison of three follow-up strategies. *School Psychology Review, 34,* 87–106.

Nolet, V. (2005). *Accessing the general curriculum: Including students with disabilities in standards-based reform* (2nd ed.). Thousand Oaks, CA: Corwin Press.

Noon v. Alaska State Board of Education & Early Development, Case No. A04-0057 CV (JKS) (Settle Agreement). 2004

Northwest Evaluation Association. (2003). *Technical manual for the NWEA measures of academic progress and achievement level tests.* Lake Oswego, OR: Author.

Northwest Evaluation Association. (2009). *Testing season checklist: A complete guide to your MAP testing season.* Retrieved from http://www.nwea.org/support/checklist.aspx?key=TestImplementation

Notari, A. R. (1988). The utility of a criterion-referenced instrument in the development of individual education plan goals for infants and young children. *Dissertation Abstracts International, 49*(07), 1767A. (University Microfilms No. AAT88-14193)

O'Brien, C. L., & O'Brien, J. (2000). *The origins of person-centered planning: A community of practice perspective.* Atlanta, GA: Responsive Systems Associates. Retrieved from http://thechp.syr.edu/PCP_History.pdf

O'Brien, J., & Lyle, C. (1987). *Framework for accomplishment.* Decatur, GA: Responsive Systems Associates.

Office of Special Education Program. (2006). *28th Annual report to Congress on the implementation of IDEA.* Retrieved from http://www.ideadata.org/tables30th/ar_1-7.htm

O'Leary, E. L., M., & Doty, D. (2001). *Transition requirements checklist.* Washington, DC: U.S. Department of Education Office of Special Education.

Oosterhof, A. (2009). *Developing and using classroom assessments* (4th ed.). Upper Saddle River, NJ: Pearson.

O'Shaughnessy, T. E., & Swanson, H. L. (2000). A comparison of two reading interventions for children with reading disabilities. *Journal of Learning Disabilities, 33,* 257–277.

Otaiba, S., & Lake, V. E. (2007). Preparing special educators to teach reading and use curriculum-based assessments. *Reading and Writing, 20,* 591–617.

Overton, T. (2009). *Assessing learners with special needs: An applied approach* (6th ed.). Upper Saddle River, NJ: Merrill/Pearson.

Owens, R. L., & Fuchs, L. S. (2002). Mathematical problem-solving strategy instruction for third-grade srtudents with learning disabilities. *Remedial & Special Education, 23,* 268–278.

Paris, S. G., & Carpenter, R. D. (2003). FAQs about IRIs. *Reading Teacher, 56,* 578–581.

Parker, R., Hasbrouck, J. E., & Tindal, G. (1992). The maze as a classroom-based reading measure: Construction methods, reliability, and validity. *The Journal of Special Education, 26,* 195–218.

Parnes, S. J. (1988). *Visionizing: State-of-the-art processes for encouraging innovative excellence.* East Aurora, NY: D.O.K. Publishing.

Parnes, S. J. (1992). *Source book for creative problem-solving: A fifty year digest of proven innovation processes.* Buffalo, NY: Creative Education Foundation Press.

Payne, L. D., Marks, L. J., & Bogan, B. L. (2007). Using curriculum-based assessment to address the academic and behavioral deficits of students with emotional and behavioral disorders. *Beyond Behavior, 16*(3), 3–6.

Pearpoint, J., O'Brien, J., & Forest, M. (1993). *PATH: A workbook for planning positive possible futures.* Toronto, Canada: Inclusion Press.

Phillips, L. M., Norris, S. P., Osmond, W. C., & Maynard, A. M. (2002). Relative reading achievement: A longitudinal study of 187 children from first through sixth grades. *Journal of Educational Psychology, 94,* 3–13.

Phillips, S. E. (1994). High stakes testing accommodations: Validity versus disabled rights. *Applied Measurement in Education, 7,* 93–120.

Pitoniak, M. J., & Royer, J. M. (2001). Testing accommodations for examinees with disabilities: A review of psychometric, legal, and social policy issues. *Review of Educational Research, 71*(1), 53–104.

Poggio, J., Glasnapp D. R., Yang, X., & Poggio, A. J. (2005). A comparative evaluation of score results from computerized and paper & pencil mathematics testing in a large scale state assessment program. *The Journal of Technology, Learning, and Assessment, 3*(6). Retrieved from http://www.jtla.org

Pomplun, M., Frey, S., & Becker, D. (2002). The score equivalence of paper-and-pencil and computerized versions of a speeded test of reading comprehension. *Educational and Psychological Measurement, 62*(2), 337–354. Retrieved from http://epm.sagepub.com

Poponi, D. M. (2009). *The relationship between student outcomes and parental involvement in multidisciplinary IEP team meetings.* Retrieved from http://digitalcommons.pcom.edu/psychology_dissertations/116

Powers, K. M., Gil-Kashiwabara, E., Geenen, S. J., Powers, L. E., Balandran, J., & Palmer, C. (2005). Mandates and effective transition planning practices reflected in IEPs. *Career Development for Exceptional Individuals, 28*(1), 47–59.

President's Commission on Excellence in Special Education. (2001). *A new era: Revitalizing special education for children and their families.* Washington, DC: Education Publications Center, U.S. Department of Education.

Pretti-Frontczak, K., & Bricker, D. (2000). Enhancing the quality of individual education plan (IEP) goals and objectives. *Journal of Early Intervention, 23*(2), 92–105.

Pretti-Frontczak, K., & Bricker, D. (2004). *An activity-based approach to early intervention* (3rd ed.). Baltimore: Brookes.

Prewitt, P. N. (1992). The relationship between the Kaufman Brief Intelligence Test (K-BIT) and the WISC-R with referred students. *Psychology in the Schools, 29,* 25–27.

Psychological Corporation. (2002). *Wechsler Individual Achievement Test* (2nd ed.). San Antonio, TX: Harcourt Assessment.

Rao, S. S. (2000). Perspectives of an African-American mother on parent-professional relationships in special education. *Mental Retardation, 38,* 475–488.

Rasheed, S. A., Fore, C., & Miller, S. (2006). Person-centered planning: Practices, promises, and provisos. *The Journal for Vocational Special Needs Education, 28*(3), 47–59.

Renaissance Learning. (1998). *STAR math.* Wisconsin Rapids, WI: Author.

Renaissance Learning. (2003). *STAR early literacy.* Wisconsin Rapids, WI: Author.

Reschly, D. J. (1996). Functional assessments and special education decision making. In W. Stainback & S. Stainback (Eds.), *Controversial issues confronting special education: Divergent perspectives* (2nd ed., pp. 115–128). Boston: Allyn & Bacon.

Reschly, D. J. (2005). Learning disabilities identification: Primary intervention, secondary intervention, and then what? *Journal of Learning Disabilities, 38*(6), 510–515.

Reschly, D. J., & Grimes, J. P. (2002). Best practices in intellectual assessment. In A. Thomas & J. Grimes (Eds.), *Best practices in school psychology* (vol. 4, pp. 1337–1350). Bethesda, MD: National Association of School Psychologists.

Reschly, D. J., & Hosp, J. L. (2004). State LD identification policies and practices. *Learning Disability Quarterly, 27*(4), 197–213.

Reschly, D. J., & Wilson, M. S. (1995). School psychology faculty and practitioners: 1986 to 1991 trends in demographic characteristics, roles, satisfaction, and system reform. *School Psychology Review, 24,* 62–80.

Reynolds, C. R., & Kamphaus, R. W. (1992). *Behavior Assessment System for Children, 2nd Edition: Manual.* Circle Pines, MN: American Guidance.

Rezaei, A., & Lovorn, M. (2010). Reliability and validity of rubrics for assessment through writing. *Assessing Writing, 15,* 18–39.

Rodger, S. (1995). Individual education plans revisited: A review of the literature. *International Journal of Disability, Development, and Education, 42,* 221–239.

Rose, D. H., & Meyer, A. (2006). *A practical reader in universal design for learning.* Cambridge, MA: Harvard Education Press.

Rothstein, R., Jacobsen, R., & Wilder, T. (2008). *Grading education: Getting accountability right.* Williston, VT: Teachers College Press.

Rozalski, M., Stewart, A., & Miller, J. (2010). How to determine the least restrictive environment for students with disabilities. *Exceptionality, 18,* 151–163.

Rust, J., & Golombok, S. (2009). *Modern psychometrics: The science of psychological assessment* (3rd ed.). New York: Routledge.

Sagan, C. (1996). *The demon-haunted world: Science as a candle in the dark.* New York: Ballantine.

Salembier, G., & Furney, K. S. (1994). Promoting self-advocacy and family participation in transition planning. *Journal for Vocational Special Needs Education, 17*(1), 12–17.

Salembier, G., & Furney, K. S. (1997). Facilitating participation: Parents' perceptions of their involvement in the IEP/transition planning process. *Career Development for Exceptional Individuals, 20*(l), 29–42.

Sandler, C., & Sugai, G. (2009). Effective behavior and instructional support: A district model for early identification of reading and behavior problems. *Journal of Positive Interventions and Supports, 11,* 35–46

Sandomierski, T., Kincaid, D., & Algozzine, B. (2007). Response to intervention and positive behavior support: Brothers from different mothers or sisters with different misters? *Positive Behavior Interventions and Supports Newsletter, 4*(2). Retrieved from http://pbis.org/news/New/Newsletters/Newsletter4-2.aspx

Sasso, G. M., Conroy, M. A., Stichter, J. P., & Fox, J. J. (2001). Slowing down the bandwagon: The misapplication of functional assessment for students with emotional or behavioral disorders. *Behavioral Disorders, 26,* 282–296.

Schulte, A., Elliott, S., & Kratochwill, T. (2001). Effects of testing accommodations on standardized mathematics test scores: An experimental analysis of the performances of students with and without disabilities. *School Psychology Review, 30,* 527–547.

Scruggs, T. M., & Mastropieri, M. A. (2000). The effectiveness of mnemonic instruction for students with learning and behavior problems: An update and research synthesis. *Journal of Behavioral Education, 10,* 163–173.

Scullin, M. H. (2006). Large state-level fluctuations in mental retardation classifications related to introduction of renormed intelligence test. *American Journal of Mental Retardation, 111*(5), 322–335.

Severson, H. H., Walker, H. M., Hope-Doolittle, J., Kratochwill, T. R., Gresham, F. M. (2007). Proactive, early screening to detect behaviorally at-risk students: Issues, approaches, emerging innovations, and professional practices. *Journal of School Psychology, 45,* 193–223.

Shapiro, E. S., Edwards, L., & Zigmond, N. (2005). Progress monitoring of mathematics among students with learning disabilities. *Assessment for Effective Intervention, 30*(2), 15–32.

Share, D. L., Jorm, A. F., MacLean, R., & Matthews, R. (1984). Sources of individual differences in reading acquisition. *Journal of Educational Psychology, 76,* 1309–1324.

Shearin, A., Roessler, R., & Schriner, K. (1999). Evaluating the transition component in IEPs of secondary students with disabilities. *Rural Special Education Quarterly, 18*(2), 22–35.

Shermer, M. (2002). *Why people believe weird things.* New York: Henry Holt.

Shin, J. S., Deno, S. L., & Espin, C. (2000). Technical adequacy of the maze task for curriculum-based measurement of reading growth. *Journal of Special Education, 34,* 164–172.

Shinn, M. R. (1989). *Curriculum-based measurement: Assessing special children.* New York: Guilford Press.

Shinn, M. R. (1998). *Advanced applications of curriculum-based measurement.* New York: Guilford Press.

Shinn, M. R., Good, R. H., Knutson, N., Tilly, W. D., & Collins, V. L. (1992). Curriculum-based measurement reading fluency: A confirmatory analysis of its relation to reading. *School Psychology Review, 21,* 459–479.

Shinn, M. R., Habedank, L., & Good, R. H. (1993). The effects of classroom reading performance data on general education teachers' and parents' attitudes about reintegration. *Exceptionality, 4,* 205–228.

Shinn, M. R., & Marston, D. (1985). Differentiating mildly handicapped, low-achieving and regular education students: A curriculum-based measurement approach. *Remedial and Special Education, 6,* 31–45.

Shinn, M. R., & McConnell, S. M. (1994). Improving general education instruction: Relevance to school psychologists. *School Psychology Review, 23*(3), 351–371.

Shinn, M. R., Ysseldyke, J. E., Deno, S. L., & Tindal, G. (1986). A comparison of differences between students labeled learning disabled and low achieving on measures of classroom performance. *Journal of Learning Disabilities, 19,* 545–552.

Shriner, J. G., Carty, S. J., Trach, J., Weber, R., & Yell, M. (April, 2008). *Research on standards-based IEPs: Development of a web-based decision model.* Paper presented at the annual meeting of the Council of Exceptional Children, Boston.

Shriner, J. G., & Destefano, L. (2003). Participation and accommodation in state assessment: The role of Individualized Education Programs. *Exceptional Children, 69,* 147–161.

Sileo, T. W., Sileo, A. P., & Prater, M. A. (1996). Parent and professional partnerships in special education: Multicultural considerations. *Intervention in School and Clinic, 31,* 145–153.

Simon, J. B. (2006). Perceptions of the IEP requirement. *Teacher Education and Special Education, 29,* 225–235.

Sireci, S. G. (2006). *Test accommodations and test validity: Issues, research findings, and unanswered questions.* Amherst, MA: University of Massachusetts [PowerPoint Slides]. Retrieved from cehd.umn.edu/NCEO/Teleconferences/tele12/TestAccommTestValidity.ppt

Sireci, S. G., Li, S., & Scarpati, S. (2003). *The effects of test accommodations on test performance: A review of the literature.* Retrieved from www.education.umn.edu/NCEO/OnlinePubs/TestAccommLitReview.pdf

Sireci, S. G., Scarpati, S., & Li, S. (2005). Test accommodations for students with disabilities: An analysis of the interaction hypothesis. *Review of Educational Research, 75,* 457–490.

Skiba, R. J., Poloni-Staudinger, L., Gallini, S., Simmons, A. B., & Feggins-Azziz, R. (2006). Disparate access: The disproportionality of African American students with disabilities across educational environments. *Exceptional Children, 72*(4), 411–424.

Skinner, D. G., Correa, V., Skinner, M., & Bailey, D. (2001). Role of religion in the lives of Latino families of young children with developmental delays. *American Journal on Mental Retardation, 106*, 297–313.

Slate, J. R., & Saudargas, R. A. (1986). Differences in the classroom behaviors of behaviorally disordered and regular class children. *Behavioral Disorders, 12*, 45–53.

Smith, A. (2003). Scientifically based research and evidence-based education: A federal policy context. *Research and Practice for Persons with Severe Disabilities, 28*, 126–132.

Smith, S. W. (1987). *Program evaluation for procedural and substantive efficacy* (PEPSE) Unpublished manuscript. University of Kansas, Special Education Department, Lawrence.

Smith, S. W. (1990a). Comparison of individualized education programs (IEPs) of students with behavioral disorders and learning disabilities. *The Journal of Special Education, 24*, 85–100.

Smith, S. W. (1990b). Individualized education programs (IEPs) in special education: From intent to acquiescence. *Exceptional Children, 57*, 6–14.

Smith, S. W., Daunic, A. P., & Taylor, G. G. (2007). Treatment validity in applied educational research: Expanding the adoption and application of measures to ensure evidence-based practices (Report). *Education and Treatment of Children, November 1.*

Smith, T. E. C., & Patton, J. R. (1998). *Section 504 and public schools: A practical guide for determining eligibility, developing accommodation plans, and documenting compliance.* Austin, TX: Pro-Ed.

Smull, M. W., & Sanderson, H. (2005). *Essential lifestyle planning for everyone.* London: Helen Sanderson.

Snow, C. E., Burns, M. S., & Griffin, P. (1998). *Preventing reading difficulties in young children.* Washington, DC: National Academies Press.

Snyder, E. P., & Shapiro, E. S. (1997). Teaching students with emotional/behavioral disorders the skills to participate in the development of their own IEPs. *Behavioral Disorders, 22*, 246–259.

Sontag, J. C., & Schacht, R. (1994). An ethnic comparison of parent participation and information needs in early

intervention. *Exceptional Children, 60*, 422–433.

Sopko, K. M. (2003). *The IEP: A synthesis of current literature since 1997* (Information Analyses). Alexandria, VA: National Association of State Directors of Special Education.

Spann, S. J., Kohler, F. W., & Soenksen, D. (2003). Examining parents' involvement in and perceptions of special education services: An interview with families in a parent support group. *FOCUS on Autism and Other Developmental Disabilities, 18*, 228–237.

Sparrow, S. S., Cicchetti, D. V., & Balla, D. A. (2005). *Vineland Adaptive Behavior Scales, 2nd Edition.* Minneapolis, MN: Pearson Assessment. Special Education Elementary Longitudinal Study. (2005). *SEELS data documentation and dictionary: Introduction.* Washington, DC: U.S. Office of Special Education Programs.

Spectrum K12 School Solutions. (2009). *Response to intervention adoption survey 2009.* Towson, MD: Author.

Speece, D. L. (2002). Classification of learning disabilities: Convergence, expansion, and caution. In R. Bradley, L. Danielson, & D. Hallahan (Eds.), *Learning disabilities: Research to practice* (pp. 279–285). Mahwah, NJ: Erlbaum.

Speece, D. L., & Case, L. P. (2001). Classification in context: An alternative approach to *Speech, and Hearing Services in Schools, 38*, 201–212.

Spicuzza, R., Ysseldyke, J., Lemkuil, A., Kosciolek, S., Boys, C., & Teeluchsingh, E. (2001). Effects of curriculum-based monitoring on classroom instruction and math achievement. *Journal of School Psychology, 39*, 521–542.

Stecker, P. M., & Fuchs, L. S. (2000). Effecting superior achievement using curriculum-based measurement: The importance of individual progress monitoring. *Learning Disability Research and Practice, 15*, 128–134.

Stecker, P. M., Fuchs, L. S., & Fuchs, D. (2005). Using curriculum-based measurement to improve student achievement: A review of research. *Psychology in the Schools, 42*, 795–818.

Stiggins, R. J. (2001). *Student-involved classroom assessment* (3rd ed.).

Upper Saddle River, NJ: Merrill/Pearson.

Stiggins, R. (2005). From formative assessment to assessment FOR learning: A path to success in standards-based schools. *Phi Delta Kappan, 87*, 324–328.

Stiggins, R. J. (2007). Five assessment myths and their consequences. *Education Week, 27*(8), 28–29. Retrieved from www.childrensprogress.com/documents/2007_10_07_EducationWeek.pdf

Stith, S., Pruitt, I., Dees, J., Fronce, M., Green, N., Som, A., & Linkh, D. (2006). Implementing community-based prevention programming: A review of the literature. *Journal of Primary Prevention, 27*, 599–617.

Straetmans, G., & Eggen, T. (1998). Comparison of test administration procedures for placement decisions in a mathematics course. *Educational Research and Evaluation, 4*, 259–275.

Stuebing, K. K., Fletcher, J. M., LeDoux, J. M., Lyon, G. R., Shaywitz, S. E., & Shaywitz, B. A. (2002). Validity of IQ-discrepancy classifications of reading disabilities: A meta-analysis. *American Educational Research Journal, 39*(2), 469–518.

Swanson, H. L., Hoskyn, M., & Lee, C. (1999). *Interventions for students with learning disabilities: A meta-analysis of treatment outcomes.* New York: Guilford Press.

Tankersley, M., Harjusola-Webb, S., & Landrum, T. J. (2008). Using single-subject research to establish the evidence base of special education. *Intervention in School and Clinic, 44*, 83–90.

Taylor, S. J. (1988). Caught in the continuum: A critical analysis of the principle of the least restrictive environment. *Journal of the Association for Persons with Severe Handicaps, 13*(1), 41–53.

Test, D. W., Mason, C., Hughes, C., Konrad, M., Neale, M., & Wood, W. M. (2004). Student involvement in Individualized Education Program meetings. *Exceptional Children, 70*(4), 391–412.

Thompson, S., Blount, A., & Thurlow, M. (2002). *A summary of research on the effects of test accommodations: 1999 through 2001* (Technical

Report 34). Minneapolis, MN: University of Minnesota, National Center on Educational Outcomes.

Thompson, S. J., Quenemoen, R. F., & Thurlow, M. L. (2006). Factors to consider in the design of inclusive online assessments. In M. Hricko (Ed.), *Online assessment and measurement: foundations and challenges* (pp. 102–117). Hershey, PA: Information Science Publishing.

Thompson, S. J., Thurlow, M. L., & Malouf, D. (2004, May). Creating better tests for everyone through universally designed assessments. *Journal of Applied Testing Technology, 10*(2). Retrieved from http://www .testpublishers.org/atp.journal.htm

Thompson, T., Symons, F. J., & Felce, D. (2000). Principles of behavioral observation: Assumptions and strategies. In T. Thompson, D. Felce, & F. J. Symons (Eds.), *Behavioral observation: Technology and applications in developmental disabilities* (pp. 3–16). Baltimore: Brookes.

Thurlow, M. L. (2000). Standards-based reform and students with disabilities: Reflections on a decade of change. *Focus on Exceptional Children, 33*(3), 1–16.

Thurlow, M. L. (2007). State policies and accommodations: Issues and implications. In C. C. Laitusis & L. L. Cook (Eds.), *Large-scale assessment and accommodations: What works?* (pp. 13–22). Arlington, VA: Council for Exceptional Children.

Thurlow, M. L., Elliott, J. E., & Ysseldyke, J. E. (2003). *Testing students with disabilities: Practical strategies for complying with district and state requirements* (2nd ed.). Thousand Oaks, CA: Corwin.

Thurlow, M. L., Lazarus, S. S., & Christensen, L. L. (2008). Role of assessment accommodations in accountability. *Perspectives on Language and Learning, 34*(4), 17–20.

Thurlow, M. L., & Thompson, S. J. (2004). Inclusion of students with disabilities in state and district assessments. In J. E. Wall & G. R. Walz (Eds.), *Measuring up: Assessment issues for teachers, counselors, and administrators* (pp. 161–176). Austin, TX: Pro-Ed.

Thurlow, M. L., Ysseldyke, J. E., & Silverstein, B. (1993). *Testing accommodations for students with disabilities: A review of the literature* (Synthesis Report 4). Minneapolis, MN: University of Minnesota, National Center on Learning Disabilities.

Thurlow, M. L., Ysseldyke, J. E., & Silverstein, B. (1995). Testing accommodations for students with disabilities. *Remedial and Special Education, 16*, 260–270.

Tilly, W. D. (2003, December). *How many tiers are needed for successful prevention and early intervention?: Heartland Area Education Agency's evolution from four to three tiers.* Paper presented at the National Research Center on Learning Disabilities Responsiveness-to-Intervention Symposium, Kansas City, MO.

Tilly, W. D., Reschly, D. J., & Grimes, J. (1999). Eligibility determination in problem solving systems: Conceptual foundations and critical components. In D. J. Reschly, W. D. Tilly, III, & J. P. Grimes (Eds.), *Special education in transition* (pp. 221–251). Longmont, CO: Sopris West.

Timmons, J. R., & Whitney-Thomas, J. (1998). The most important member: Facilitating the focus person's participation in person centered planning. *Research in Practice, 4*(1), 3–6.

Tindal, G. A. (1992). Evaluating instructional programs using curriculum-based measurement: *Preventing School Failure, 36*, 39–44.

Tindal, G., & Fuchs, L. (2000). *A summary of research on test changes: An empirical basis for defining accommodations.* Lexington, KY: Mid-South Regional Resource Center. (ERIC Document Reproduction Service No. ED 442 245)

Tindal, G., Fuchs, L., Fuchs, D. Shinn, M., Deno, S., & Germann, G. (1983). *The technical adequacy of a basal reading series mastery test: The Scott-Foresman reading program* (Research Report No. 128). Minneapolis: University of Minnesota Institute for Research on Learning Disabilities.

Tindal, G., Germann, G., & Deno, S. L. (1983). *Descriptive research on the Pine County norms: A compilation of findings* (Research Report No. 132). Minneapolis: University of Minnesota Institute for Research on Learning Disabilities.

Tindal, G., & Nolet, V. (1995). Curriculum-based measurement in middle and high schools: Critical thinking skills in content areas. *Focus on Exceptional Children, 27*, 1–22.

Tindal, G. A., & Parker, R. (1991). Identifying measures for evaluating written expression. *Learning Disabilities Research and Practice, 6*, 211–218.

Tomlinson, C. A. (2003). *Fulfilling the promise of the differentiated classroom: Strategies and tools for responsive teaching.* Alexandria, VA: Association for Supervision and Curriculum Development.

Tone, B., & Farr, R. C. (1998). *Portfolio and performance assessment: Helping students evaluate their progress as readers and writers.* Fort Worth, TX: Harcourt Brace.

Torgesen, J. K., Alexander, A. W., Wagner, R. K., Rashotte, C. A., Voeller, K. K. S., & Conway, T. (2001). Intensive remedial instruction for children with severe reading disabilities: Immediate and long-term outcomes for two instructional approaches. *Journal of Learning Disabilities, 34*, 33–58.

Torgesen, J. K., & Bryant, B. R. (1994). *Test of Phonological Awareness.* Burlingame, CA: Psychological and Educational Publications.

Towles-Reeves, E., Kleinert, H., & Muhomba, M. (2009). Alternate assessment: Have we learned anything new? *Exceptional Children, 75*, 233–252.

Trainor, A. A. (2007). Person-centered planning in two culturally distinct communities: Responding to divergent needs and preferences. *Career Development for Exceptional Individuals, 30*, 92–103.

Turnbull, A. P., & Turnbull, H. R. (1990). *Families, professionals, and exceptionality: A special partnership.* Upper Saddle River, NJ: Merrill/ Pearson.

Turnbull, A., Turnbull, R., Erwin, E. J., Soodak, L. C., & Shogren, K. A. (2011). *Families, professionals, and exceptionality: Positive outcomes through partnerships and trust* (6th ed.). Upper Saddle River, NJ: Pearson.

Turnbull, A. P., Zuna, N., Hong, J. Y., Hu, X., Kyzar, K., Obremski, S., . . . Stowe, M. (2010). Knowledge-to-action guides: Preparing families to be partners in making educational decisions. *Teaching Exceptional Children, 42*(3), 42–53.

Turnbull, H. R., III. (2005). Individuals with Disabilities Education Act Reauthorization: Accountability and personal responsibility. *Remedial and Special Education, 26*, 320–326.

Turnbull, H. R., Turnbull, A., & Wheat, M. (1982). Assumptions about parent participation: A legislative history. *Exceptional Education Quarterly, 3*(2), 1–8.

Tylenda, B., Beckett, J., & Barrett, R. P. (2007). Assessing mental retardation using standardized intelligence tests. In J. L. Matson (Ed.), *Handbook of assessment in persons with intellectual disability* (vol. 34, pp. 27–97). Boston: Elsevier. U.S. Department of Education. (2001). *The No Child Left Behind Act of 2001.* Retrieved from http://www.ed.gov/legislation/ESEA02/

U.S. Department of Education. (2004). *The Individuals with Disabilities Education Improvement Act of 2004.* Retrieved from http://idea.ed.gov

U.S. Department of Education. (2010). *Memo: A Response to Intervention (RTI) process cannot be used to delay-deny an evaluation of eligibility under the Individuals with Disabilities Education Act (IDEA).* Retrieved from http://www5.esc13.net/thescoop/special/files/2011/01/RTI-Memo-1-21-111.pdf.

Vacc, N. A., Vallecorsa, A. L., Parker, A., Bonner, S., Lester, C., Richardson, S., & Yates, C. (1985). Parents' and educators' participation in IEP conferences. *Education and Treatment of Children, 8*(2), 153–162.

Vandercook, T., York, J., & Forest, M. (1989). The McGill Action Planning System (MAPS): A strategy for building the vision. *Journal of the Association for Persons with Severe Handicaps, 14*, 205–215.

VanDerHeyden, A. M., & Burns, M. K. (2005). Using curriculum-based assessment and curriculum-based measurement to guide elementary mathematics instruction: Effect on individual and group accountability scores. *Assessment for Effective Intervention, 30*(3), 15–29.

VanDerHeyden, A. M., & Burns, M. K. (2010). *Essentials of Response to Intervention.* New York: Wiley.

VanDerHeyden, A. M., Witt, J. C., & Gilbertson, D. A. (2007). Multiyear evaluation of the effects of a response to intervention (RtI) model on identification of children for special education. *Journal of School Psychology, 45,* 225–256.

VanDerHeyden, A. M., Witt, J. C., & Naquin, G. (2003). Development and validation of a process for screening referrals to special education. *School Psychology Review, 32,* 204–227.

Van Reusen, A. K., & Bos, C. S. (1990). IPLAN: Helping students communicate in planning conferences. *Teaching Exceptional Children, 22*(4), 30–32.

Vansickle, T. (2004). Types and uses of tests. In J. E. Wall & G. R. Walz (Eds.), *Measuring up: Assessment issues for teachers, counselors, and administrators* (pp. 21–31). Austin, TX: Pro-Ed.

Varnhagen, S., & Gerber, M. M. (1984). Use of microcomputers for spelling assessment: Reasons to be cautious. *Learning Disability Quarterly, 7,* 266–270.

Vaughn, S., Bos, C. S., Harrell, J. E., & Lasky, B. A., (1988). Parent participation in the initial placement/IEP conference: Ten years after mandated involvement. *Journal of Learning Disabilities, 21,* 82–89.

Vaughn, S., & Klingner, J. K. (1998). Students' perceptions of inclusion and resource room settings. *The Journal of Special Education, 32,* 79–88.

Venn, J. J. (2007). *Assessing students with special needs* (4th ed.). Upper Saddle River, NJ: Merrill/Pearson Education.

Volz, M. (2004, August 3). *Disabled students in Alaska to get special accommodations during high school exit exams in settlement.* Retrieved from www.SignOnSanDiego.com.

Wagner, M., Kutash, K., Duchnowski, A. J., Epstein, M. H., & Sumi, W. C. (2005). The children and youth we serve: A national picture of the characteristics of students with emotional disturbances receiving special education. *Journal of Emotional and Behavioral Disorders, 13*(2), 79–96.

Walker, H. M., Nishioka, V. M., Zeller, R., Severson, H. H., & Feil, E. G. (2000). Causal factors and potential solutions for the persistent underidentification of students having emotional or behavioral disorders in the context of schooling. *Assessment for Effective Intervention, 26*(1), 29–39.

Walker, H. M., & Severson, H. H. (1992). *Systematic screening for behavior disorders (SSBD) technical manual.* Longmont, CO: Sopris West.

Walker, H. M., Severson, H. H., & Feil, E. G. (1995). *User manual. Early Screening Project: A proven child find process.* Longmont, CO: Sopris West.

Walker, H. M., Severson, H. H., Feil, E. G., Stiller, B., & Golly, A. (1998). First step to success: Intervening at the point of school entry to prevent antisocial behavior. *Psychology in the Schools, 35*(3), 259–269.

Walker, H. M., Severson, H., & Haring, N. (1985). *Standardized screening and identification of behavior disordered pupils in the elementary age range: Rationale, procedure, and guidelines.* Eugene, OR: Oregon Research Institute.

Walker, H. M., Severson, H., Nicholson, F., Kehel, T., Jenson, W. R., & Clark, E. (1994). Replication of the Systematic Screening for Behavior Disorders (SSBD) procedure for the identification of at-risk children. *Journal of Emotional and Behavioral Disorders, 2*(2), 66–77.

Walker, H. M., Severson, H., Stiller, B., Williams, G., Haring, N., Shinn, M., & Todis, B. (1988). Systematic screening of pupils in the elementary age range at risk for behavior disorders: Development and trial testing of a Multiple Gating model. *Remedial and Special Education, 9*(3), 8–14.

Wallace, T., Espin, C. A., McMaster, K., Deno, S. L., & Foegen, A. (2007). CBM progress monitoring within a standards-based system. *The Journal of Special Education, 41,* 66–67.

Warren, S. F., Fey, M. E., & Yoder, P. J. (2007). Differential treatment intensity research: A missing link to creating optimally effective communication interventions. *Mental Retardation and Developmental Disabilities, 13,* 70–77.

Watson, C., & Willows, D. M. (1995). Information-processing patterns in specific reading disability. *Journal of Learning Disabilities, 28,* 216–231.

Wayman, M. M., Wallace, T., Wiley, H. I., Ticha, R., & Espin, C. A. (2007). Literature synthesis on curriculum-based measurement in reading. *Journal of Special Education, 41,* 85–120.

Weber, M. C. (2009). The IDEA eligibility mess. *Buffalo Law Review, 57,* 83–160.

Wechsler, D. (2004). *The Wechsler Intelligence Scale for Children–4th Edition.* London: Pearson Assessment. Wehmeyer, M. (2005). Self-determination and individuals with severe disabilities: Re-examining meanings and misinterpretations. *Research and Practice in Severe Disabilities, 30,* 113–120.

Wehmeyer, M. L. (1996). Self-determination as an educational outcome: Why is it important to children, youth and adults with disabilities? In D. J. Sands & M. L. Wehmeyer (Eds.), *Self-determination across the lifespan: Independence and choice for people with disabilities* (pp. 15–34). Baltimore: Brookes.

Weiss, M. P., & Lloyd, J. W. (2001). Structure and effective teaching. In D. P. Hallahan & B. K. Keogh (Eds.), *Research and global perspectives in learning disabilities: Essays in honor of William M. Cruickshank* (pp. 131–145). Mahwah, NJ: Erlbaum.

Weissberg, R. P., Kumpfer, K. L., & Seligman, M. E. P. (2003). Prevention that works for children and youth. *American Psychologist, 58,* 425–432.

Whitbread, K. M., Bruder, M. B., Fleming, G., & Park, H. J. (2007). Collaboration in special education: Parent-professional training. *TEACHING Exceptional Children, 39*(4), 6–14.

White, K. R., Taylor, M. J., & Moss, V. D. (1992). Does research support claims about the benefits of involving parents in early intervention programs? *Review of Educational Research, 62,* 91–125.

Whittington, D. (1999). Making room for values and fairness: Teaching reliability and validity in the classroom context. *Educational Measurement, 18,* 14–21.

Wiley, A. L., Siperstein, G. N., Bountress, K. E., Forness, S. R., & Brigham, F. J. (2009). School context and the academic achievement of students with emotional disturbance. *Behavioral Disorders, 33,* 198–210.

Wiley, A. L., Siperstein, G. N., Forness, S. R., & Brigham, F. J. (2010). School context and the problem behavior and social skills of students with emotional disturbance. *Journal of Child and Family Studies, 19,* 451–461.

Wilkinson, G. S. (1993). *Wide Range Achievement Test.* Wilmington, DE: Wide Range.

Willingham, W. W., Ragosta, M., Bennett, R. E., Braun, H., Rock, D. A., & Powers, D. E. (1988). *Testing handicapped people.* Needham Heights, MA: Allyn & Bacon.

Witt, J. C., Elliott, S. N., Daly, E. J., III, Gresham, F. M., & Kramer, J. J. (1998). *Assessment of at-risk and special needs children* (2nd ed.). Boston: McGraw-Hill.

Witt, J. C., & VanDerHeyden, A. M. (2007). The System to Enhance Educational Performance (STEEP): Using science to improve achievement. In S. R. Jimerson, M. K., Burns, & A. M. VanDerHeyden (Eds.), *Handbook of Response to Intervention* (pp. 148–171). New York: Springer.

Wolfensberger, W. (1972). *The principle of normalization in human services.* Downsview, Ontario: National Institute on Mental Retardation.

Woodcock, R. W. (1987). *Woodcock Reading Mastery Tests–Revised.* Circles Pines, MN: American Guidance Service.

Woodcock, R. W., & Johnson, M. B. (1990). *Woodcock-Johnson Psycho-Educational Battery-Revised.* Allen, TX: DLM Teaching Resources.

Woodcock, R. W., McGrew, K. S., & Mather, N. (2001). *Woodcock-Johnson—III Tests of Achievement.* Itasca, IL: Riverside Publishing.

Woods, M. L., & Moe, A. J. (2006). *Analytical reading inventory* (8th ed.). Upper Saddle River, NJ: Merrill/Pearson Education.

Yell, M. L. (2006). *The law and special education* (2nd ed.). Upper Saddle River, NJ: Merrill/Pearson Education.

Yell, M. L. (2009). Developing educationally meaningful and legally correct Individualized Education Programs. In M. L. Yell, N. B. Meadows, E. Dragsow, & J. G. Shriner, *Evidence based practices for educating students with emotional and behavioral disorders* (pp. 190–214). Upper Saddle River, NJ: Merrill/Pearson Education.

Yell, M. L., & Crockett, J. B. (2011). Free Appropriate Public Education. In J. M. Kauffman & D. P. Hallahan (Eds.), *Handbook of special education* (pp. 77–99). New York: Routledge.

Yell, M. L., & Drasgow, E. (2000). Litigating a free appropriate public education: The Lovaas hearings and cases. *Journal of Special Education, 33,* 206–215.

Yell, M. L., Drasgow, E., & Oh, I. (April, 2008). *Development of an evaluation instrument to assess the procedural and substantive quality of IEPs: The IEP Quality Indicator Scale (IQUIS).* Paper presented at the annual meeting of the Council of Exceptional Children, Boston.

Yell, M. L., Rogers, D., & Rogers, E. L. (1998). The legal history of special education: What a long, strange trip it's been! *Remedial and Special Education, 19,* 219–238.

Yell, M. L., & Stecker, P. M. (2003). Developing legally correct and educationally meaningful IEPs using curriculum-based measurement. *Assessment for Effective Intervention, 28*(3/4), 73–88.

Yoshida, R. K., Fenton, K. S., Kaufman, M. J., & Maxwell, J. (1978). Parental involvement in the special education pupil planning process: The school's perspective. *Exceptional Children, 44,* 531–534.

Ysseldyke, J. E. (2005). Assessment and decision making for students with learning disabilities: What if this is as good as it gets? *Learning Disability Quarterly, 28,* 125–128.

Ysseldyke, J. E., & McLeod, S. (2007). Using technology tools to monitor Response to Intervention. In S. Jimerson, M. K. Burns, & A. M. VanDerHeyden (Eds.), *Handbook of Response to Intervention: The science and practice of assessment and intervention* (pp. 396–407). New York: Springer.

Ysseldyke, J., Thurlow, M., Bielinski, J., House, A., Moody, M., & Haigh, J. (2001). The relationship between instructional and assessment accommodations in an inclusive state accountability system. *Journal of Learning Disabilities, 34,* 212–220.

Zenisky, A. L., & Sireci, S. G. (2007). *A summary of the research on the effects of test accommodations: 2005–2006* (Technical Report 47). Minneapolis, MN: University of Minnesota, National Center on Educational Outcomes.

Zettel, J. J., & Ballard, J. (1982). The Education for All Handicapped Children Act of 1975 (P.L. 94-142): Its history, origins, and concepts. In J. Ballard, B. Ramirez, & F. Weintraub (Eds.), *Special education in America: Its legal and governmental foundations* (pp. 11–22). Reston, VA: Council for Exceptional Children.

Zigmond, N., Kloo, A., & Volonino, V. (2009). What, where, and how? Special education in the climate of full inclusion. *Exceptionality, 17,* 189–204.

Zigmond, N., & Magiera, K. (2001). *Co-teaching* (Current Practice Alerts No. 6). Reston, VA: Division for Learning Disabilities & Division for Research of the Council for Exceptional Children.

Name Index

Abbott, M., 6
Achenbach, T., 34
Ahearn, E. M., 39
Ahonen, T., 76
Albers, C. A., 42
Albus, D., 97
Algozzine, B., 9
Allen, N., 46
Allen, S. K., 65, 66
Allen-Meares, P., 38
Alonzo, J., 61, 63
Altman, J., 103
Analysis of Comments and Changes, 60
Anderson, N. E., 97
Applegate, A. J., 88
Applegate, M. D., 88
Appleton, J. A., 8, 18
Archer, J., 90
Ard, W. R., 47
Arguelles, M. E., 6
Artiles, A. J., 34
Arunachalam, V., 2
Ashworth, S., 53

Bachmeier, R. J., 40
Bail, E. W., 13
Bailey, D., 46
Baker, S., 25
Ball, A., 37
Balla, D. A., 34
Ballard, J., 56
Banbury, M. M., 45
Bannerjee, M., 102, 109
Barnett, D., 14, 15
Barrett, R. P., 38
Barton, K. E., 102
Bateman, B. D., 44, 57, 58, 59, 60, 67, 68, 72
Bates, P. E., 48, 49, 50, 66
Beare, P. L., 60, 61, 62, 64
Beckett, J., 38
Beebe-Frankenberger, M., 74
Beegle, G., 45
Behar, L., 37
Bennett, R. E., 77
Bentz, J., 25
Berger, M., 45
Bergeron, R., 38
Bielinski, J., 63
Billingsley, F., 54
Binkley, E., 63, 98, 99, 105
Bird, H. R., 38
Blachman, B. A., 13
Black, R., 13

Blount, A., 102
Blue-Banning, M., 45, 46
Blumberg, R., 47
Boardman, A. G., 6
Board of Education v. Rowley (1982), 56
Bogan, B. L., 85
Boice, C. H., 12
Bolt, S., 94
Bolt, S. E., 97
Bongers, J., 35
Boone, R., 47
Bordin, J., 46
Bos, C. S., 45, 66
Botvin, G., 8
Bountress, K. E., 78
Braden, J. P., 94
Brady, S. A., 61, 62, 64, 67
Braun-Monegan, J., 63
Bremer, C., 97
Brengelman, S. U., 79
Bricker, D., 64, 65, 69
Brigham, F. J., 72, 78, 79, 85
Brigham, M. M., 72
Brigham, M. S. P., 79
Brophy, J., 5
Brown, J., 87
Brown-Chidsey, R., 19, 20
Bruder, M. B., 45, 46
Bruininks, R. H., 38
Bryant, B. R., 22
Bryant, J. D., 27
Burk, M., 102
Burke, C., 87
Burke, C. L., 87
Burke, M. D., 22
Burns, M. K., 6, 8, 9, 10, 11, 12, 13, 14, 15, 16, 17, 18, 40
Burns, M. S., 9
Busch, T. W., 21, 79, 88
Busse, R. T., 77

Caldarella, P., 37
Calhoon, M. B., 102, 109
Callicot, K. J., 50
Campbell, H., 21, 23, 31
Canter, A., 35
Carnine, D., 6
Carpenter, R. D., 88
Carr-George, C., 72, 81
Carson, P. M., 10
Carty, S. J., 67
Case, B. J., 91, 97
Case, L. P., 15, 16

Cassidy, D., 79
Catone, W. V., 61, 62, 64, 67
Cestone, C. M., 7
Chabris, C., 1–2
Chambers, C. R., 50
Chandler, M. A., 73
Chard, D. J., 20
Charlebois, P., 37
Chatel, R. G., 87, 88
Chiang, B., 22, 35
Childre, A., 50
Christ, T. J., 10, 14, 25
Christensen, L. L., 94, 96, 98, 100, 102, 104
Christensen, W. R., 65
Chun, E., 102, 109
Cicchetti, D. V., 34
Claes, C., 43, 47, 49
Clark, E., 22
Clements, M. A., 42
Cloninger, C. J., 43, 51, 52, 53, 54, 62
Codding, R. S., 105
Cohen, A. S., 98, 99, 105
Cohen, L., 92
Cohen, P., 79
Coie, J. D., 8
Coladarci, T., 85
Cole, N. S., 86
Collins, V. L., 22
Compton, D. L., 13, 27
Cone, J. D., 45
Connell, J. E., 16
Conroy, M. A., 77
Cook, B. G., 1, 4, 5, 6, 7, 43
Cook, L., 4
Cook, L. L., 94
Cook, V. J., 38
Coolong-Chaffin, M., 9
Correa, V., 46
Cortiella, C., 74, 95
Coulter, W. A., 20
Council for Exceptional Children (CEC), 2–3
Cox, M. L., 97
Coyne, M., 35
Crawford, L., 98, 99, 104, 105
Crockett, J. B., 2, 56, 71, 72
Crone, M., 96, 98
Cronis, T. G., 60
Cross, C. T., 20, 39, 42
Crossland, C. L., 102, 103, 109
Crouch, R., 98, 99, 105
Curran, C. M., 60, 67, 68
Curry, L., 45
Cutler, W. W., 44

Dabkowski, D. M., 46
Dacy, B. J. S., 7
Daly, E. J., III, 10, 84
Dammann, J. E., 2, 6
Daniel, P. T. K., 81
Daunic, A. P., 40
Davey, B., 102, 103, 109
Davis, J. L., 72
Dean, V. J., 9
Deatline-Buchman, A., 24
De Groot, E. V., 79
De La Paz, S., 21
Delawyer, D. D., 45
Della Toffalo, D. A., 75
Demaray, M. K., 35
Demczyk, M. J., 97
Deng, M., 98, 105
Dennis, R. E., 53, 54, 62
Deno, S. L., 5, 8, 9, 19, 21, 22, 23, 24, 26, 29,
        40, 60, 68, 79, 88
Deshler, D. D., 40
Desimone, L., 60, 64, 66, 67
DeStefano, L., 44, 65, 104
Deville, C., 100, 108
Dickson, D., 2
Disability Rights Advocates, 96
Dishion, T. J., 37
Dolan, R. P., 102, 103, 109
Donovan, M. S., 20, 39, 42
Dool, E. J., 10
Doty, D., 65
Doyle, M. B., 54
Doyle, W., 5
Drasgow, E., 57, 58, 67
Duchnowski, A. J., 36
Duhon, G. J., 16

Eaton, S., 75
Eaton, S. B., 63, 98, 99, 100, 101,
        105, 107
Eckert, T. L., 10
Edelman, S., 53, 54
Edelman, S. W., 53, 62
Edwards, L., 24
Edwards, P. A., 41
Ehri, L. C., 87
Elbaum, B., 72, 100, 101, 107
Elliot, N., 15, 91
Elliot, S., 100, 108
Elliott, J., 17, 22
Elliott, J. E., 95
Elliott, J. L., 95, 96, 104
Elliott, S. N., 61, 63, 64, 77, 84, 91, 92, 94, 98,
        99, 100, 101, 105, 107
Ellis, A. K., 15
Engelmann, S., 73
Epstein, J. S., 44
Epstein, M. H., 36, 61, 62, 64, 67, 77
Erwin, E. J., 17, 43
Espin, C., 21, 23, 31, 88
Espin, C. A., 14, 21, 79
Espin, C. L., 25
Etscheidt, S., 60, 67, 68
Evans-Fernandez, S., 77

Farr, R., 93
Farr, R. C., 89
Faykus, S. P., 88
Feggins-Azziz, R., 36
Feil, E. G., 36, 37
Felce, D., 77
Fenton, K. S., 45
Ferguson, C., 44
Fey, M. E., 14

Finell, B., 9
Finn, J. E., 65
Fitzgerald, M., 47
Fitzgerald, S., 6
Fitzsimmons, D., 90
Flannery, K. B., 47, 49, 50
Fleming, G., 46
Fletcher, J. M., 16, 20
Flowers, C., 66
Floyd, R. G., 38
Foegen, A., 23, 24, 31, 79
Foley, R., 62
Foley, S., 10
Foorman, B. R., 16
Fore, C., 47
Forest, M., 48
Forgan, J. W., 79
Forness, S. R., 73, 76, 78
Foster, M., 45
Fowler, S., 46
Fox, J. J., 77
Frame, J., 10
Francis, D. J., 16, 20
Frankland, H. C., 45
Freedman, D. H., 2
Frisbie, D., 100, 108
Fuchs, D., 9, 12, 13, 16, 18, 19, 20, 21, 22,
        23, 25, 27, 30, 40, 61, 63, 64, 75,
        79, 85, 96, 98, 99, 100, 101,
        105, 107
Fuchs, L., 22, 75, 100, 101, 102, 103
Fuchs, L. S., 9, 11, 12, 13, 16, 18, 19, 20, 21,
        22, 23, 24, 25, 27, 30, 61, 63, 64,
        75, 79, 80, 85, 96, 98, 99, 100, 101,
        102, 105, 107, 109
Fulk, B. M., 79
Furney, K. S., 44, 46, 50

Galagan, J. E., 75
Gallagher, J., 60, 64, 66, 67
Gallagher, W., 73
Gallini, S., 36
Gansle, K. A., 13, 16, 21, 86
Garcia, T., 86
Gardner, J. E., 65
Gatti, S. L., 16
Geenan, S., 46, 47
Gerber, M. M., 17, 78, 102, 110
Gerber, P. L., 45
Germann, G., 21, 22
Gersten, R., 79
Giangreco, M. F., 43, 47, 51, 52, 53, 54,
        61, 62
Gibbons, K., 9
Gibbs, H., 45
Gickling, E., 9
Gilbertson, D. A., 8
Gilbertson, D. N., 86
Glasgow, A., 102, 109
Glasnapp, D. R., 102, 110
Glover, T. A., 42
Goldenberg, D. S., 34
Goldman, R. W., 73
Goldstein, S., 45
Golly, A., 37
Good, R. H., 19, 22, 26, 97
Good, R. H., III, 19, 21
Good, T. L., 5
Goodman, K. S., 87
Goodman, S., 17
Goodman, Y., 87
Gordon, M., 105
Gordon, S., 73, 83
Gould, K., 35

Graden, J., 15
Graden, J. L., 16
Graff, J. J., 33
Gravois, T. A., 9, 17
Greene, B. A., 65, 66
Greene, G., 46
Greenspan, S., 38
Greenwood, C. R., 6
Gregg, N., 98, 99, 105, 106
Gresham, F. M., 9, 16, 36, 39, 40, 77, 84
Griffin, P., 9
Grimes, J., 17, 42
Grimes, J. P., 38
Grisham-Brown, J., 69
Gronlund, N., 90
Gustafson, J. K., 16, 39, 41

Habedank, L., 19
Hafner, J. C., 91
Hafner, P. M., 91
Hage, S. M., 8
Hagen-Burke, S., 22
Haigh, J., 63
Hale, J. A., 86
Hale, J. B., 17
Hall, T., 84
Hall, T. E., 102, 109
Hallenbeck, B. A., 73
Halpern, A. S., 66
Hamlett, C. L., 9, 19, 25, 63, 75, 98, 99, 100,
        101, 102, 105, 107, 109
Hammer, M. R., 65, 66
Hampton, D., 9, 24
Hanich, L., 24
Harbin, G. L., 46
Haring, N., 36
Harjusola-Webb, S., 4, 5
Harrell, J. E., 45
Harris-Murri, N., 36, 41
Harrison, P., 38
Harry, B., 36, 43, 46, 55
Hartshorne, T. S., 34
Hasazi, S., 44
Hasbrouck, J., 12
Hasbrouck, J. E., 88
Hasselbring, T. S., 102, 103, 109
Hauser, A., 10
Hauser, R. M., 96
Hay, S. E., 86
Heflinger, C. R., 38
Helwig, R., 98, 100, 101, 105, 107
Hemmeter, M. L., 69
Henderson, A. T., 44
Hendricker, E., 9
Henry, M., 44
Herner, J. G., 97
Hess, F., 3
Hess, F. M., 78
Heubert, J. P., 96
Hill, B. K., 38
Hill, C. C., 66
Hintze, J. M., 10, 25, 86
Hoge, R. D., 85
Hogue, A., 5
Holdnack, J. A., 32
Hollenbeck, K., 102, 109
Hollinger, C., 16
Hoover-Dempsey, K. V., 46
Hope-Dolittle, J., 36
Horn, E., 65, 66
Horner, R. H., 47
Horton, S. V., 102, 109
Hoskyn, M., 73
Hosp, J. L., 10, 36, 39

Hosp, M. K., 9, 22, 36
House, A., 63
Howlett, K. W., 10
Hudson, P. J., 65
Hudson, R. F., 89
Huebner, E. S., 35
Huefner, D. S., 57, 67
Hughes, C. A., 45
Hughes, M. T., 6, 72

Ihlo, T., 15
Ikeda, M. J., 16, 39, 41
Impecoven-Lind, L., 31
Individuals with Disabilities Education Act
    (IDEA), 56, 57, 60, 66
Iverson, V. S., 43, 51, 52

Jackson, L., 54
Jacob, S., 34, 40
Jacobsen, R., 92
Jarmulowicz, L., 86
Jegatheesan, B., 46
Jenkins, F. F., 97
Jenkins, J. R., 23, 33
Jerman, R. L., 66
Jewell, M., 23
Jeynes, W. H., 44
Jiban, C., 12, 14, 23, 24
Jimerson, S. R., 40
Jitendra, A. K., 24
Johns, J. L., 88
Johnson, E., 79, 100, 101, 107
Johnson, M. B., 22
Johnstone, C. J., 103
Joint Committee on Testing Practices, 86
Jones, E. D., 85
Jones, K. P., 46
Jones, M. L., 6
Jonsson, A., 90, 91
Jordan, N. C., 24
Jorm, A. F., 22
Juel, C., 20
Justen, J. E. I., 60

Kaestle, C. F., 44
Kaloi, L., 95
Kalyanpur, M., 46
Kalymon, K. M., 42
Kame'enui, E. J., 19, 20
Kaminski, R. A., 22, 26, 97
Kamphaus, R. W., 34
Karns, K. M., 63, 98, 99, 100, 101,
    105, 107
Kauffman, J. M., 6, 35, 40, 73, 74, 76
Kaufman, A. S., 17, 75
Kaufman, M. J., 45
Kaufman, N., 39
Kaufman, N. L., 75
Kavale, K. A., 17, 40, 73
Kay, P. L., 47
Kayzar, B., 44
Kazdin, A. E., 60
Keen, S., 102, 103, 109
Keller, L. A., 10, 25
Ketterlin-Geller, L., 100, 101, 107
Ketterlin-Geller, L. R., 61, 63
Kettler, R. J., 63, 92
Keyes, M. W., 47
Kiefer-O'Donnell, R., 53
Kilpatrick, J., 9, 12
Kincaid, D., 9
King, K., 36
Kirby v. Cabell County Board of Education
    (2006), 59

Klar, S., 9
Kleinert, H., 92
Klingner, J., 6
Klingner, J. K., 36, 41, 79
Kloo, A., 72
Knutson, J., 54
Knutson, N., 22
Koenig, A. J., 86
Kohler, F. W., 46
Kohler, P. D., 65
Konold, T. R., 74, 76
Kortteinen, H., 76
Kosciolek, S., 15
Kramer, J. J., 84
Kratochwill, T., 100, 108
Kratochwill, T. R., 36, 42
Krom, D. M., 61, 62, 64
Kruschwitz, R., 21
Kucer, S. B., 87
Kuehnle, K., 21
Kumpfer, K. L., 20
Kurns, S., 17
Kutash, K., 36

Lail, K. E., 94
Laitusis, C. C., 94, 96
Lake, S. E., 57, 58
Lake, V. E., 86
Lambert, N., 38
LaMonte, M., 79
Lamory, S., 46
Lancaster, P., 66
Lancaster, S., 66
Landrum, T. J., 2, 4, 6, 7, 36, 43
Lane, H. B., 89
Lane, K. L., 74
Larsen, J. A., 86
Lasky, B. A., 45
Lau, M., 35
Lau, M. Y., 16
Layton, C. A., 86
Lazarus, S. S., 94, 96, 98, 101
Leafstedt, J. M., 79
Leblanc, M., 37
Lee, C., 73
Lee, S. W., 22
LeFever, G. B., 40
Leland, H., 38
Lembke, E., 9
Lembke, E. S., 21, 23, 24, 88
Lembke, R., 23, 31
Levine, D. U., 17
Lewandowski, L. J., 98, 99, 105, 106
Lewis, R. B., 86, 89
Lezotte, L. W., 17
Li, S., 66, 91, 92, 96
Lieber, J., 66
Linden, M. A., 57, 58, 59, 60, 67, 68
Lindstrom, J. H., 98, 99, 106
Linn, R., 90
Linn, R. L., 95
Livingston, S., 15
Lloyd, J. W., 3, 34, 35, 72, 73, 75
Lloyd, P. A., 3
Loeber, R., 37
Lohman, D., 79
Long, J. D., 21, 23, 31
Lopez-Vasquez, A., 46
Lovett, B. J., 98, 105, 106
Lovett, D. L., 65
Lovitt, T. C., 102, 109
Lovorn, M., 90
Lowry, L., 21
Lusthaus, C. S., 45

Lusthaus, E., 48
Lusthaus, E. W., 45
Lyle, C., 48
Lynch, E. C., 60, 61, 62, 64
Lynch, E. W., 46
Lyon, G. R., 20
Lytle, R. K., 46

MacLean, R., 22
MacMann, G., 15
MacMillan, D., 45
MacMillan, D. L., 33, 42, 76
Madelaine, A., 3
Mager, R., 59
Magiera, K., 75
Malecki, C. K., 35
Malouf, D., 103
Malouf, D. B., 2
Mapp, K. L., 44
Marcotte, A. M., 86
Mardell, C., 34
Marek, A. M., 87
Marks, L. J., 85
Marquart, A. M., 98, 99, 105
Marshall, L. H., 65, 66
Marston, D., 19, 21, 22, 35, 39, 40
Marston, D. B., 21, 22
Martens, B. K., 10
Martin, J. E., 65, 66
Martin, K. F., 35
Mastropieri, M. A., 5
Mather, N., 34, 39, 75
Mathes, P. G., 12
Matthews, A., 17
Matthews, R., 22
Mattingly, D. J., 44
Maxson, L. M., 66
Maxwell, J., 45
Maxwell, S., 22
May, K., 33
Maynard, A. M., 20
McComas, J. J., 10
McConaughy, S. H., 47
McConnell, S. M., 35
McConnell, S. R., 62
McCormick, S., 87
McCurdy, B. L., 88
McDuffie, K. A., 2
McGahee-Kovac, M., 81
McGlinchey, M., 17
McGraw, C. K., 13
McGrew, K. S., 34, 75
McGuinness, D., 86
McKenna, M. C., 87
McKenzie, T. L., 44
McKevitt, B. C., 63, 91, 92, 100, 101, 107
McKinnon, A., 73
McLaughlin, M.J., 46, 61
McLean, M., 45
McLeod, S., 10
McLoughlin, J. A., 86, 89
McMaster, K., 79
McMaster, K. L., 5, 13, 15, 16
McNair, J., 46
McNamara, K., 16
McWilliam, R. A., 46
Mead, J. F., 81
Mehta, P., 16
Mellard, D. F., 79
Meloy, L., 100, 101, 108
Mengel, M., 84
Menlove, R. R., 65
Mercer, C. D., 88
Merulla, E., 73

Messick, S., 14, 15
Meyer, A., 72
Michnowicz, L. L., 61, 62
Miglioretti, D. L., 33
Milke, R. M., 75
Miller, D., 90
Miller, J., 72
Miller, J. H., 45
Miller, K. E., 97
Miller, P., 46
Miller, S., 47
Miner, C. A., 48, 49, 50, 66
Minnesota Department of Education, 96
Mirkin, P. K., 9, 19, 21, 22, 23, 29
Mock, D., 80
Moe, A. J., 88
Moody, M., 63
Moody, S. W., 72
Moore, R. F., 36
Morgan, P. L., 80
Morrison, D., 17
Moss, V. D., 44
Mostert, M. P., 2
Mount, B., 48
Mueller, P., 53
Muhomba, M., 92
Muyskens, P., 35

Naglieri, J. A., 17, 34
Naquin, G., 12
Naquin, G. M., 21
Närhi, V., 76
National Council for Accreditation
      for Teacher Education, 86
National Reading Panel (NRP), 10, 12
National Universal Design for Learning
      Task Force, 92
Natnais, M., 15
Neil, M., 92
Nelson, C., 53
Nelson, L. L., 45
Newborg, J., 34, 38
Newton, S., 47
Nicholson, F., 37
Nickles, J. L., 60, 61, 62, 64, 67
Nieberding, J. L., 97
Nihalani, P. K., 7
Nihira, K., 38
Nilsson, N. L., 88
Nippold, M. A., 86
Nishioka, V., 42
Nishioka, V. M., 36
No Child Left Behind Act of 2001, 18
Noell, G. H., 13, 16, 21
Nolet, V., 10, 21, 74
Norris, S. P., 20
Northwest Evaluation Association,
      9, 97

Oakland, T., 38
O'Brien, C. L., 48
O'Brien, J., 48
Odom, S. L., 62
Office of Special Education, 36
Oh, I., 67
O'Leary, E. L. M., 65
Olson, J. R., 31
Oosterhof, A., 89
Osborn, D., 54
O'Shaughnessy, T. E., 13
Osmond, W. C., 20
Otaiba, S., 86
Owens, R. L., 24
Owens-Johnson, L., 47

Paris, S. G., 88
Park, H. J., 46
Parker, R., 21, 88
Parnes, S. J., 53
Parolin, R., 105
Patterson, G. R., 37
Patton, J. R., 62, 95
Payne, L. D., 85
Pearpoint, J., 48
Peters, R., 16
Peterson, C. A., 62
Petrilli, M., 3
Phillips, N. B., 25
Phillips, S. E., 20, 95
Picard, M., 87
Pitoniak, M. J., 91
Poggio, A. J., 102, 110
Poggio, J., 102, 103, 110
Polloway, E. A., 62
Poloni-Staudinger, L., 36
Poponi, D. M., 47
Poth, R. L., 16
Powers, K. M., 61, 64
Powers, L. E., 46
Prasse, D., 15
Prater, M. A., 46, 61, 62, 64
President's Commission on Excellence
      in Special Education, 57
Pretti-Frontczak, K., 64, 65, 69
Prewitt, P. N., 22
Prislin, R., 44
Psychological Corporation, 34
Pullen, P. C., 3, 88, 89

Quenemoen, R. F., 103
Quinn, K. B., 88

Rao, S. S., 46
Rasheed, S. A., 47
Reed, R. P., 46
Reschly, D. J., 8, 20, 35, 38, 39, 40, 42
Reynolds, C. R., 34
Rezaei, A., 90
Richards, C., 79
Richardson, M. J., 37
Ridgley, R., 69
Roach, A. T., 94
Robinson, D. H., 7
Robinson, T. R., 57
Rodger, S., 61
Rodriguez, J. L., 44
Roelofs, L., 21
Roessler, R., 64
Rogers, C. L., 98, 106
Rogers, D., 44, 73
Rogers, E. L., 44, 73
Rose, D. H., 72
Rosenfield, S. A., 17
Rostenberg, D., 36
Rothstein, R., 92
Royer, J. M., 91
Rozalski, M., 72
Rozek-Tedesco, M., 100, 107
Rozek-Tedesco, M. A., 102, 109
Ruhl, K. L., 45
Rusch, F. R., 46
Russ, S., 35
Rylance, B. J., 35
Ryndak, D. L., 54

Sagan, C., 5
Sale, P., 65
Salembier, G., 46, 50
Sandall, S., 66

Sanderson, H., 48
Sandler, C., 17
Sandomierski, T., 9
Sasso, G. M., 77
Saudargas, R. A., 77
Scarpati, S., 91, 92, 96
Schacht, R., 46
Schalock, R. L., 43
Schatschneider, C., 16
Schaughency, E., 17
Schiller, E. P., 2
Schirmer, B. R., 6
Scholin, S. E., 15
Schriner, K., 64
Schulte, A., 100, 101, 108
Schumm, J. S., 72, 79
Schwartz, I., 66
Scierka, B. J., 21
Scruggs, T. E., 5
Scullin, M. H., 38
Sczesniak, E., 24
Seligman, M. E. P., 20
Semmel, M. I., 78
Senesac, B. K., 11, 17
Severson, H., 36, 37
Severson, H. H., 36, 37, 77
Shands, E. I., 38
Shapiro, E. S., 24, 25, 81
Share, D. L., 22
Sharma, H. M., 77
Shaywitz, B. A., 20
Shaywitz, S. E., 20
Shearin, A., 61, 64
Sheinker, A., 102
Shermer, M., 5
Shin, J., 19, 21, 79
Shin, J. S., 88
Shinn, M., 22
Shinn, M. R., 19, 21, 22, 35
Shogren, K. A., 43
Shriner, J. G., 65, 67, 104
Sileo, A. P., 46
Sileo, T. W., 46
Silverstein, B., 96
Simmons, A. B., 36
Simmons, D. C., 12, 19
Simon, J. B., 60, 65
Simons, D., 1–2
Siperstein, G. N., 33, 42, 78
Sireci, S. G., 91, 92, 96, 97, 103
Skiba, R. J., 36, 38
Skinner, D. G., 46
Skinner, M., 46
Slate, J. R., 77
Slider, N. J., 21
Slovic, R., 47
Smith, A., 3
Smith, A. C., 66
Smith, G. J., 1, 60
Smith, S., 25
Smith, S. W., 40, 43, 45, 60, 61, 62, 67
Smith, T. E. C., 95
Smull, M. W., 48
Snow, C. E., 9, 12
Snyder, E. P., 81
Soenksen, D., 46
Sontag, J. C., 46
Soodak, L. C., 43
Sopko, K. M., 61
Southern, W. S., 85
Spann, S. J., 46
Sparrow, S. S., 34
Spectrum K12 School Solutions, 15
Speece, D. L., 15, 16, 39

Spenciner, L., 92
Spicuzza, R., 25
Stecker, P. M., 19, 21, 23, 24, 25, 60, 61
Steege, M. W., 19, 20
Stehouwer, J. D., 8, 18
Stein, R., 46
Stewart, A., 72
Stichter, J. P., 77
Stiggins, R., 8
Stiggins, R. J., 86, 91
Stiller, B., 37
Stith, S., 8
Stollar, S. A., 16
Strangman, N., 102, 109
Strickland, B., 45
Stringfield, S., 37
Stuebing, K. K., 20, 39
Sturges, K. M., 36
Sugai, G., 17
Sumi, W. C., 36
Summers, J. A., 45
Suter, D., 65
Svingby, G., 90, 91
Swafford, J., 9
Swanson, H. L., 13, 73
Symington, T., 16
Symons, F. J., 77

Tangel, D. M., 13
Tankersley, M., 3, 4, 5, 6, 7, 43
Tankersley, M. T., 6
Taylor, G. G., 40
Taylor, M. J., 44
Taylor, S. J., 73
Test, D. W., 65, 66
Thackery, M., 38
Thompson, S., 102, 103
Thompson, S. J., 74, 103, 104
Thompson, T., 77
Thurlow, M., 63, 97, 102, 103
Thurlow, M. L., 74, 75, 94, 95, 96, 97, 98,
    103, 104
Ticha, R., 14, 21
Tilly, W. D., 17, 22, 40, 42
Tilly, W. D., III, 17
Timmons, J. R., 66
Tindal, G., 12, 21, 22, 63, 88, 98, 100, 101,
    102, 103, 105, 107, 109
Tindal, G. A., 21, 22
Tocci, L., 46
Tollefson, N., 22
Tomlinson, C. A., 72

Tone, B., 89
Torgesen, J. K., 16, 22
Towles-Reeves, E., 92
Trach, J., 67
Trainor, A. A., 50
Tucker, J. A., 10
Turnbull, A., 43, 44, 46, 54
Turnbull, A. P., 45
Turnbull, H. R., 3, 43, 45
Turnbull, R., 43
Tylenda, B., 38

Umbreit, J., 74
U.S. Department of Education, 18, 20, 80

Vacc, N. A., 45
Vandercook, T., 48
VanDerHeyden, A. M., 8, 12, 13, 14, 16, 17,
    21, 41, 86
Vandevelde, S., 43
Van Dycke, J. L., 65, 66
Van Hove, G., 43
Van Loon, J., 43
Vannest, K. J., 72
Van Reusen, A. K., 66
Vansickle, T., 77
Varnhagen, S., 102, 110
Vaughn, S., 2, 6, 20, 45, 72, 79
Venn, J. J., 84, 87, 88, 89, 90, 91
Viglietta, E., 13
Volonino, V., 72
Volz, M., 96

Wagner, A. R., 40
Wagner, D., 10, 13
Wagner, M., 36
Walker, H., 37
Walker, H. M., 36, 37, 77
Walker, J. M. T., 46
Wallace, T., 14, 21, 23, 25, 31, 79
Wang, T., 104
Warren, S. H., 61
Warren, S. F., 14
Watson, C., 86
Watson, D., 87
Wayman, M. M., 14
Weatherman, R. F., 38
Weber, M. C., 41
Weber, R., 67
Wechsler, D., 34
Wehmeyer, M., 66
Wehmeyer, M. L., 48

Weiss, L. G., 32
Weiss, M. P., 73, 75
Weissberg, R. P., 20
Wheat, M., 43
Wheldall, K., 3
Whitbread, K. M., 46, 47
White, J., 94
White, K. R., 44
Whiteford, L., 54
Whiteford, T., 54
Whitney-Thomas, J., 66
Whittaker, T. A., 24
Whittington, D., 86
Wilder, T., 92
Wiley, A. L., 78
Wiley, H. I., 13, 14
Wilkinson, G. S., 24
Williams, W., 53
Willingham, W. W., 104
Willows, D. M., 86
Willson, V., 72
Wilson, M. S., 35
Witt, J. C., 8, 10, 12, 41, 84, 85
Wolfe, V. V., 45
Wolfensberger, W., 48
Wood, W. M., 66
Woodcock, R. W., 22, 34, 38, 75
Woods, M. L., 88

Yang, X., 102
Yell, M., 67
Yell, M. L., 44, 56, 57, 58, 59, 60, 61, 67,
    68, 69, 72, 73, 80
Yoder, P. J., 14
York, J., 48
Yoshida, R. K., 45
Young, B. J., 37
Young, C. L., 80
Young, E. L., 37
Young, K. R., 37
Young, M. R., 53
Yovanoff, P., 100, 101, 107
Ysseldyke, J., 61, 63
Ysseldyke, J. E., 6, 10, 13, 21, 95, 96
Yuan, S., 53

Zeller, R., 36
Zenisky, A. L., 103
Zettel, J. J., 56
Zieky, M. J., 86
Zigmond, N., 24, 72, 75
Zwernik, K., 48

Subject Index

AAMR Adaptive Behavior Scale, 38
Academic achievement
  curriculum-based measurement and, 18–31
  placement decisions and, 72
  reading proficiency and, 22
Academic skills outcomes
  curriculum-based assessment and, 85
  research-based practices in, 7
  research-to-practice gap and, 6
Accommodations. *See also* Assessment
    accommodations
  curriculum-based assessment, 91–92
  false negatives and, 75
  individualized education programs and, 61,
    62–63, 65, 67, 95
  placement decisions and, 74
Accommodations Bibliography, 98
Accountability, No Child Left Behind Act
    of 2001, 18
Achievement tests. *See specific tests*
Adaptive behavior, 38
Adaptive Behavior Assessment System-Second
    Edition (ABAS-II), 38
Adequate yearly progress (AYP), 95
ADHD. *See* Attention deficit hyperactivity
    disorder (ADHD)
Adverse impact on classmates, placement
    decisions, 81–82
Alphabetic principle, Response to
    Intervention, 13
Alternative assessments. *See* Modifications
*Alvin Independent School Dist. v. A.D. ex rel.
    Patricia F* (2007), 74, 81
Amanda J. v. Clark County School District
    (2001), 57
Analytic rubrics, 90–91
Appropriate services, placement decisions, 71
Assessment. *See also* Curriculum-based
    assessment (CBA);
    Curriculum-based measurement
    (CBM); Response to Intervention (RtI)
  curriculum-based measurement and, 19–31,
    99, 101
  eligibility identification, 32–42
  hypotheses for student failure, 10
  individualized education programs and,
    59, 63
  Individuals with Disabilities Act of 2004
    and, 8–9
  oral reading fluency assessments, 22,
    27–29, 31, 89, 90
  parental involvement in, 43–55
  placement decisions and, 70–83

  research-based practices in, 7
  self-assessment, 90–91
  tools for placement decisions, 74–80
  using in making placement decisions,
    70, 80–82
Assessment accommodations
  computer-based testing and, 97, 100,
    101–103, 109–110
  extended time, 94, 97, 98–99, 103,
    105–106
  historical context for, 94–95
  implications for practice, 104
  legal and policy context for, 96–97
  read aloud/oral presentation, 97, 100–101,
    103, 107–108
  research on, 95–96, 97–104
  theoretical context for, 95–96
Assessment modifications, 94
At-risk students
  curriculum-based measurement and, 26, 31
  progress monitoring and, 20
Attention, illusions of, 1–2
Attention deficit hyperactivity disorder
    (ADHD)
  assessment accommodations, 98, 99
  eligibility identification and, 38
Audio recordings, miscue and error analysis, 86
Autism
  as disability category, 33
  eligibility identification and, 38
  parental involvement and, 46
AYP (adequate yearly progress), 95

BASC-2 (Behavior Assessment System
    for Children), 34
Battelle Developmental Inventory (BDI-2),
    34, 38
Behavioral and Emotional Rating Scale
    (BERS), 77
Behavioral outcomes, research-based
    practices in, 7
Behavioral supports. *See* Positive behavior
    support (PBS)
Behavior Assessment System for Children
    (BASC-2), 34
Behavior rating scales, 76–77, 82
Benchmarking, 19
BERS (Behavioral and Emotional Rating
    Scale), 77
Blindness. *See* Deaf-blindness (DB); Visual
    impairments (VI)
Board of Education v. Rowley (1982),
    56, 71, 81

California High School Exit Exam, 96
Case studies, 26–30, 50
Causality, 1–2, 4
CBA. *See* Curriculum-based assessment
    (CBA)
CBA-ID (curriculum-based assessment
    of instructional design), 9–10
CBCL (Child Behavior Checklist), 34
CEC (Council for Exceptional Children), 2
Checklists
  checklists for literacy assessment, 34, 36,
    86, 89
  Child Behavior Checklist, 34
  Critical Life Events checklist, 36
  Developing Skills Checklist, 22
  oral reading fluency assessments, 89, 90
  Transition Requirements Checklist, 65
Child Behavior Checklist (CBCL), 34
Choosing Outcomes and Accommodations
    for Children (COACH)
  conceptual basis for, 51–52
  as family-centered practice, 43, 47
  overview of, 50–51
  parental involvement and, 50–55
  research on, 53–54
  unique elements of, 52–53
Classroom-based measures, assessment
    accommodations, 98
Classroom grades, for placement decisions,
    78, 81
Class-wide problems, identifying, 11, 12–13
Cloze diagnostic tool, 86, 87–88
COACH. *See* Choosing Outcomes and
    Accommodations for Children
    (COACH)
Cognitive disabilities. *See* Intellectual
    disabilities
Cognitive strategy instruction (CSI), placement
    decisions, 72
Colleagues, personal experiences of, 1, 3
Combined Frequency Index for adaptive and
    maladaptive behaviors, 36
Community Survey form, 50
Compliance issues, individualized education
    programs, 60–67
Comprehension. *See* Reading comprehension
Computation assessment test, 24
Computer-based testing, 97, 100, 101–103,
    109–110
Concepts/Applications assessment test, 24
Confidence, illusions of, 1–2
Congruence, individualized education
    programs, 62

Content mapping, 86
Control groups, 4
Co-teaching, placement decisions, 75
Council for Exceptional Children (CEC), 2
CPS (Osborn-Parnes Creative Problem-Solving Process), 53
Creative problem solving, 53
Credible measures, 3–4
Critical Life Events checklist, 36
CSI. *See* Cognitive strategy instruction (CSI)
Cultural diversity
    disproportionate representation and, 36
    eligibility identification and, 38
    parental involvement and, 46, 50, 54, 55
Curriculum-based assessment (CBA)
    accommodations and modifications and, 91–92
    barriers to high-quality, 91
    characteristics of, 85
    checklists and rating scales for literacy assessment, 86, 89
    cloze diagnostic tool, 87–88
    definition of, 84–85
    informal reading inventories, 88–89
    miscue and error analysis, 86–87
    placement decisions, 79, 81
    portfolio assessment, 86, 89–91
    recommendations for teachers, decision makers, and researchers, 92–93
    research on, 92–93
Curriculum-based assessment of instructional design (CBA-ID), 9–10
Curriculum-based evaluation, Response to Intervention, 10, 16
Curriculum-based measurement (CBM)
    assessment accommodations and, 99, 101
    implementation, 26–31
    placement decisions and, 77, 79, 81
    progress monitoring and, 18–31
    in reading and mathematics, 9, 21–25, 31
    Response to Intervention and, 9, 11–12, 20, 23, 24, 31
    student outcomes and, 25

Daniel Two-Part Test, 72
Data-based academic decision making
    progress monitoring and, 18–21, 26–31
    using curriculum-based measurement in reading and mathematics, 21–25
Data management teams, 12
Data sources, eligibility identification, 34
Deaf-blindness (DB)
    individualized education programs and, 62
    parental involvement and, 54
Deafness. *See* Deaf-blindness (DB); Hearing impairment
Decoding, informal reading inventories, 88
Determining a Student's Educational Program, COACH, 51
Developing Skills Checklist, 22
Developmental disabilities
    individualized education programs and, 64
    parental involvement and, 46
Developmental Indicators for the Assessment of Learning (DIAL-R), 34
Diagnostic assessments, 8
DIBELS (Dynamic Indicators of Basic Early Literacy), 22, 25, 26–28, 97
Differential boost, 96–103, 105, 109
Digital portfolios, 89–90
Digital textbooks, 92
Direct observation, for placement decisions, 77–78, 82

Disproportionate representation, diversity, 36–40, 42
Disruptive students, placement decisions, 81–82
Diversity, disproportionate representation, 36–40, 42
Down Syndrome, parental involvement, 54
Dreams form, 50
Dynamic Assessment of Test Accommodations, 75
Dynamic Indicators of Basic Early Literacy (DIBELS), 22, 25, 26–28, 97

Early intervention, eligibility identification, 36, 39, 42
Early literacy instruction, progress monitoring, 22
Early Screening Project (ESP), 37
EBDs. *See* Emotional and behavioral disorders (EBDs)
EBIS (Effective Behavior and Instructional Support), 17
ED. *See* Emotional disturbance (ED)
Educational Testing Services, 104
Education for All Handicapped Children Act (EHA)
    assessment accommodations and, 95
    individualized education programs and, 56
    parental involvement and, 43, 44, 45
    placement decisions and, 73
Effective Behavior and Instructional Support (EBIS), 17
Effective practices
    caveats regarding, 5
    limitations of traditional determining factors, 1–2
    need for in-depth information on, 1
    relation between reality and educator's judgments, 3
    research as basis for, 2–5
    research-to-practice gap, 5–7
Effective teaching, research-based practices, 5
EHA. *See* Education for All Handicapped Children Act (EHA)
Electronic portfolios, 89–90
Elementary and Secondary Education Act (ESEA), 44, 71, 95. *See also* No Child Left Behind Act (NCLB)
Eligibility identification
    assessment procedures for, 34–35, 36
    early intervention and, 36, 39, 42
    emotional disturbance and, 33, 34, 35–38, 41
    high-incidence disabilities and, 35–41
    historical, legal, and ethical context of, 32–34
    internalizing and externalizing behaviors and, 37
    orthopedic impairment and, 35, 49, 50
    research on, 40, 41–42
ELLs. *See* English Language Learners (ELLs)
Emergent reading. *See* Early literacy instruction
Emotional and behavioral disorders (EBDs)
    assessment accommodations and, 98
    individualized education programs and, 62
    placement decisions and, 70–71, 79
Emotional disabilities, individualized education programs, 64
Emotional disturbance (ED), eligibility identification, 33, 34, 35–38, 41
English Language Learners (ELLs), eligibility identification, 34
ERIC online catalog, 98
Error analysis, 86–87

Errors, miscue analysis, 86–87
ESEA (Elementary and Secondary Education Act), 44, 71, 95. *See also* No Child Left Behind Act (NCLB)
ESP (Early Screening Project), 37
Ethical context, eligibility identification, 32–34
Eugenics movement, 44
Evaluation, eligibility identification, 34
Expectations, 2
Experimental groups, 4
Experimental research, person-centered planning, 49
Expert opinion, 1–2, 3, 4, 6
Extended time, as accommodation, 94, 97, 98–99, 103, 105–106
Externalizing behaviors, eligibility identification, 37

Fact Retrieval, 24
Failing scores, large-scale state assessments, 74–75
Fairness, curriculum-based assessment, 86
False negatives
    large-scale state assessments, 74–75
    safeguards against, 3–6
False positives, safeguards against, 3–6
Family-centered practice, 43, 47–54
Family Interview, 51, 52, 53
Family professional partnerships, 46
FAPE. *See* Free appropriate public education (FAPE)
Florida Comprehensive Assessment Test (FCAT), 99
Flynn effect, 38
Free appropriate public education (FAPE)
    individualized education programs and, 56–57, 69, 72
    parental involvement and, 44
    placement decisions and, 70–71, 73, 75, 76, 79, 81
Frustration level, informal reading inventories, 88

Geffre et al. v. Leola School District 44-2 (2009), 78
Geffre ex rel. S.G. v. Leola Sch. Dist. (2009), 81
Gender bias
    disproportionate representation and, 36, 37
    Response to Intervention and, 15
General education, parental involvement, 44
General education classrooms, special education placement decisions, 70–71, 72–73, 75, 80
General education teachers, role in eligibility identification, 35
Glossaries, digital textbooks, 92
Goals, individualized education programs, 59, 60, 61–62, 64–69
Goals and Dreams form, 50
Goals form, 50
Grade-level teams, Response to Intervention, 11–12, 13
Graphs, curriculum-based measurement, 19, 27–31
Group experimental research, 4

Hartman Three-Part Test, 72
Hearing impairment
    as disability category, 35
    person-centered planning and, 49
    placement decisions and, 71
Heartland Educational Agency Model, 40–41
Hierarchical Linear Modeling, 24

High-incidence disabilities. *See also specific disabilities*
  eligibility identification and, 35–41
High scores, on achievement tests, 76
High-stakes assessment tests, 19, 90–93, 96
Historical context
  for assessment accommodations, 94–95
  eligibility identification, 32–34
  parental involvement, 44–45
  person-centered planning, 48
  progress monitoring, 20–21
Holistic rubrics, 90–91

IDEA. *See* Individuals with Disabilities Education Improvement Act (IDEA)
Identification. *See also* Eligibility identification
  Response to Intervention and, 8–9, 16, 17
IDM (Instructional Decision Making) framework, 40–41
IEPs. *See* Individualized education programs (IEPs)
Implementation
  assessment accommodations, 104
  curriculum-based measurement, 26–31
  individualized education programs, 61–64, 66, 67, 69
  person-centered planning, 48–49
  Response to Intervention, 13, 15–16, 17
Improving America's Schools Act of 1994, 95
Independent level, informal reading inventories, 88
Individualized education program participation training, 66–67
Individualized education programs (IEPs)
  accommodations and, 61, 62–63, 65, 67, 95
  assessment accommodations and, 96
  assessment and, 59, 63
  curriculum-based assessment and, 84, 85
  curriculum-based measurement and, 19–20, 31
  development of, 58–61, 64–67
  eligibility identification and, 35
  free appropriate public education and, 56–57, 69, 72
  legal requirements, 56–58
  parental involvement and, 43, 44, 45–46, 48–55, 57, 60
  placement decisions and, 70–72, 74–75, 77, 80, 81, 82
  recommendations for practice, 67–69
  research on, 60, 61–67
  self-determination and, 66
  special education and, 49–50, 57–60, 62
  special education services and, 60
  substantive requirements, 57–59, 62, 69
  summary of literature, 67
Individually administered tests, for placement decisions, 75–76
Individuals with Disabilities Education Act Amendments of 1997, 59, 95
Individuals with Disabilities Education Improvement Act (IDEA)
  accommodations and, 95
  assessment and, 8–9
  development of individualized education programs, 58–61
  Education for All Handicapped Children Act and, 56
  eligibility identification and, 32–36, 39, 41
  individualized education program implementation and, 67–69
  legal requirements for individualized education programs, 56–58

modifications and, 95
parental involvement in special education and, 43–45, 54
  placement decisions and, 70–71, 76, 80, 82
  progress monitoring and, 20
  research-based practices and, 3
  research on individualized education programs and, 63–67
Informal assessment measures, placement decisions, 77–79
Informal reading inventories (IRIs), 86, 88–89
In-service training, 68
Instructional Decision Making (IDM) framework, 40–41
Instructional leadership, 17
Instructional level, informal reading inventories, 88
Instructional objectives, individualized education programs, 59
Instructional practices. *See also* Effective practices
  research-to-practice gap and, 5–7
Intellectual disabilities
  individualized education programs and, 62, 64, 66
  parental involvement and, 54
  person-centered planning and, 49, 50
Intelligence quotient (IQ)
  eligibility identification and, 38, 39
  IQ-achievement discrepancy, 33, 39, 41, 42
  testing, 76
Interaction hypothesis, 96
Internalizing behaviors, eligibility identification, 37
Internet, parental involvement, 55
Interventions. *See also* Response to Intervention (RtI)
  curriculum-based assessment and, 84, 92
  curriculum-based measurement and, 19–31
  delay and, 36, 39, 42
  individualized education programs and, 66, 67
  placement decisions and, 73, 80
  progress monitoring and, 20
  Response to Intervention, 8–17
  single-subject research and, 4
Interviews, for placement decisions, 79, 81
IPLAN strategy, 66–67
IQ. *See* Intelligence quotient (IQ)
IRIs (informal reading inventories), 86, 88–89

Jordan's Story Problems, 24
Juleus Chapman et al. v. California Department of Education (2001), 96

Kaufman Brief Intelligence Test, 22
Kaufman Test of Educational Achievement, 75
Kirby v. Cabell County Board of Education (2006), 59
Knowledge, illusions of, 1–2

Large-scale state assessments
  assessment accommodations and, 96, 102
  placement decisions and, 74–75, 80–81
LD. *See* Learning disabilities (LD)
Learning disabilities (LD)
  assessment accommodations and, 98, 99, 100, 101, 102, 103
  eligibility identification and, 33, 34, 35, 38, 39–42
  individualized education programs and, 62, 63, 64
  placement decisions and, 70–71, 79
  progress monitoring and, 20, 24

research on person-centered planning, 49
Response to Intervention and, 16, 17
Least restrictive environment (LRE), placement decisions, 70–73, 74, 76, 78–83
Legal context
  for assessment accommodations, 96–97
  eligibility identification, 32–34
  parental involvement, 44–45
  for placement decisions, 71–72
  for progress monitoring, 20–21
Linguistic diversity
  disproportionate representation and, 36
  parental involvement and, 46, 50
Local education agencies, individualized education programs, 60
Logical basis, for progress monitoring, 20–21
Low-incidence disabilities, 51
Low scores, on achievement tests, 76
LRE. *See* Least restrictive environment (LRE)

MAP (Measures of Academic Progress), 9, 97
Mathematical reasoning, Tier-2 assessment, 10
Mathematics
  curriculum-based measurement and, 9, 21–25, 31
  research on assessment accommodations and, 98, 99
  transition to adulthood and, 63
Maze task, 23, 31, 88
Measurable annual goals, individualized education programs, 59, 60, 61–62, 64–69
Measures
  baseline measures, 4
  credibility of, 3–4
Measures of Academic Progress (MAP), 9, 97
Medically identifiable disability categories, 35
Memory, illusions of, 1–2
Mental retardation, eligibility identification, 33, 34, 35, 37–38
Mild cognitive disabilities, assessment accommodations, 98
Mild intellectual disabilities
  individualized education programs and, 62
  placement decisions and, 70–71
Mild mental retardation (MMR), eligibility identification, 38, 40, 41
Miscue and error analysis, 86–87
Missing Number, 23–24
Modifications
  accommodations and, 63, 95
  curriculum-based assessment and, 91–92
Multiple disabilities, parental involvement, 53–54
Multi-tiered system of supports (MTSS). *See* Three-tiered models of prevention

Naglieri Nonverbal Cognitive Test, 34
National Center on Educational Outcomes, 96
National Center on Response to Intervention, 14, 26, 31
National Center on Student Progress Monitoring, 28
National Secondary Transition Technical Assistance Center, 49
NCLB. *See* No Child Left Behind Act (NCLB)
No Child Left Behind Act (NCLB)
  accommodations and, 95
  accountability and, 18
  parental involvement and, 44
  placement decisions and, 71, 76, 80
  progress monitoring and, 20
  research-supported effective practices and, 3
Nonresponders, 5

Nonstandard accommodations, 95
Noon v. Alaska State Board of Education &
    Early Development (2004), 96
Norm referenced tests, 84, 92
Northwest Educational Assessments
    (NWEA), 97
Now form, 50
Number Identification, 23–24
Number Identification/Counting, 24
NWEA (Northwest Educational
    Assessments), 97

Office of Special Education 28th Annual
    Report to Congress, 36
Office of Special Education Programs, 36
Oral reading fluency (ORF) assessments
    checklists and, 89, 90
    curriculum-based measurement and, 22,
        27–29, 31
Oregon Transition Systems Change Project, 49
ORF. *See* Oral reading fluency (ORF)
    assessments
Orthopedic impairment
    eligibility identification and, 35, 49, 50
    person-centered planning, 49, 50
Osborn-Parnes Creative Problem-Solving
    Process (CPS), 53
Outcome measures
    curriculum-based measurement and, 25
    individualized education programs and, 67

PALS. *See* Peer-Assisted Learning Strategies
    (PALS)
Paper-and-pencil tests, 102–103
Parental involvement
    in assessment, 43–55
    barriers to, 45–46, 54–55
    characterizations of, 45
    Choosing Outcomes and Accommodations
        for Children and, 50–55
    family and professional partnerships, 46
    family-centered practices, 47–54
    general education and, 44
    historical, legal, and theoretical
        underpinnings of, 44–45
    individualized education programs and, 43,
        44, 45–46, 48–55, 57, 60
    introduction, 43
    levels of, 45–47
    person-centered planning, 47–50, 55
    placement decisions and, 71
    research on, 44, 45–47
    Response to Intervention and, 16
    role in eligibility identification, 35
Passing scores, large-scale state assessments, 74
PBS. *See* Positive behavior support (PBS)
PCP. *See* Person-centered planning (PCP)
Peer-Assisted Learning Strategies (PALS),
    Response to Intervention, 12
Peer-reviewed research
    individualized education programs and, 69
    special education services, 60
Perceptual motor training, 73
Personal experiences, 1–5, 6
Personal Futures Planning model, 49
Personal profiles, 48
Person-centered planning (PCP)
    attributes of, 47
    case studies, 50
    as family-centered practice, 43, 47
    historical and theoretical underpinnings of, 48
    implementation, 48–49
    individualized education programs and, 66
    introduction, 47–48

parental involvement and, 47–50, 55
    research on, 49–50
Phonological awareness, Response to
    Intervention, 13
Physical disabilities
    assessment accommodations and, 98
    individualized education programs and, 64
PLAAFP (Present Level of Academic
    Achievement and Functional
    performance), 57, 59–60
Placement decisions
    assessment and, 70–83
    conceptual contextual base for, 73
    curriculum-based assessment and, 79, 81
    curriculum-based measurement and, 77,
        79, 81
    empirical contextual base for, 72–73
    general education classrooms and, 70–71,
        72–73, 75, 80
    informal assessment measures, 77–79
    legal contextual base for, 71–72
    research on, 72–73
    Response to Intervention and, 79–80
    standardized tests and, 74–77
PLCs (professional learning communities),
    11–12
Policy context, for assessment
    accommodations, 96–97
Portfolio assessment, 86, 89–91
Positive behavior support (PBS), school-wide, 9
Posture of listening, 52
Practitioners, training to develop and
    implement individualized education
    programs, 64–67
Present Level of Academic Achievement and
    Functional performance (PLAAFP),
    57, 59–60
Present levels of performance, individualized
    education program goals, 62
Pre-service training, 67–69
Prevention science, 8
Problem solving
    Choosing Outcomes and Accommodations
        for Children and, 53
    problem-solving teams, 27–29, 31
Problem-Solving Model, 40
Procedural requirements, individualized
    education programs, 57–59, 62, 69
Process portfolios, 89
Product portfolios, 89
Professional development, individualized
    education programs, 69
Professional learning communities (PLCs),
    11–12
Progress monitoring
    case study, 26–30
    curriculum-based assessment and, 85, 92
    curriculum-based measurement and, 18–31
    data-based academic decision making and,
        18–21, 26–31
    decision-making rubric, 30
    definition of, 18–19
    historical, legal, and logical basis for, 20–21
    individualized education programs and, 59,
        60–61, 68
    mathematics and, 23–25
    placement decisions and, 79
    reading and, 22–23
    research-based practices and, 5
    Response to Intervention and, 9, 18
    selecting students for, 27
    Tier-3 interventions and, 10
    uses of, 19–20
Public examination, scientific research, 4

Qualitative research, person-centered
    planning, 50
Quantity Array, 23–24
Quantity Discrimination, 23–24

Race/ethnicity
    disproportionate representation and,
        36–40, 42
    individualized education programs and, 63
    person-centered planning and, 50
    Response to Intervention, 15
Rachel H. Four Part Test, 72
Rating scales for literacy assessment, 86, 89
Read aloud/oral presentation, 97, 100–101,
    103, 107–108
Reading. *See also* Early literacy instruction;
        Reading comprehension
    assessment accommodations and, 98, 103
    curriculum-based measurement and, 9,
        21–23, 31
    progress monitoring and, 22–23
    research on, 63
Reading comprehension
    assessment accommodations and, 99
    cloze and, 88
    informal reading inventories and, 88–89
Reading disabilities
    assessment accommodations and, 102
    individualized education programs and, 62
Reading Miscue Inventory, 87
Reading performance, curriculum-based
    assessment, 86–89
Reading proficiency, academic
    achievement, 22
Reasonable accommodations, 95
Referral, 34, 39
Rehabilitation Act Section 504, 95, 96
Relationship Circle form, 50
Reliability
    checklists and, 89
    curriculum-based assessment and, 86, 88
    of measures, 3
    portfolios and, 90–91
Research
    on assessment accommodations, 95–96,
        97–104
    on checklists, 89
    on Choosing Outcomes and
        Accommodations for Children,
        53–54
    on curriculum-based assessment, 92–93
    directions for future research, 17, 31,
        41–42, 55, 67
    effective practices based on, 2–5
    on eligibility identification, 40, 41–42
    on individualized education programs, 60,
        61–67
    on math, 63
    on maze procedures, 88
    on miscue analysis, 87
    open and iterative nature of science
        and, 4–5
    on parental involvement, 44, 45–47
    on person-centered planning, 49–50
    on placement decisions, 72–73
    on reading, 63
    research-to-practice gap, 6–7
    on Response to Intervention, 11, 13, 14–17
    safeguards in, 3–5
    on training to develop and implement
        individualized education programs,
        64–67
Research-based practices, as basis for effective
        practices, 2–5

Research Institute on Progress Monitoring, 25, 31
Research-to-practice gap, 6–7
Response to Intervention (RtI)
    curriculum-based measurement and, 9, 11–12, 20, 23, 24, 31
    data management teams, 12
    effect on special education, 17
    eligibility identification and, 33, 35, 39–42
    grade-level teams, 11–12, 13
    identifying class-wide problems, 12–13
    implementation, 13
    intervention intensity and, 14
    limitations of empirical research base, 16–17
    placement decisions and, 79–80
    progress monitoring and, 9, 18
    research on, 11, 13, 14–17
    school-wide prevention, 8–17
    Tier-1 instruction and screening, 9, 80
    Tier-2 interventions, 9–10, 11, 12, 13–14, 80
    Tier-3 interventions, 10, 11, 13, 80
Review, Interview, Observe, Test-Instruction, Curriculum, Environment, and Learner (RIOT-ICEL), 10
Roncker Portability Test, 72
RtI. *See* Response to Intervention (RtI)

Samples, size and composition of, 4
Scales of Independent Behavior-Revised, 38
Scholastic Aptitude Reasoning Test, 99
School psychologists, eligibility identification, 35
School-wide positive behavior support (SW-PBS), 9
School-wide prevention, Response to Intervention, 8–17
School-wide screening, 27
SCIEP (Student-Centered Individualized Education Planning), 50
Scoring rubrics, portfolio assessment, 90–91
Screening tools
    curriculum-based measurement and, 19
    Response to Intervention and, 9
Self-Advocacy Strategy, 66
Self-assessment/evaluation, portfolio assessment, 90–91
Self-determination
    individualized education programs and, 66
    person-centered planning and, 48
Self-Reported Delinquency Questionnaire, 37
Self-reporting measures, for placement decisions, 77
SEL (Star Early Literacy), 9–10
Sensory disabilities
    assessment accommodations and, 97
    parental involvement and, 53–54
SES. *See* Socioeconomic status (SES)
Severe mental retardation, as disability category, 35
Single-subject research, 4
SLDs. *See* Speech and language disorders (SLDs)
Social Security Act of 1956, 32–33
Social validity. *See also* Validity
    assessment accommodations and, 103
    curriculum-based assessment and, 86
    maze and, 88
Socioeconomic status (SES), disproportionate representation, 36, 37
Special education
    accommodations and, 94–95
    curriculum-based measurement and, 19, 20, 24, 26

eligibility determination and, 32–35, 39
individualized education programs and, 49–50, 57–60, 62
parent involvement, 43
placement decisions, 71, 72–74, 79
Response to Intervention and, 8–9, 16, 17
Special education practices. *See* Effective practices
Special education teachers
    individualized education programs and, 58–59, 68
    personal experiences of, 1–5
    research-based practices and, 2–3
    research-to-practice gap and, 6–7
    Response to Intervention and, 11, 12, 14
Speech and language disorders (SLDs)
    assessment accommodations and, 98
    person-centered planning and, 49
Speech-to-text, 100
SSBD. *See* Systematic Screening for Behavior Disorders (SSBD)
SSCS (Student Self-Concept Scale), 77
Standard accommodations, 95
Standardized tests, for placement decisions, 74–77
Star Early Literacy (SEL), 9–10
State assessments. *See* Large-scale state assessments
Strategies and Processes to Implement a COACH-Generated Educational Program, 51
Strengths and Preferences form, 50
Student-Centered Individualized Education Planning (SCIEP), 50
Student outcomes. *See also* Academic skills outcomes
    curriculum-based measurement and, 25
Student performance, credible measures of, 3
Student Self-Concept Scale (SSCS), 77
Students with disabilities
    accommodations for assessment, 94–104, 105–110
    curriculum-based assessment and, 91
    curriculum-based measurement and, 25
    free appropriate public education and, 56
    individualized education programs and, 57–69
    modifications and, 63, 91–92, 95
    need for effective practices, 1–2, 3
    No Child Left Behind Act of 2001, 95
    parental involvement and, 49, 54
    placement decisions and, 70–71, 73–74
    Response to Intervention and, 8
Study descriptions
    computer-based testing, 109–110
    extended time, 105–106
    read aloud/oral presentation, 107–108
Study design
    assessment accommodations, 97–98, 103–104
    COACH and, 54
    Response to Intervention and, 16
Substantive requirements, individualized education programs, 57–59, 62, 69
SW-PBS (school-wide positive behavior support), 9
Systematic Screening for Behavior Disorders (SSBD)
    eligibility identification and, 36–37, 42
    placement decisions and, 77

Target groups. *See also specific types of disabilities*
    research-based practices and, 5, 7

Teacher behaviors, 5
Teacher judgment, in placement decisions, 78, 82
Teacher opinions, in placement decisions, 78, 81
Teacher-preparation programs, for individualized education programs, 67–69
Teacher Rating Questionnaire, 22
Teaching practices. *See* Effective practices; Instructional practices
Technically adequate measures, 18–19, 22–23
Testing accommodations, 63
Test interpretation, 75–76
Test of Phonological Awareness, 22
Text-to-speech (TTS), 92, 102
Three-tiered models of prevention
    curriculum-based measurement and, 20
    placement decisions and, 79–80
    Response to Intervention and, 9
Tier 1
    curriculum-based measurement and, 9, 20
    eligibility identification and, 35, 40
    placement decisions and, 80
    Response to Intervention and, 9, 80
Tier 2
    curriculum-based measurement and, 10, 20
    eligibility identification and, 35, 40
    placement decisions and, 80
    Response to Intervention and, 9–10, 11, 12, 13–14, 80
Tier 3
    curriculum-based measurement and, 20
    eligibility identification and, 35, 40
    placement decisions and, 80
    Response to Intervention and, 10, 11, 13, 80
Tiered intervention approaches. *See* Three-tiered models of prevention
Traditions, 1–2, 3
Transition Outcomes Project, 65
Transition plans, individualized education programs, 61, 63–65, 67
Transition Requirements Checklist, 65
Transition to adulthood, individualized education programs, 61, 63–65, 67
Traumatic brain injury, as disability category, 33, 35
Treatment delays, 36, 39, 42
Treatment integrity, Response to Intervention, 16
Treatment resistors, 5

UDL. *See* Universal Design for Learning (UDL)
Underidentification, emotional disturbance, 35–36
Universal Design for Learning (UDL)
    curriculum-based assessment and, 92
    placement decisions and, 72
U.S. Supreme Court decisions, 71

Validity. *See also* Social validity
    of assessment accommodations, 94, 97, 103
    of curriculum-based assessment, 86, 87, 88, 89, 92, 93
    of curriculum-based measurement, 19, 21, 22, 23, 24, 25, 26
    of eligibility identification, 32, 37, 39, 40, 42
    of individualized education programs, 63, 64
    of measures, 3
    of Response to Intervention, 14–15, 16

Valued life outcomes, 52–53
Variability, research on assessment
    accommodations, 103
VI. *See* Visual impairments (VI)
Vineland Adaptive Behavior Scales II,
    34, 38
Visual impairments (VI). *See also*
    Deaf-blindness (DB)
  as disability category, 35
Vocational training, 63–64

Weschler Individual Achievement Test-II
    (WIAT-II), 34, 39
Weschler Intelligence Scale for Children
    (WISC-IV), 34, 38
What Works form, 50
Who and When form, 50
WIAT-II (Weschler Individual Achievement
    Test-II), 34, 39
WISC-IV (Weschler Intelligence Scale for
    Children), 34, 38

Within-group comparison research,
    person-centered planning, 49
Woodcock Johnson III Test of Achievement
    (WJ III), 34, 40, 75
Woodcock Johnson Psycho-Educational
    Achievement Battery-Revised, 22
Woodcock Reading Mastery Test-Revised, 22
WRAT 3-Arithmetic, 24
Writing assessment, assessment
    accommodations, 98